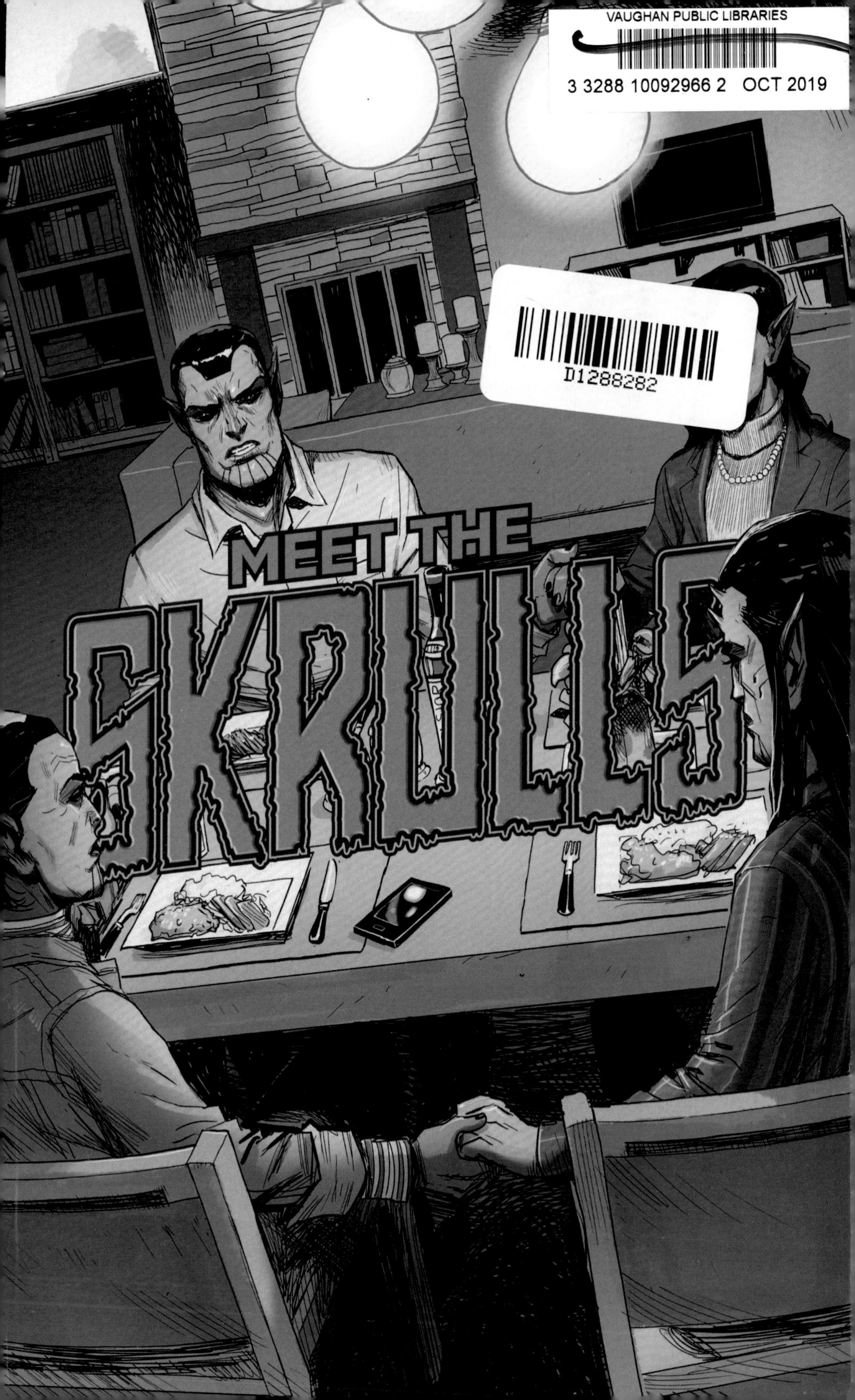
MEET THE
SKRULLS

collection editor JENNIFER GRÜNWALD ✦ assistant editor CAITLIN O'CONNELL

associate managing editor KATERI WOODY ✦ editor, special projects MARK D. BEAZLEY

vp production & special projects JEFF YOUNGQUIST ✦ book designer ADAM DEL RE

svp print, sales & marketing DAVID GABRIEL ✦ director, licensed publishing SVEN LARSEN

editor in chief C.B. CEBULSKI ✦ chief creative officer JOE QUESADA

president DAN BUCKLEY ✦ executive producer ALAN FINE

MEET THE SKRULLS. Contains material originally published in magazine form as MEET THE SKRULLS #1-5. First printing 2019. ISBN 978-1-302-91713-5. Published by MARVEL WORLDWIDE, INC., a subsidiary of MARVEL ENTERTAINMENT, LLC. OFFICE OF PUBLICATION: 135 West 50th Street, New York, NY 10020. © 2019 MARVEL No similarity between any of the names, characters, persons, and/or institutions in this magazine with those of any living or dead person or institution is intended, and any such similarity which may exist is purely coincidental. **Printed in Canada.** DAN BUCKLEY, President, Marvel Entertainment; JOHN NEE, Publisher; JOE QUESADA, Chief Creative Officer; TOM BREVOORT, SVP of Publishing; DAVID BOGART, Associate Publisher & SVP of Talent Affairs; DAVID GABRIEL, SVP of Sales & Marketing, Publishing; JEFF YOUNGQUIST, VP of Production & Special Projects; DAN CARR, Executive Director of Publishing Technology; ALEX MORALES, Director of Publishing Operations; DAN EDINGTON, Managing Editor; SUSAN CRESPI, Production Manager; STAN LEE, Chairman Emeritus. For information regarding advertising in Marvel Comics or on Marvel.com, please contact Vit DeBellis, Custom Solutions & Integrated Advertising Manager, at vdebellis@marvel.com. For Marvel subscription inquiries, please call 888-511-5480. **Manufactured between 6/28/2019 and 7/30/2019 by SOLISCO PRINTERS, SCOTT, QC, CANADA.**

10 9 8 7 6 5 4 3 2 1

MEET THE SKRULLS

ROBBIE THOMPSON
writer

NIKO HENRICHON
artist

LAURENT GROSSAT
color assistant

VC's TRAVIS LANHAM
letterer

MARCOS MARTIN
cover art

KATHLEEN WISNESKI
assistant editor

NICK LOWE
editor

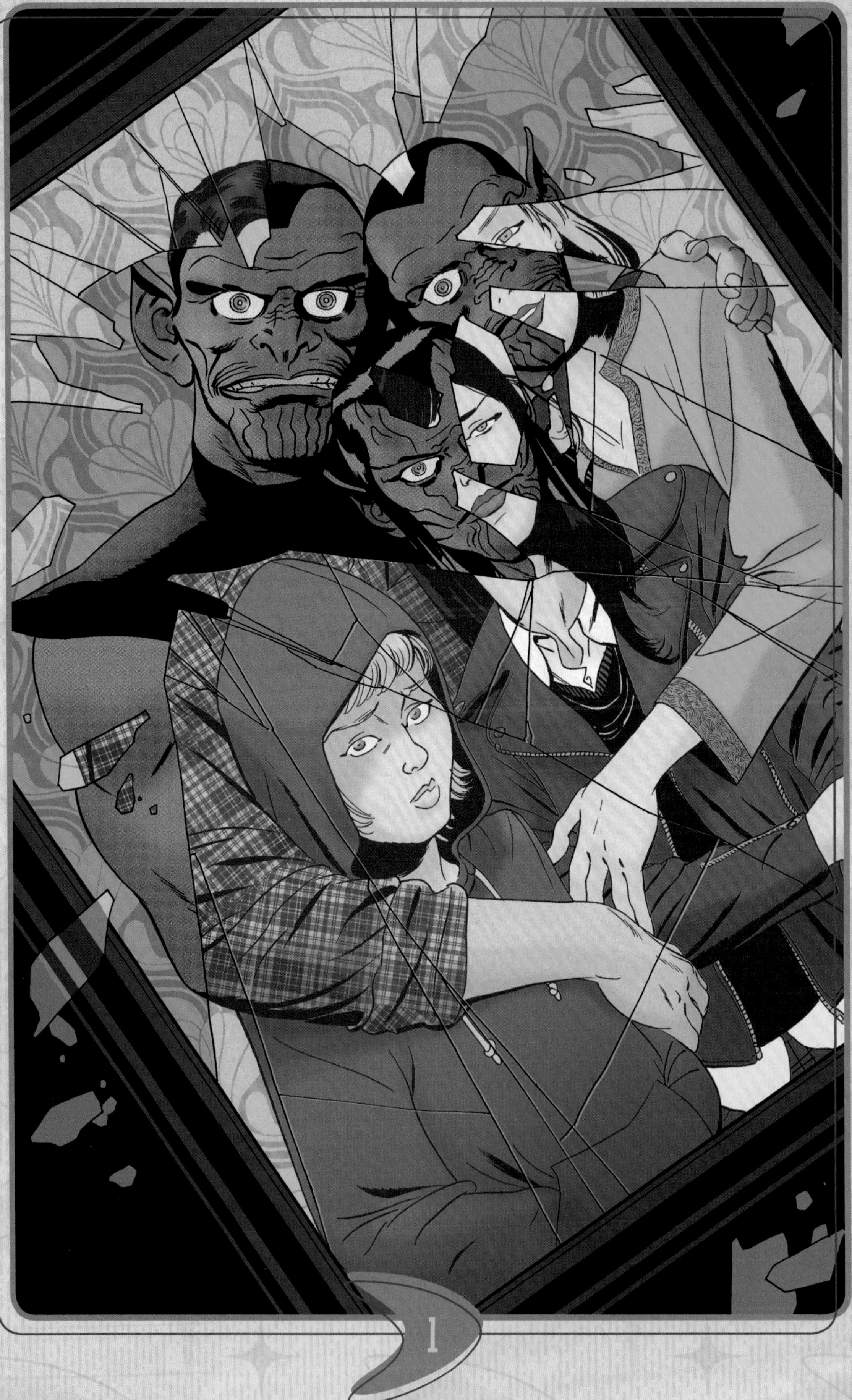

1

SKRULL ['skrəl] noun

A member of an alien people whose empire once spanned the Andromeda Galaxy. Unstable molecules in their bodies allow them to take any shape. The slow collapse of their empire was hastened by a failed invasion of the planet Earth.

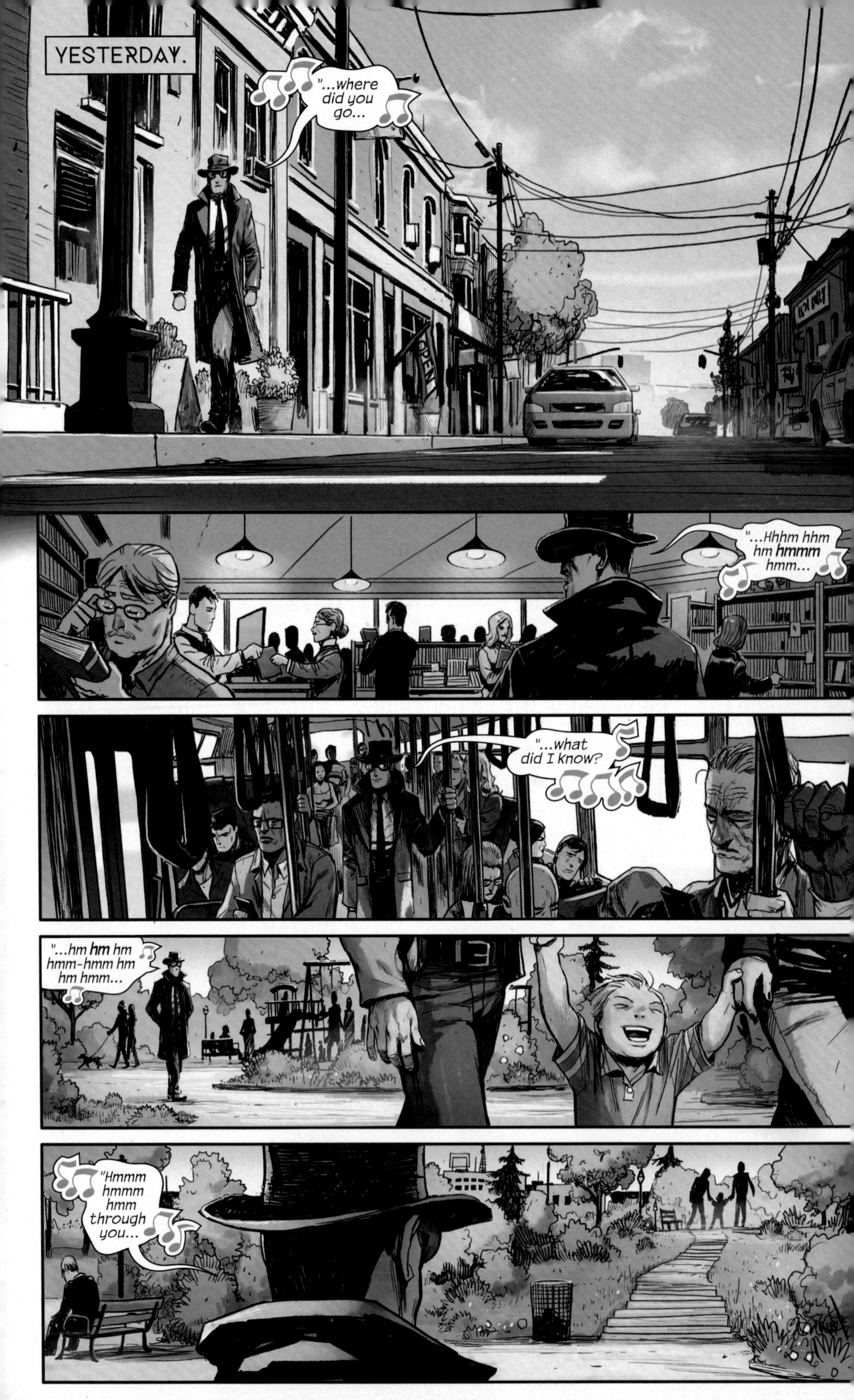
YESTERDAY.
"...where did you go...
"...Hhhm hhm hm hmmm hmm...
"...what did I know?
"...hm hm hm hmm-hmm hm hm hmm...
"Hmmm hmmm hmm through you...

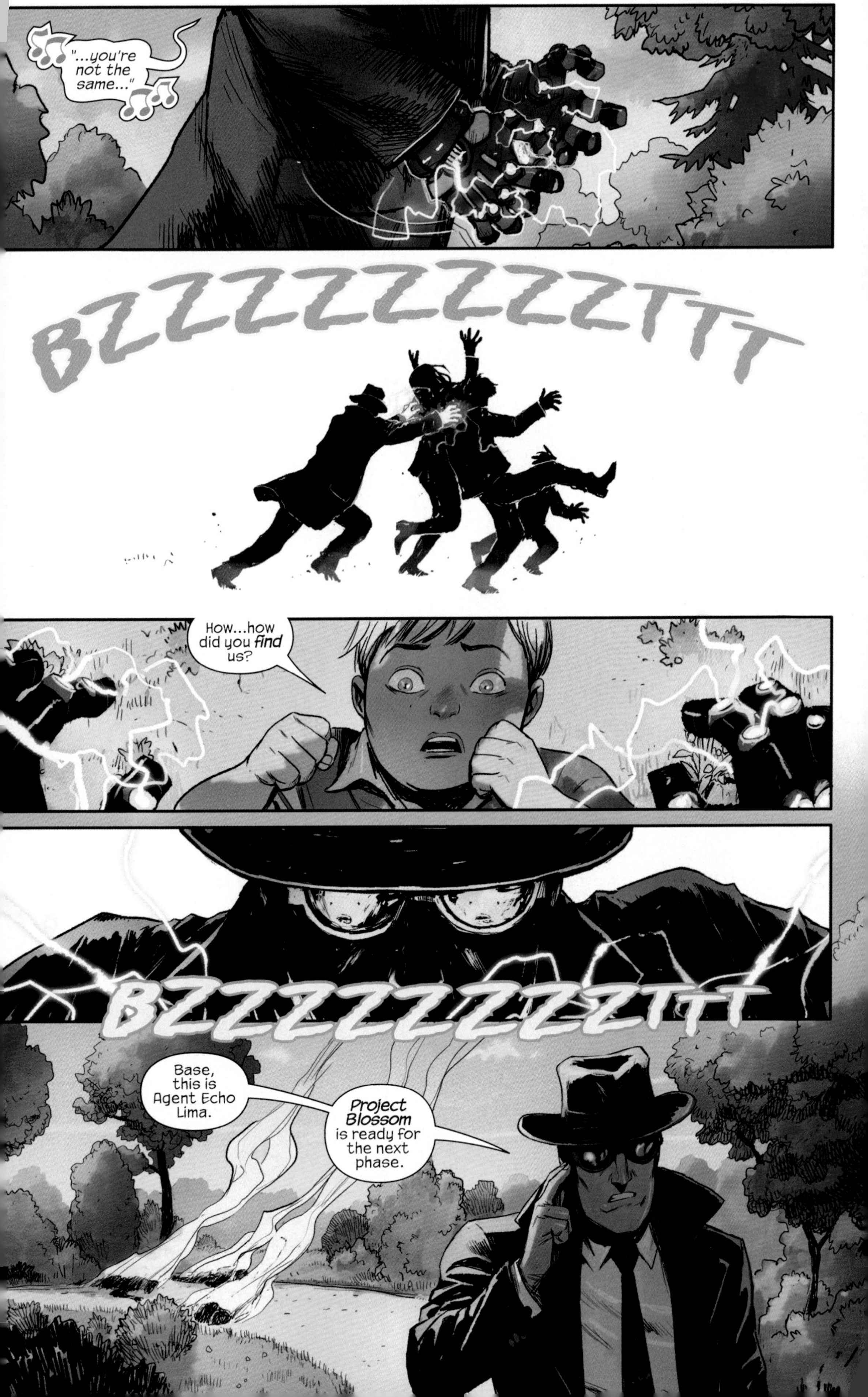
"...you're not the same..."
BZZZZZZZZZTTT
How...how did you *find* us?
BZZZZZZZZZTTT
Base, this is Agent Echo Lima.
Project Blossom is ready for the next phase.

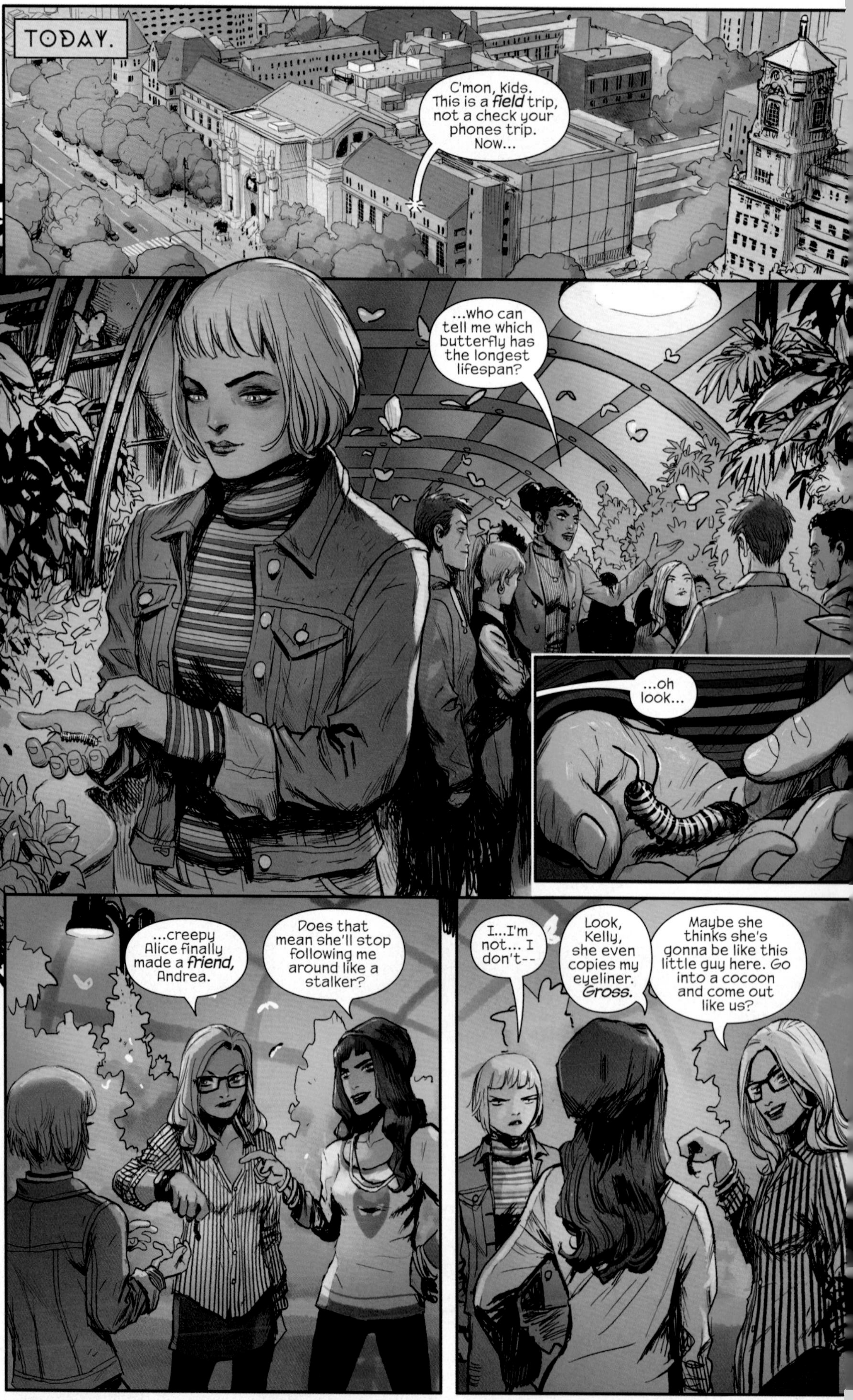
TODAY.
C'mon, kids. This is a field trip, not a check your phones trip. Now...
...who can tell me which butterfly has the longest lifespan?
...oh look...
...creepy Alice finally made a friend, Andrea.
Does that mean she'll stop following me around like a stalker?
I...I'm not... I don't--
Look, Kelly, she even copies my eyeliner. Gross.
Maybe she thinks she's gonna be like this little guy here. Go into a cocoon and come out like us?

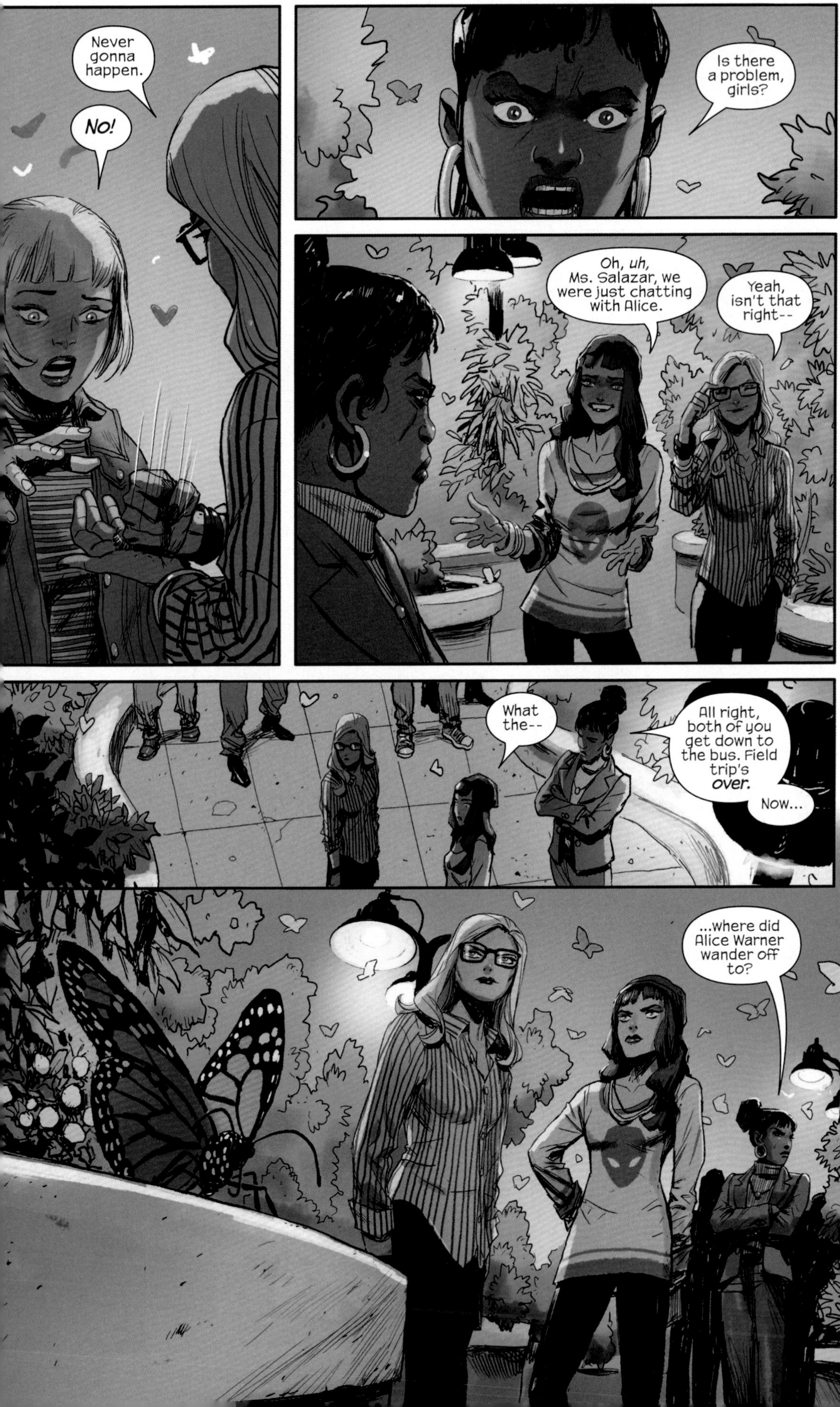
Never gonna happen.
No!
Is there a problem, girls?
Oh, uh, Ms. Salazar, we were just chatting with Alice.
Yeah, isn't that right--
What the--
All right, both of you get down to the bus. Field trip's over.
Now...
...where did Alice Warner wander off to?

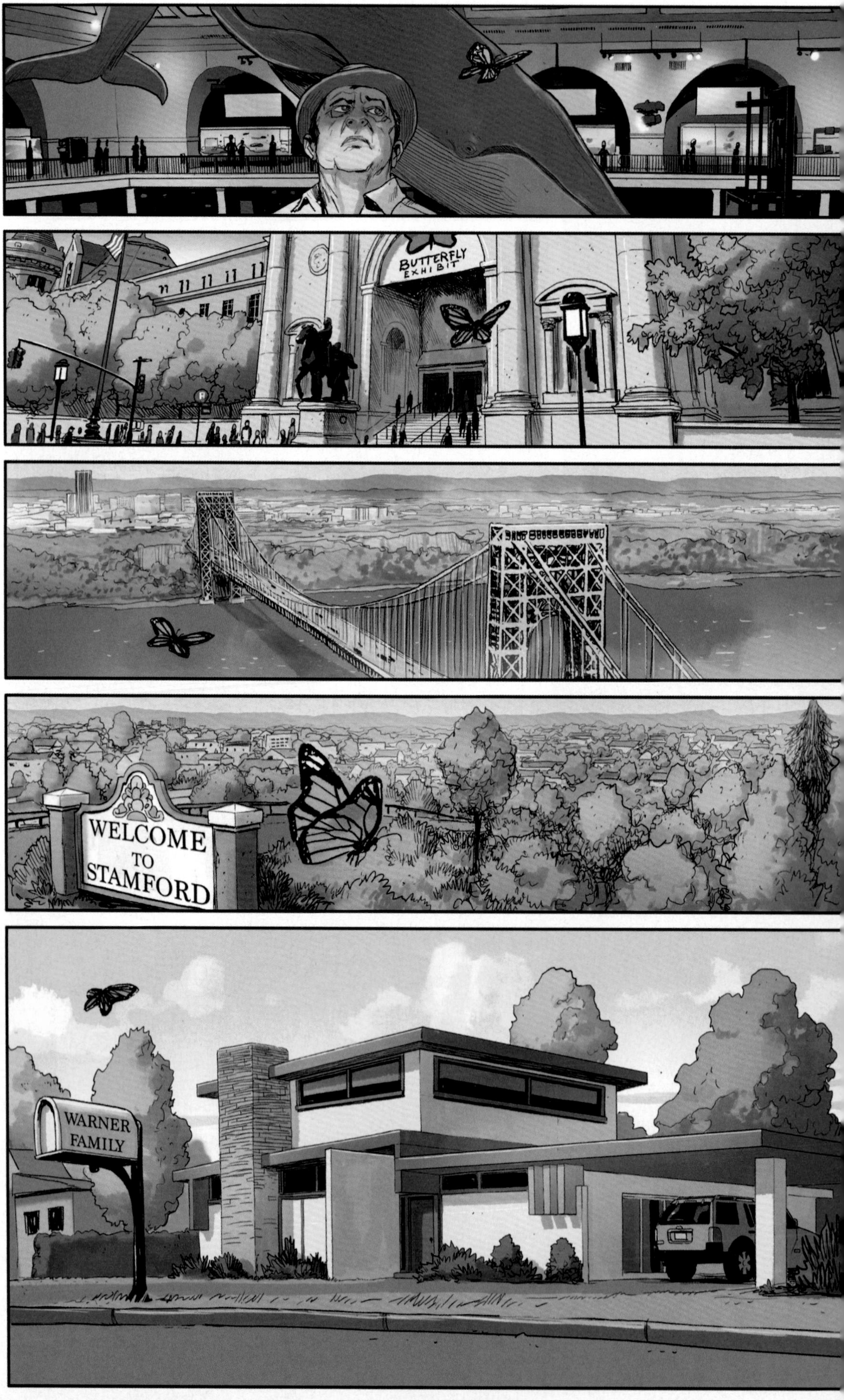
BUTTERFLY EXHIBIT
WELCOME TO STAMFORD
WARNER FAMILY

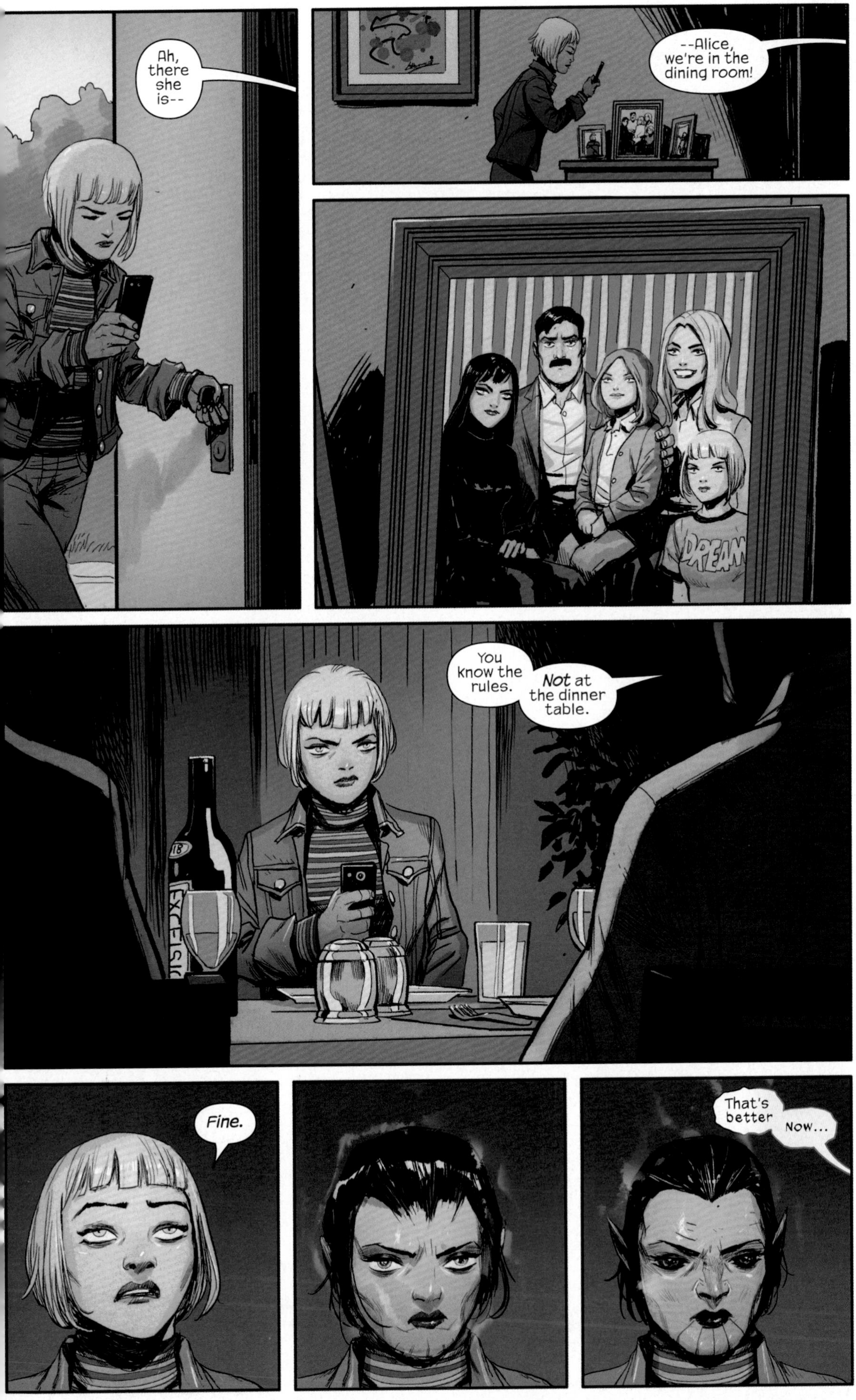

Ah, there she is--
--Alice, we're in the dining room!
DREAM
You know the rules.
Not at the dinner table.
Fine.
That's better
Now...

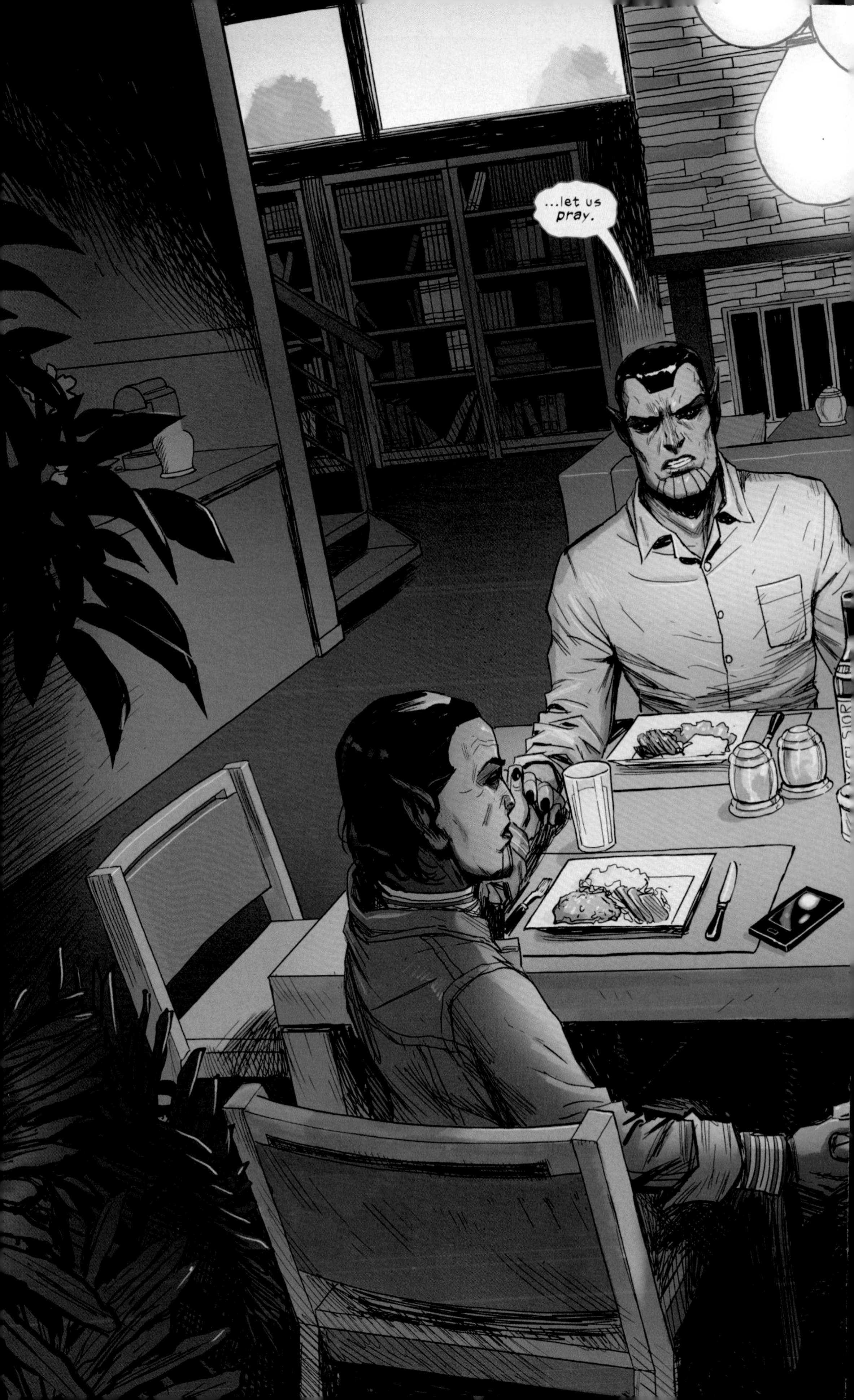
...let us pray.

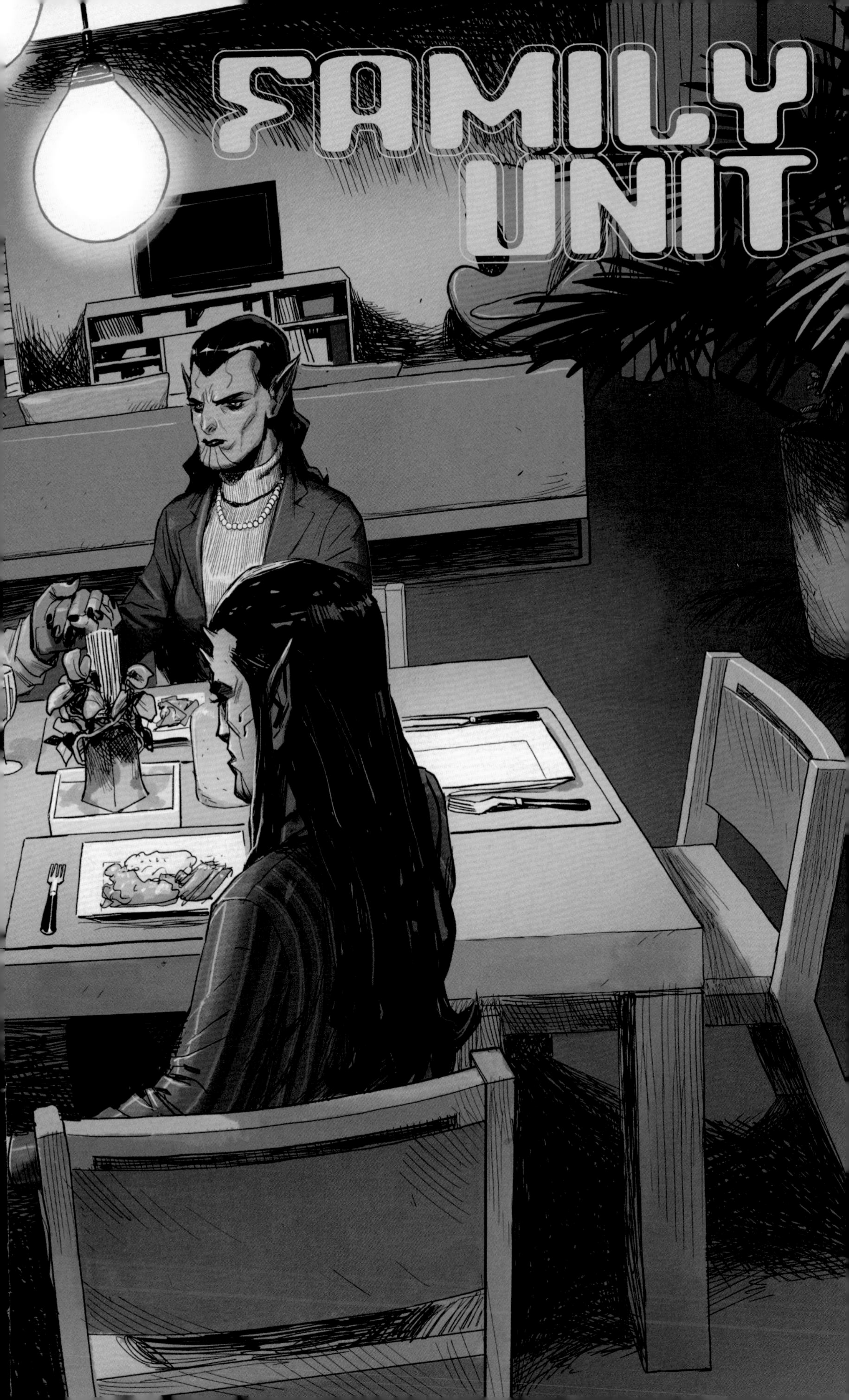
FAMILY
UNIT

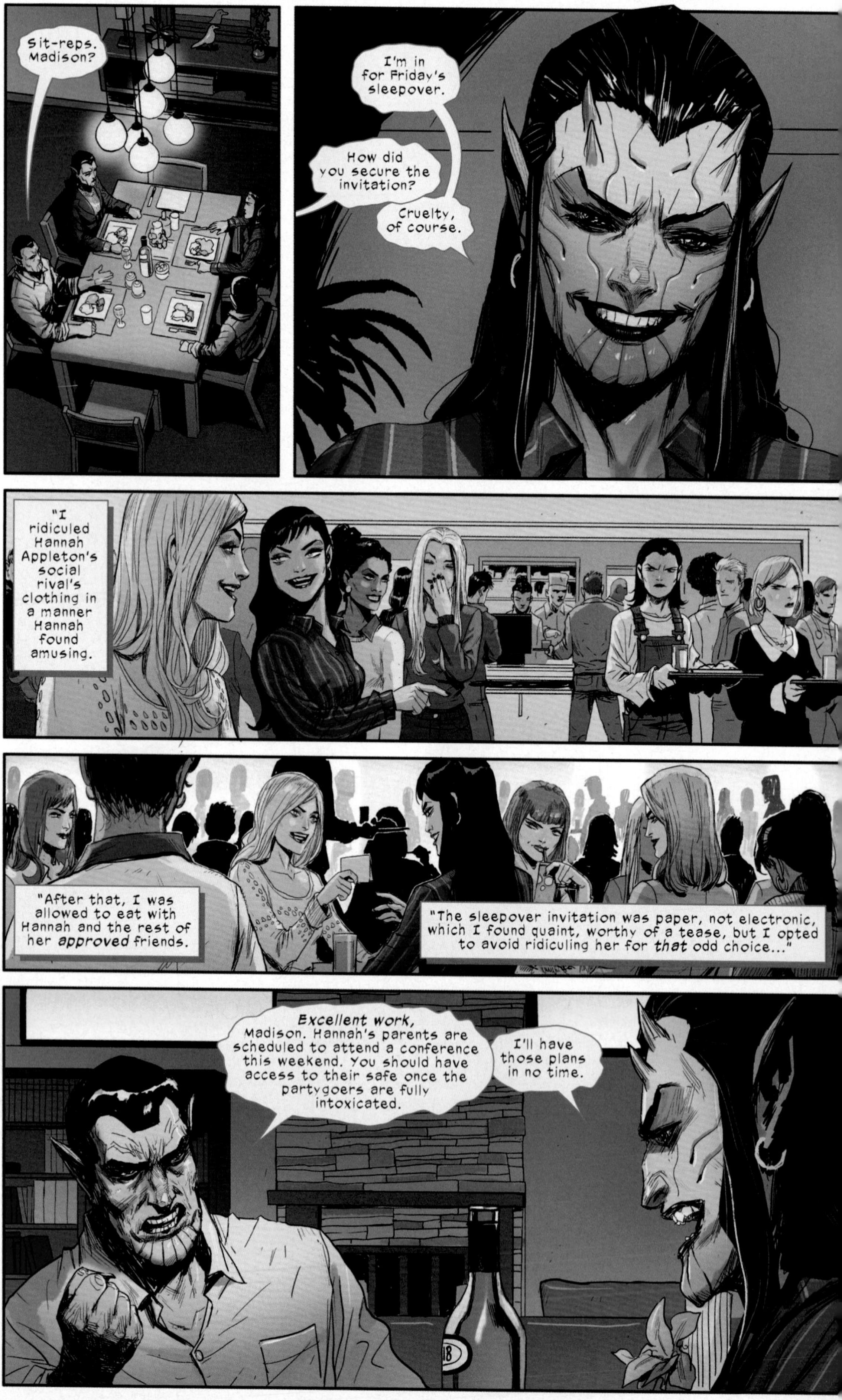

Sit-reps. Madison?
I'm in for Friday's sleepover.
How did you secure the invitation?
Cruelty, of course.
"I ridiculed Hannah Appleton's social rival's clothing in a manner Hannah found amusing.
"After that, I was allowed to eat with Hannah and the rest of her *approved* friends.
"The sleepover invitation was paper, not electronic, which I found quaint, worthy of a tease, but I opted to avoid ridiculing her for *that* odd choice..."
Excellent work, Madison. Hannah's parents are scheduled to attend a conference this weekend. You should have access to their safe once the partygoers are fully intoxicated.
I'll have those plans in no time.

Perfect. Gloria?

After my meeting today, Congresswoman Baker will be getting some much-needed good news...

...Baker doesn't have the votes, Gloria. We both know it. Now, why you had me drive all the way out to the boring-ass *suburbs* to tell you this is--

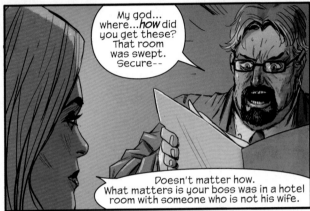

My god... where... *how* did you get these? That room was swept. Secure--

Doesn't matter how. What matters is your boss was in a hotel room with someone who is not his wife.

Blackmail? Does Congresswoman Baker know--

She pays me to *fix* things. She doesn't need to know *how* I fix them. And frankly she doesn't care.

"I secured the votes needed to get Baker on the Special Projects Committee..."

...she'll be meeting with Project Blossom's various subcontractors next week.

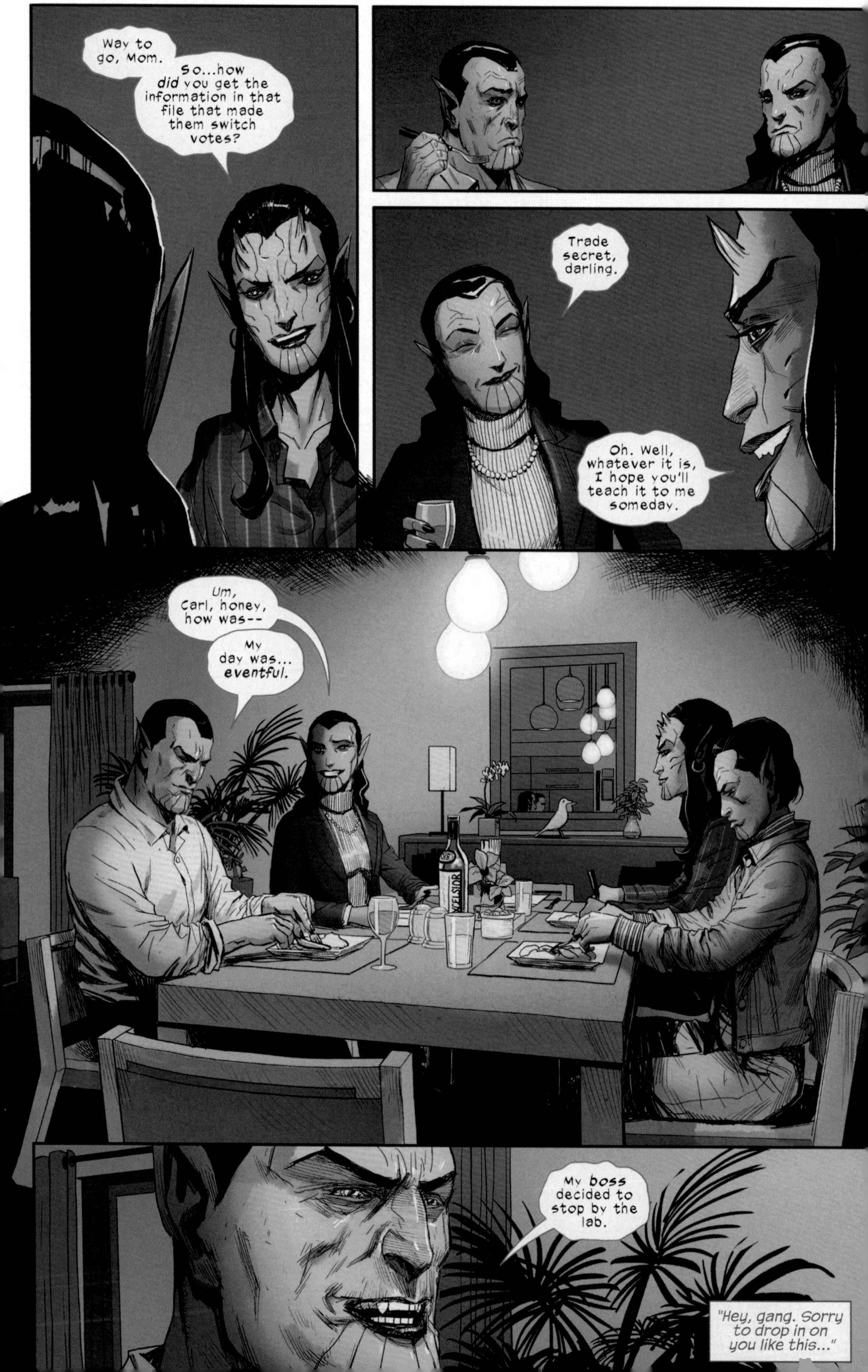
Way to go, Mom.
So...how *did* you get the information in that file that made them switch votes?
Trade secret, darling.
Oh. Well, whatever it is, I hope you'll teach it to me someday.
Um, Carl, honey, how was--
My day was... *eventful.*
EXCELSIOR
My *boss* decided to stop by the lab.
"Hey, gang. Sorry to drop in on you like this..."

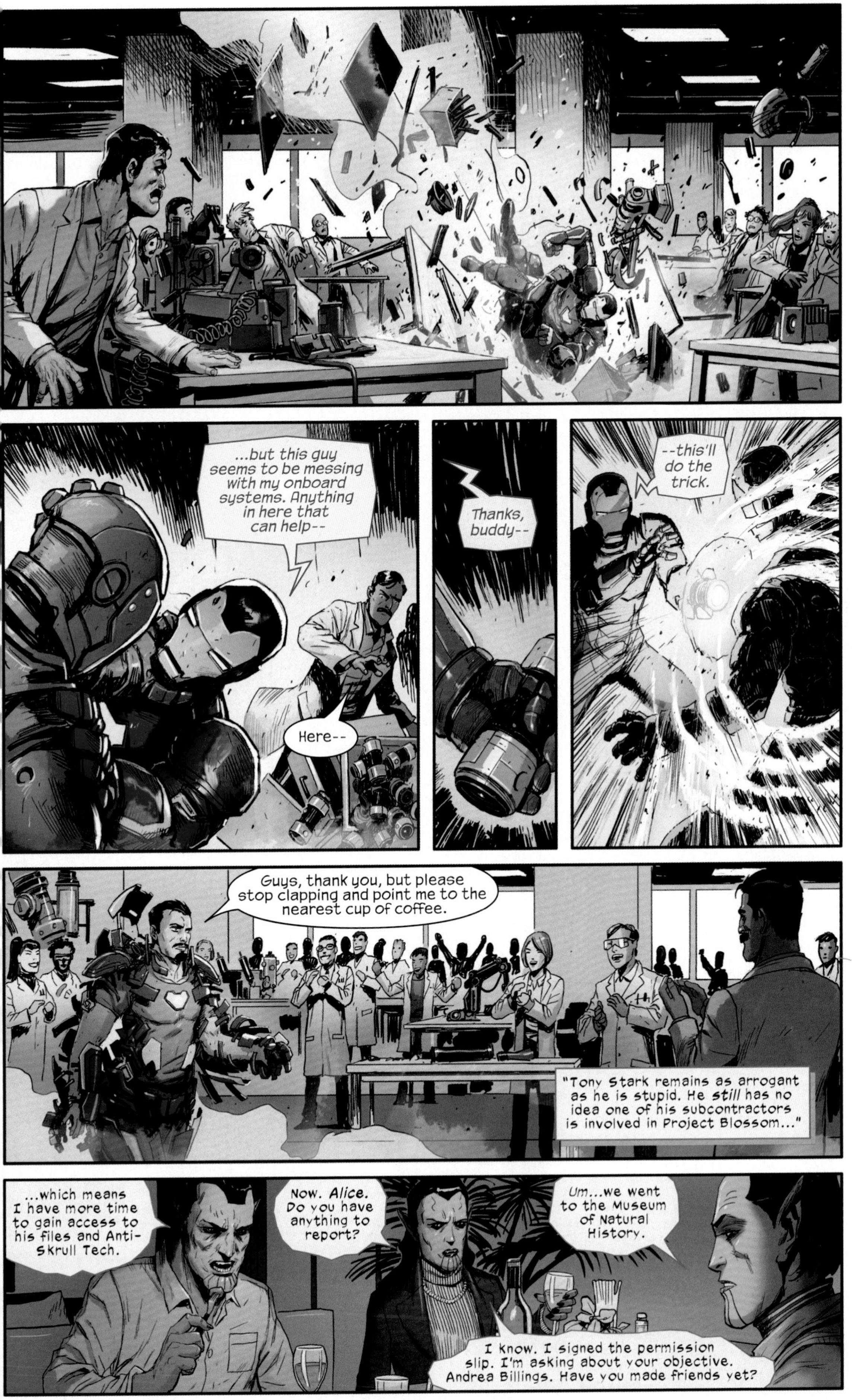
...but this guy seems to be messing with my onboard systems. Anything in here that can help--
Here--
Thanks, buddy--
--this'll do the trick.
Guys, thank you, but please stop clapping and point me to the nearest cup of coffee.
"Tony Stark remains as arrogant as he is stupid. He *still* has no idea one of his subcontractors is involved in Project Blossom..."
...which means I have more time to gain access to his files and Anti-Skrull Tech.
Now. *Alice.* Do you have anything to report?
Um...we went to the Museum of Natural History.
I know. I signed the permission slip. I'm asking about your objective. Andrea Billings. Have you made friends yet?

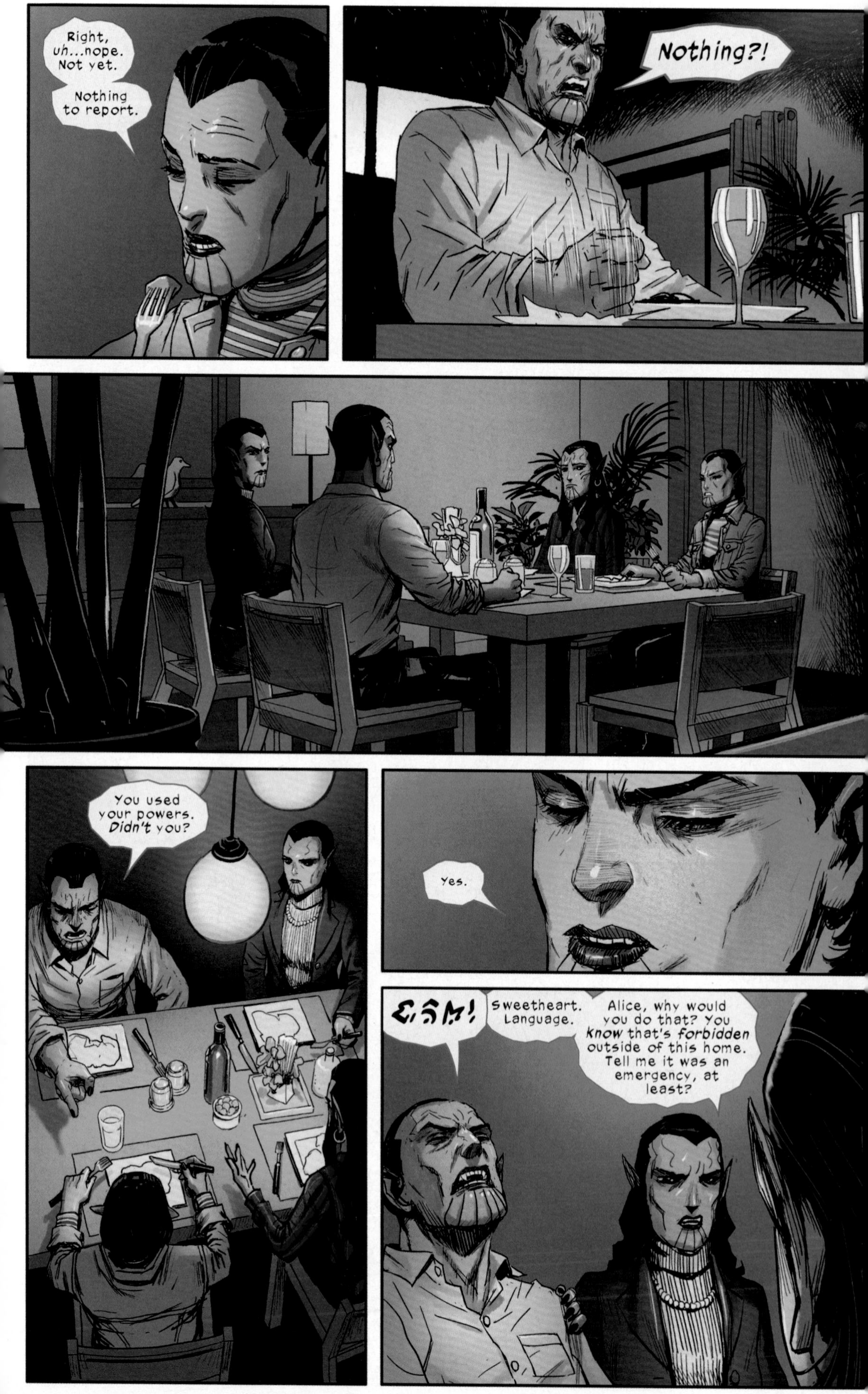

Right, uh...nope. Not yet.
Nothing to report.
Nothing?!
You used your powers. Didn't you?
Yes.
£∆ℳ!
Sweetheart. Language.
Alice, why would you do that? You know that's forbidden outside of this home. Tell me it was an emergency, at least?

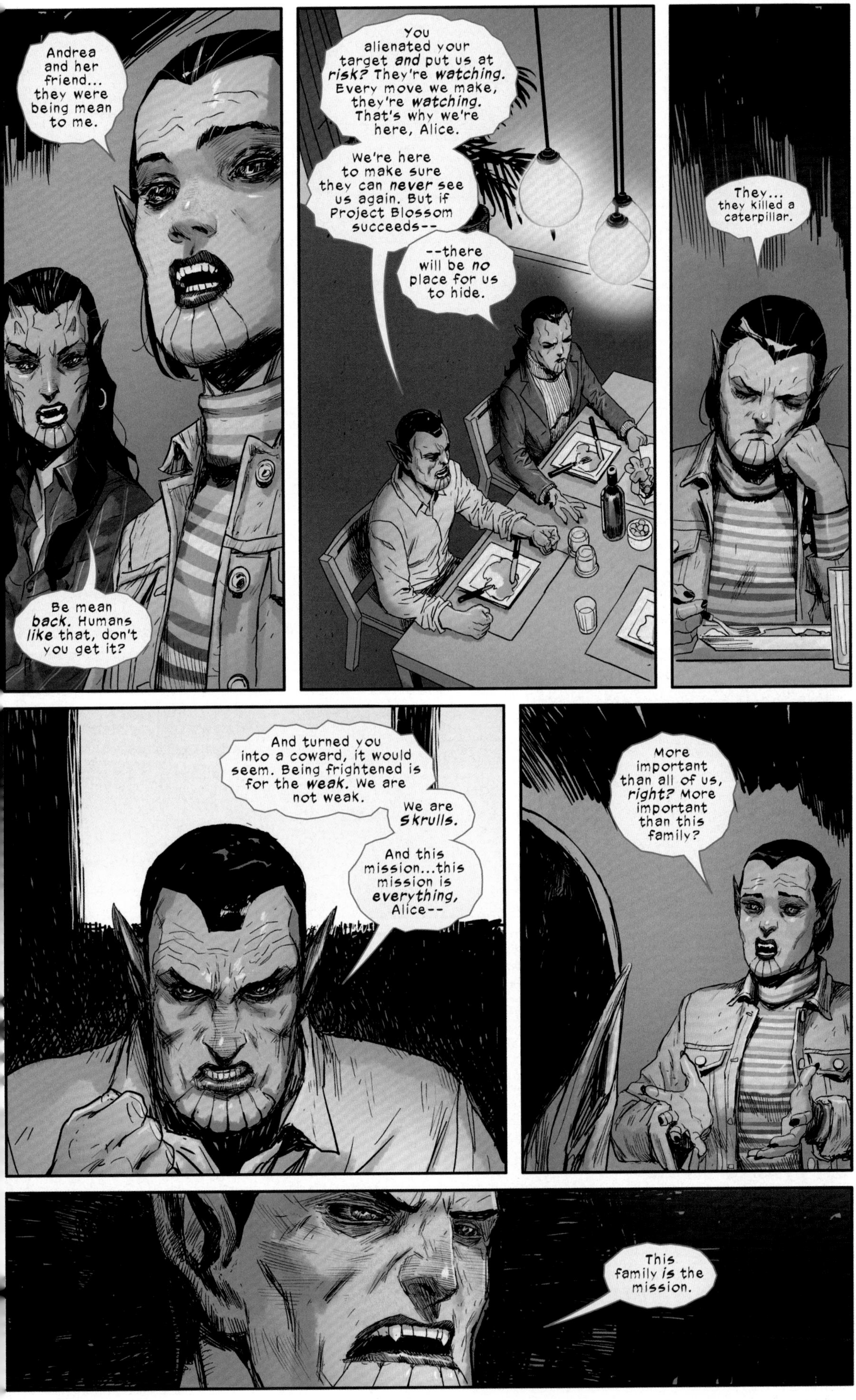
Andrea and her friend... they were being mean to me.
Be mean back. Humans like that, don't you get it?
You alienated your target and put us at risk? They're watching. Every move we make, they're watching. That's why we're here, Alice.
We're here to make sure they can never see us again. But if Project Blossom succeeds--
--there will be no place for us to hide.
They... they killed a caterpillar.
And turned you into a coward, it would seem. Being frightened is for the weak. We are not weak.
We are Skrulls.
And this mission...this mission is everything, Alice--
More important than all of us, right? More important than this family?
This family is the mission.

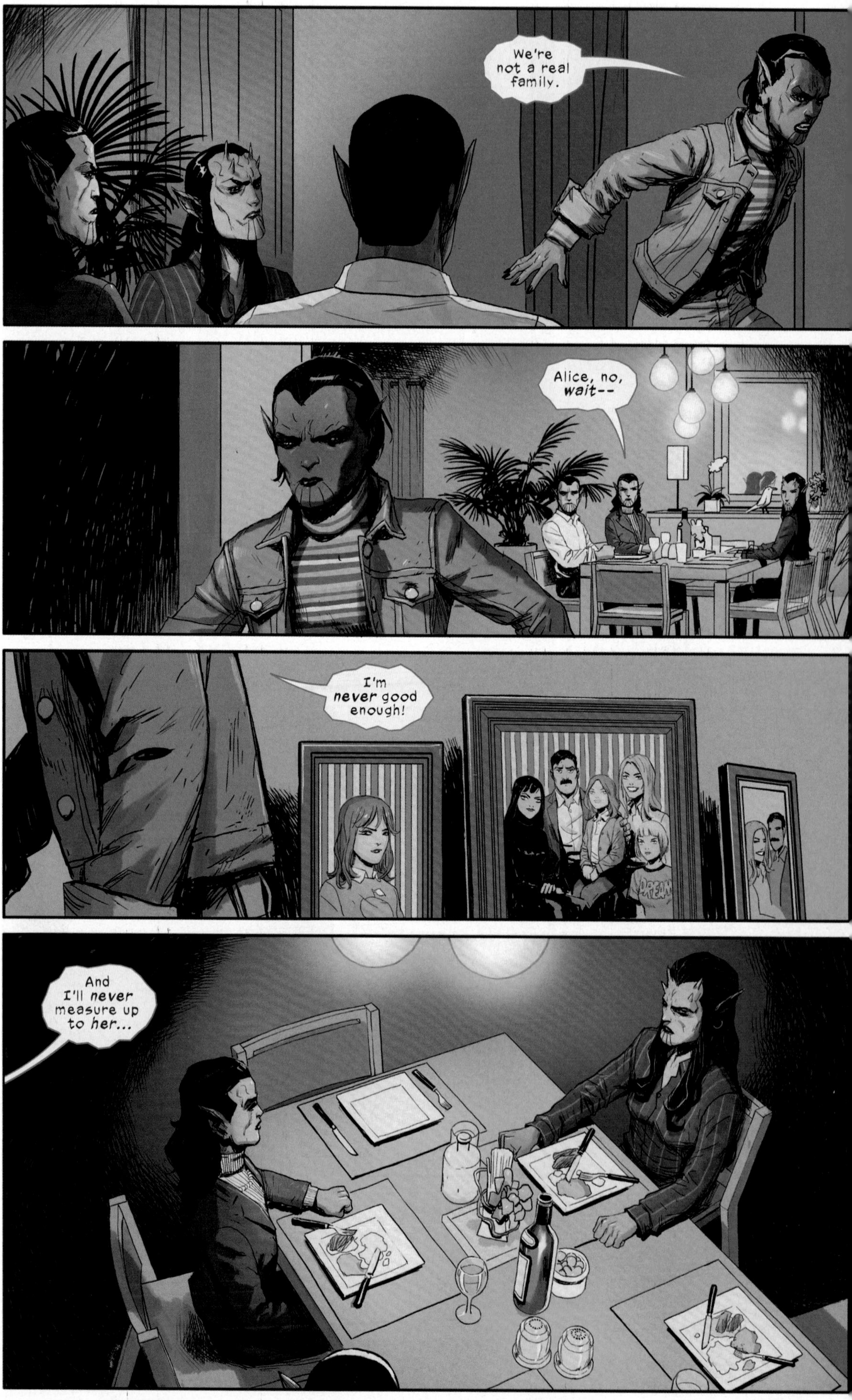
We're not a real family.
Alice, no, *wait--*
I'm *never* good enough!
And I'll *never* measure up to *her*...

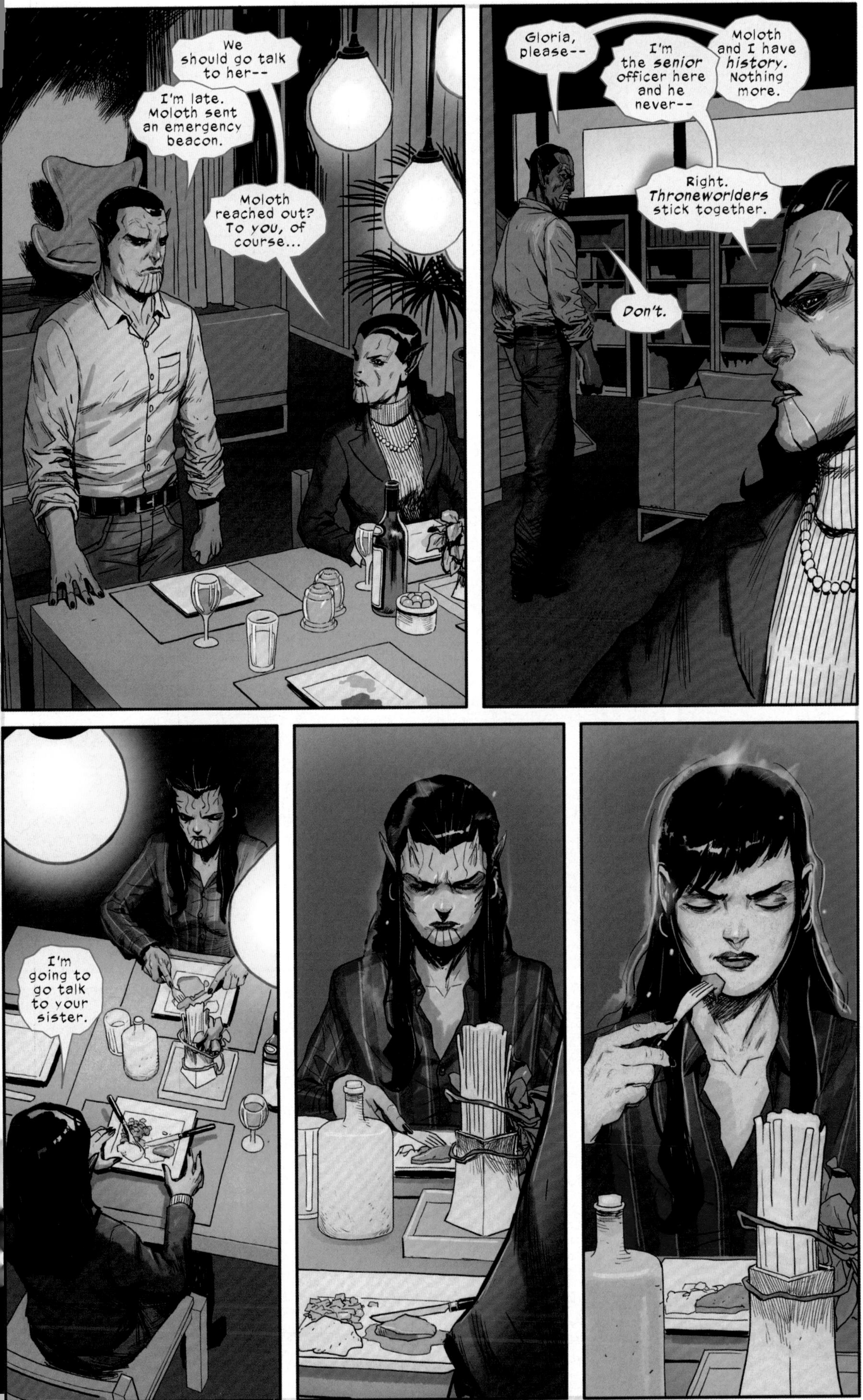
I'm late. Moloth sent an emergency beacon.
We should go talk to her--
Moloth reached out? To *you*, of course...
Gloria, please--
Moloth and I have *history*. Nothing more.
I'm the *senior* officer here and he never--
Right. *Throneworlders* stick together.
Don't.
I'm going to go talk to your sister.

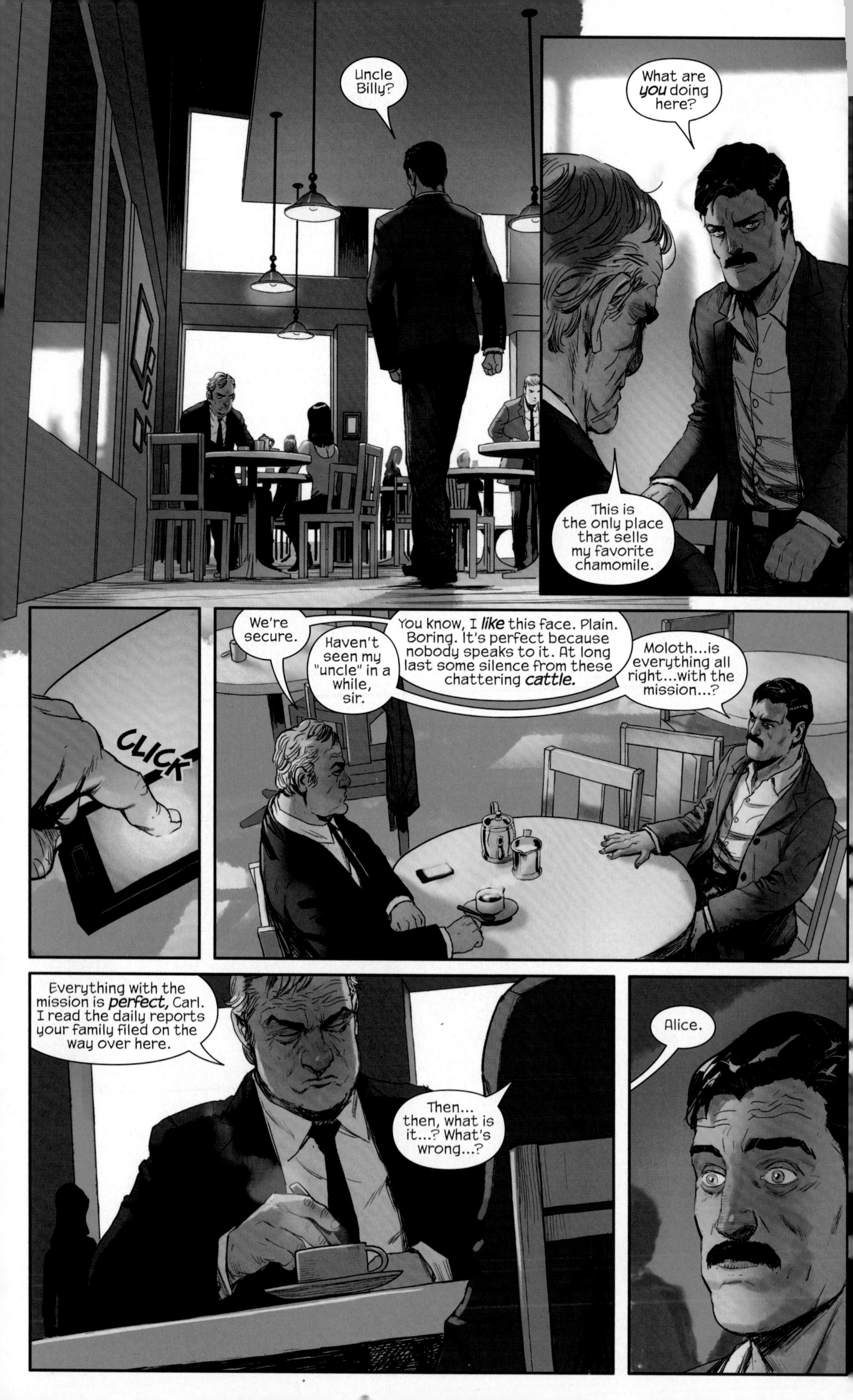
Uncle Billy?
What are *you* doing here?
This is the only place that sells my favorite chamomile.
CLICK
We're secure.
Haven't seen my "uncle" in a while, sir.
You know, I *like* this face. Plain. Boring. It's perfect because nobody speaks to it. At long last some silence from these chattering *cattle.*
Moloth...is everything all right...with the mission...?
Everything with the mission is *perfect,* Carl. I read the daily reports your family filed on the way over here.
Then... then, what is it...? What's wrong...?
Alice.

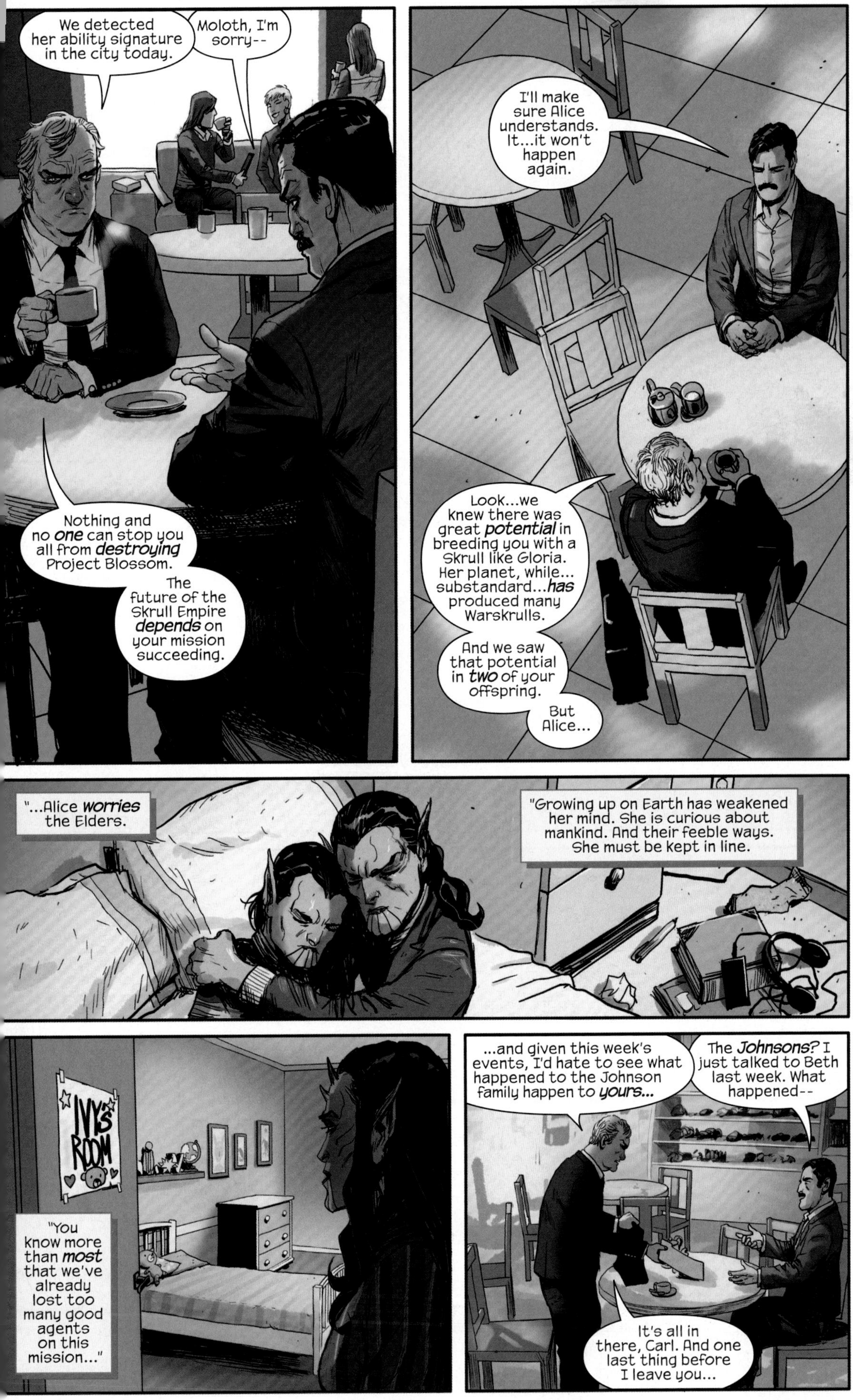
We detected her ability signature in the city today.
Moloth, I'm sorry--
Nothing and no *one* can stop you all from *destroying* Project Blossom.
The future of the Skrull Empire *depends* on your mission succeeding.
I'll make sure Alice understands. It...it won't happen again.
Look...we knew there was great *potential* in breeding you with a Skrull like Gloria. Her planet, while... substandard...*has* produced many Warskrulls.
And we saw that potential in *two* of your offspring.
But Alice...
"...Alice *worries* the Elders.
"Growing up on Earth has weakened her mind. She is curious about mankind. And their feeble ways. She must be kept in line.
IVY'S ROOM
"You know more than *most* that we've already lost too many good agents on this mission..."
...and given this week's events, I'd hate to see what happened to the Johnson family happen to *yours...*
The *Johnsons?* I just talked to Beth last week. What happened--
It's all in there, Carl. And one last thing before I leave you...

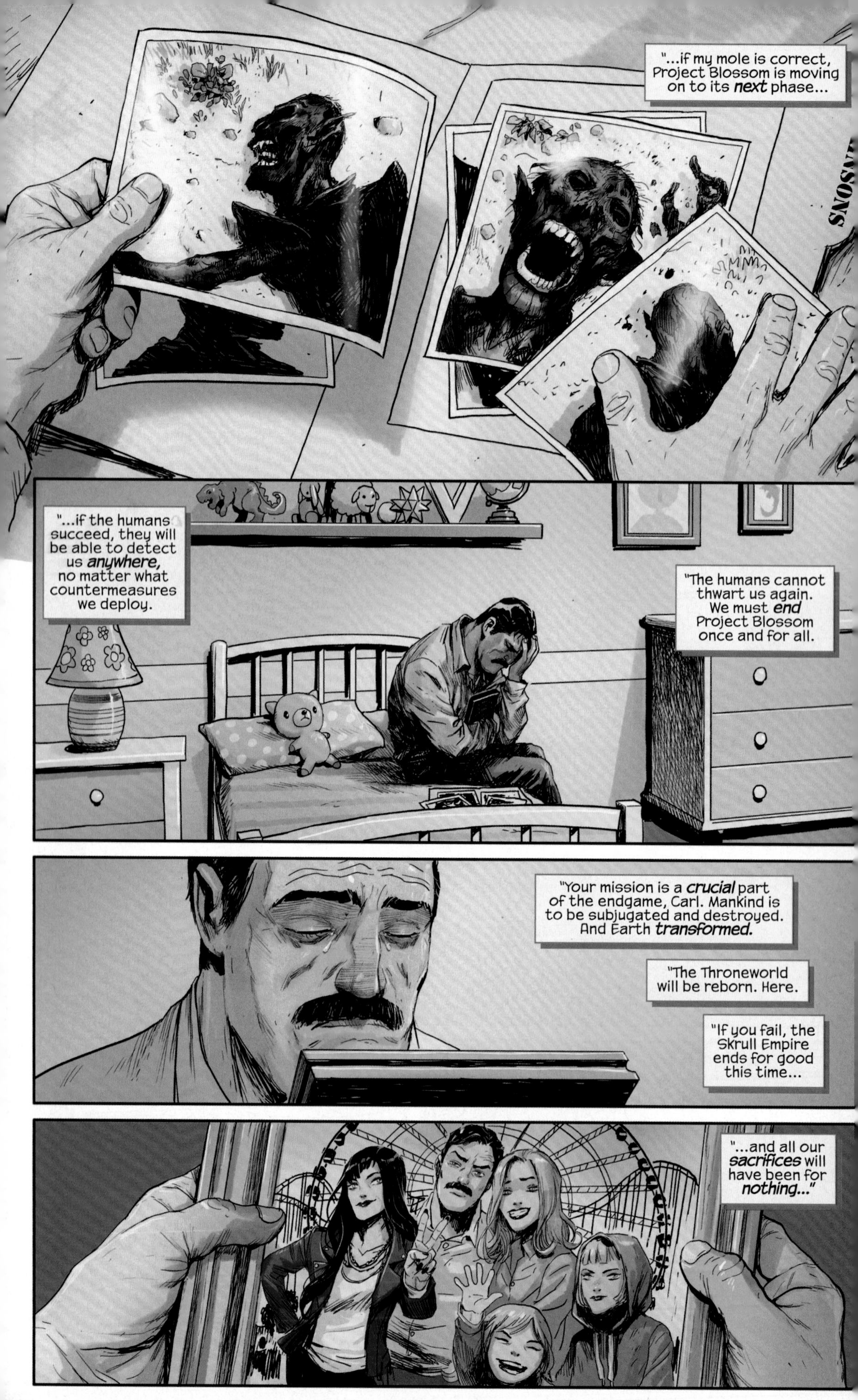
"...if my mole is correct, Project Blossom is moving on to its *next* phase...
"...if the humans succeed, they will be able to detect us *anywhere,* no matter what countermeasures we deploy.
"The humans cannot thwart us again. We must *end* Project Blossom once and for all.
"Your mission is a *crucial* part of the endgame, Carl. Mankind is to be subjugated and destroyed. And Earth *transformed.*
"The Throneworld will be reborn. Here.
"If you fail, the Skrull Empire ends for good this time...
"...and all our *sacrifices* will have been for *nothing...*"

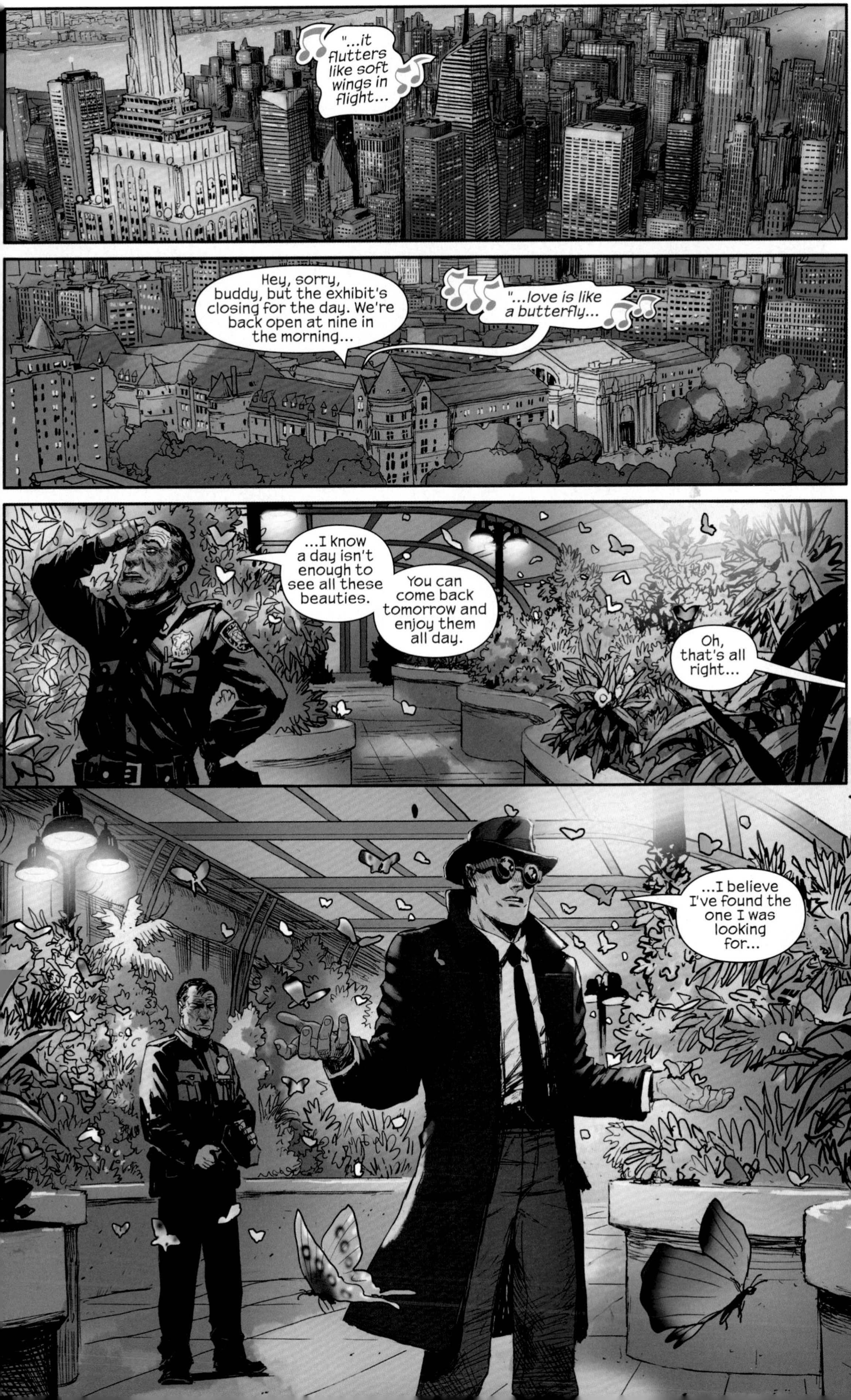
"...it flutters like soft wings in flight...
Hey, sorry, buddy, but the exhibit's closing for the day. We're back open at nine in the morning...
"...love is like a butterfly...
...I know a day isn't enough to see all these beauties.
You can come back tomorrow and enjoy them all day.
Oh, that's all right...
...I believe I've found the one I was looking for...

HOMECOMING 2019

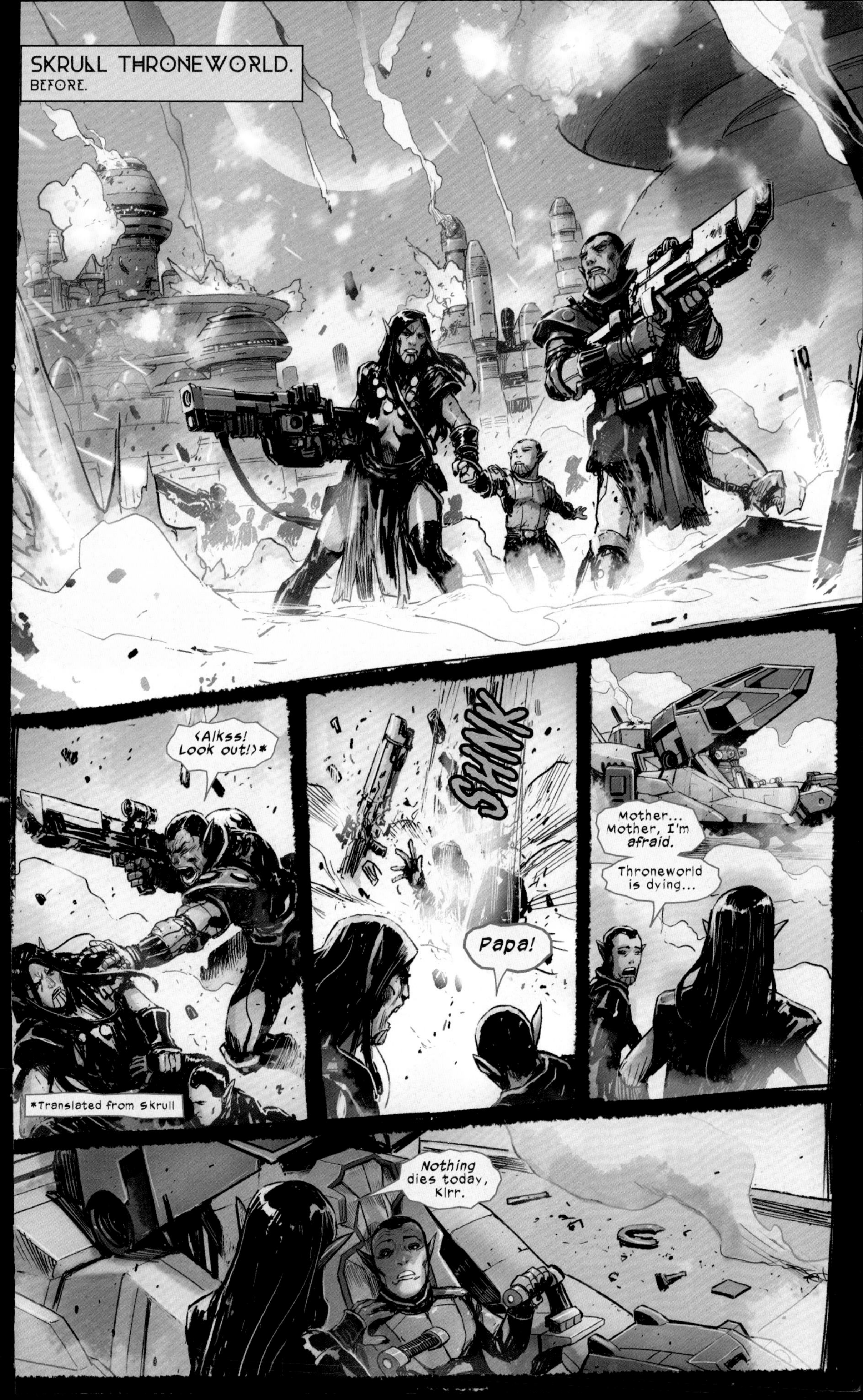
SKRULL THRONEWORLD.
BEFORE.
‹Alkss! Look out!›*
*Translated from Skrull
SHINK
Papa!
Mother... Mother, I'm afraid.
Throneworld is dying...
Nothing dies today, Klrr.

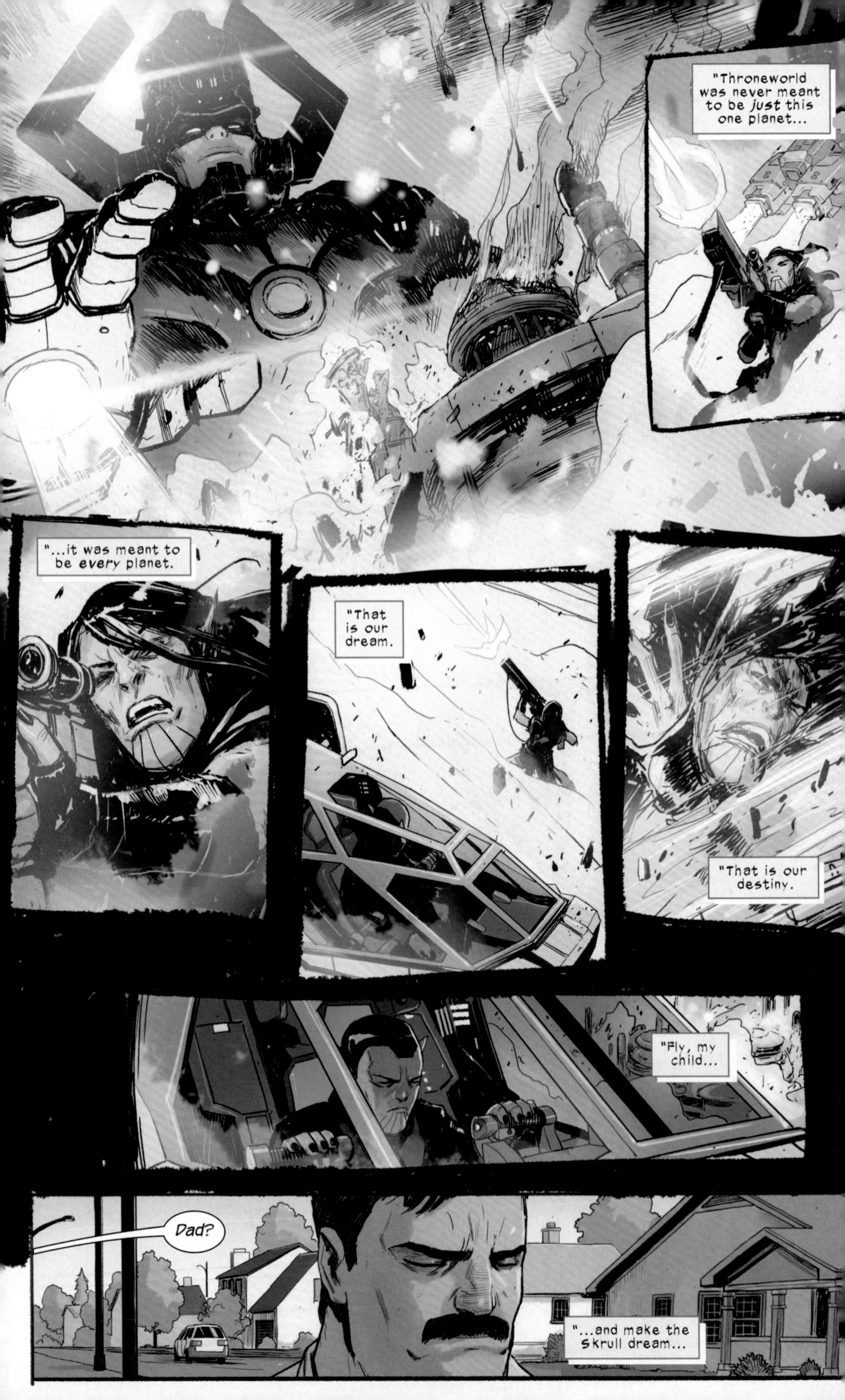
"Throneworld was never meant to be *just* this one planet...
"...it was meant to be *every* planet.
"That is our dream.
"That is our destiny.
"Fly, my child...
Dad?
"...and make the Skrull dream...

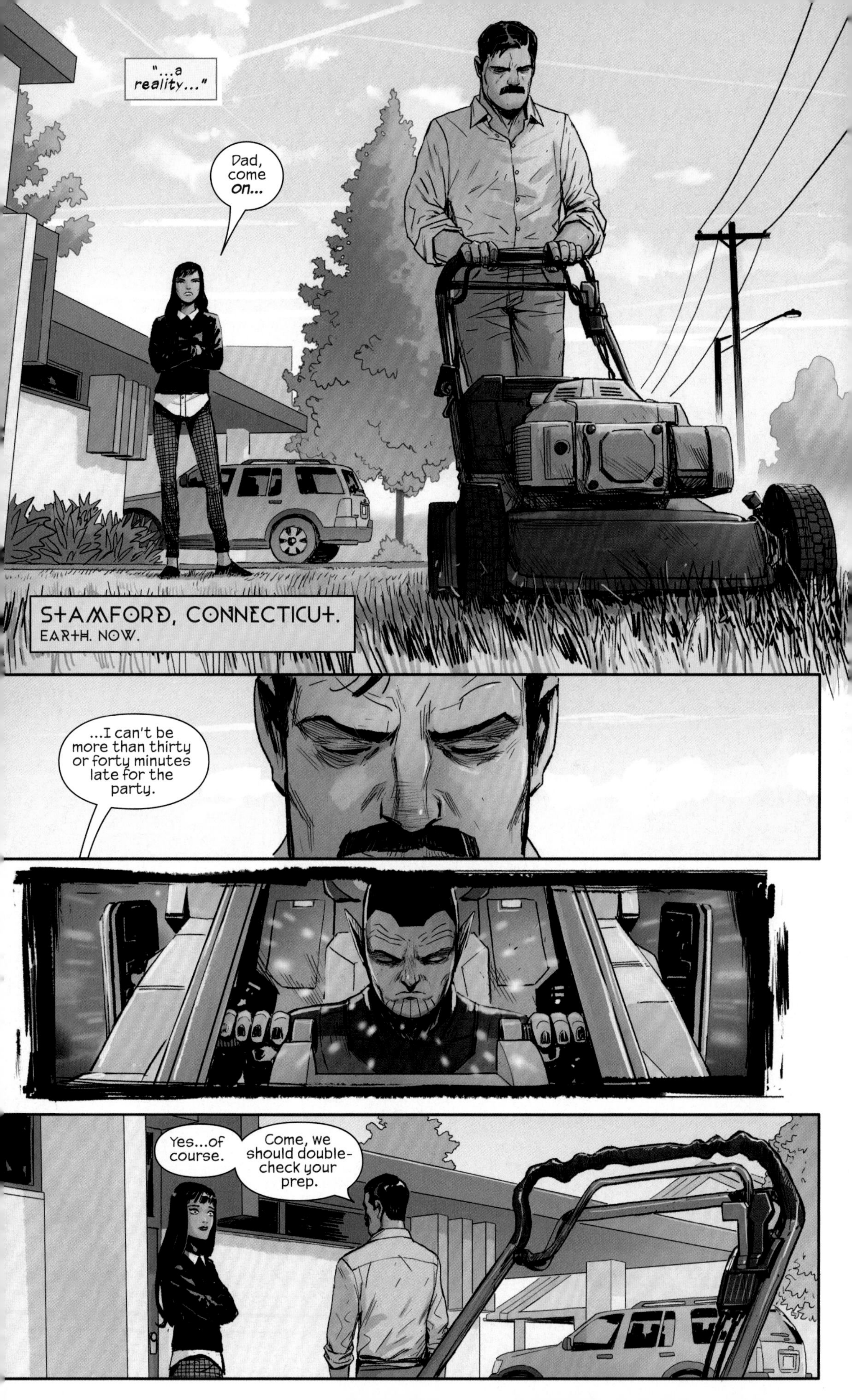
"...a reality..."
Dad, come on...
STAMFORD, CONNECTICUT.
EARTH. NOW.
...I can't be more than thirty or forty minutes late for the party.
Yes...of course.
Come, we should double-check your prep.

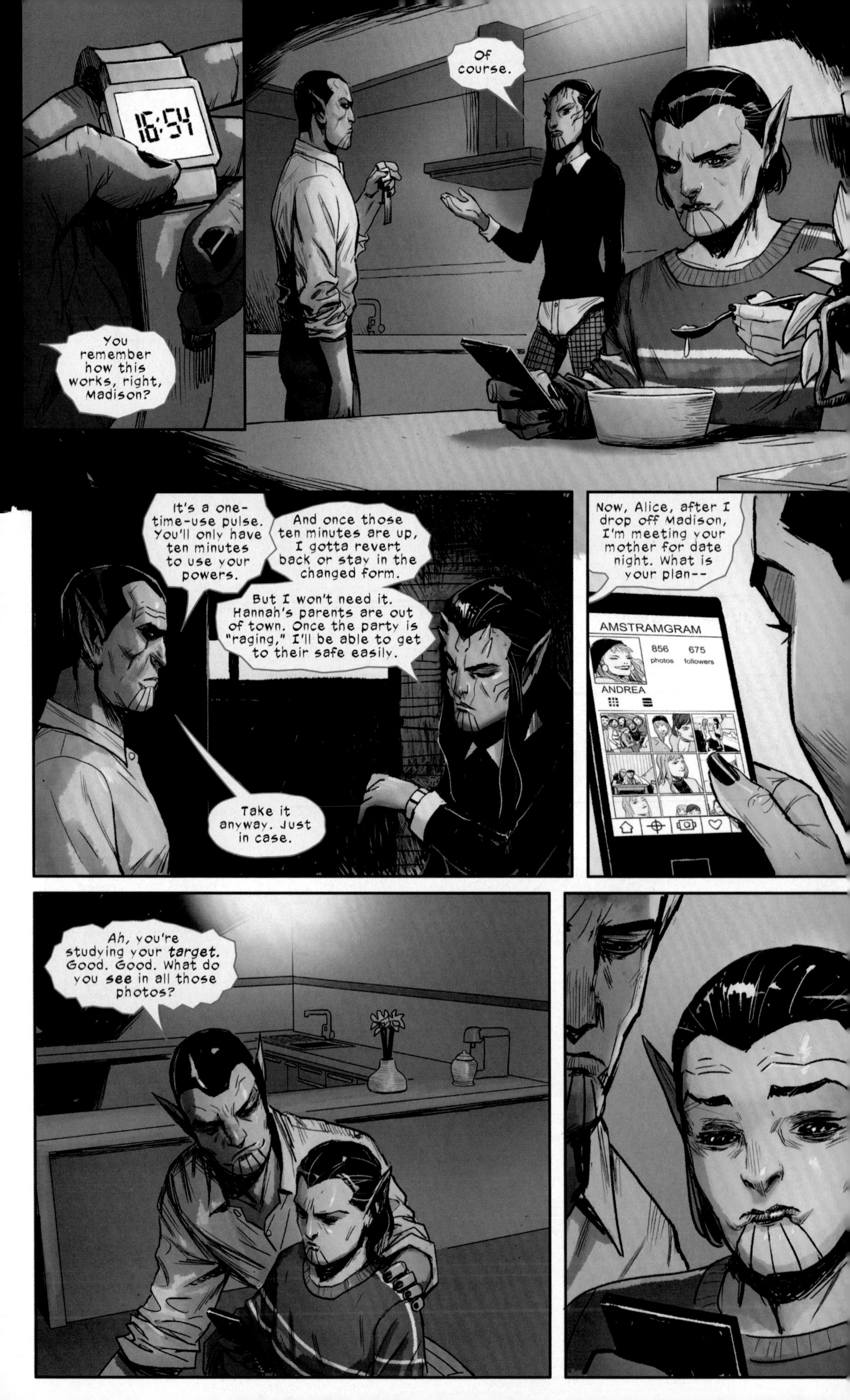
16:54
You remember how this works, right, Madison?
Of course.
It's a one-time-use pulse. You'll only have ten minutes to use your powers.
And once those ten minutes are up, I gotta revert back or stay in the changed form.
But I won't need it. Hannah's parents are out of town. Once the party is "raging," I'll be able to get to their safe easily.
Take it anyway. Just in case.
Now, Alice, after I drop off Madison, I'm meeting your mother for date night. What is your plan--
AMSTRAMGRAM
856 photos
675 followers
ANDREA
Ah, you're studying your *target.* Good. Good. What do you *see* in all those photos?

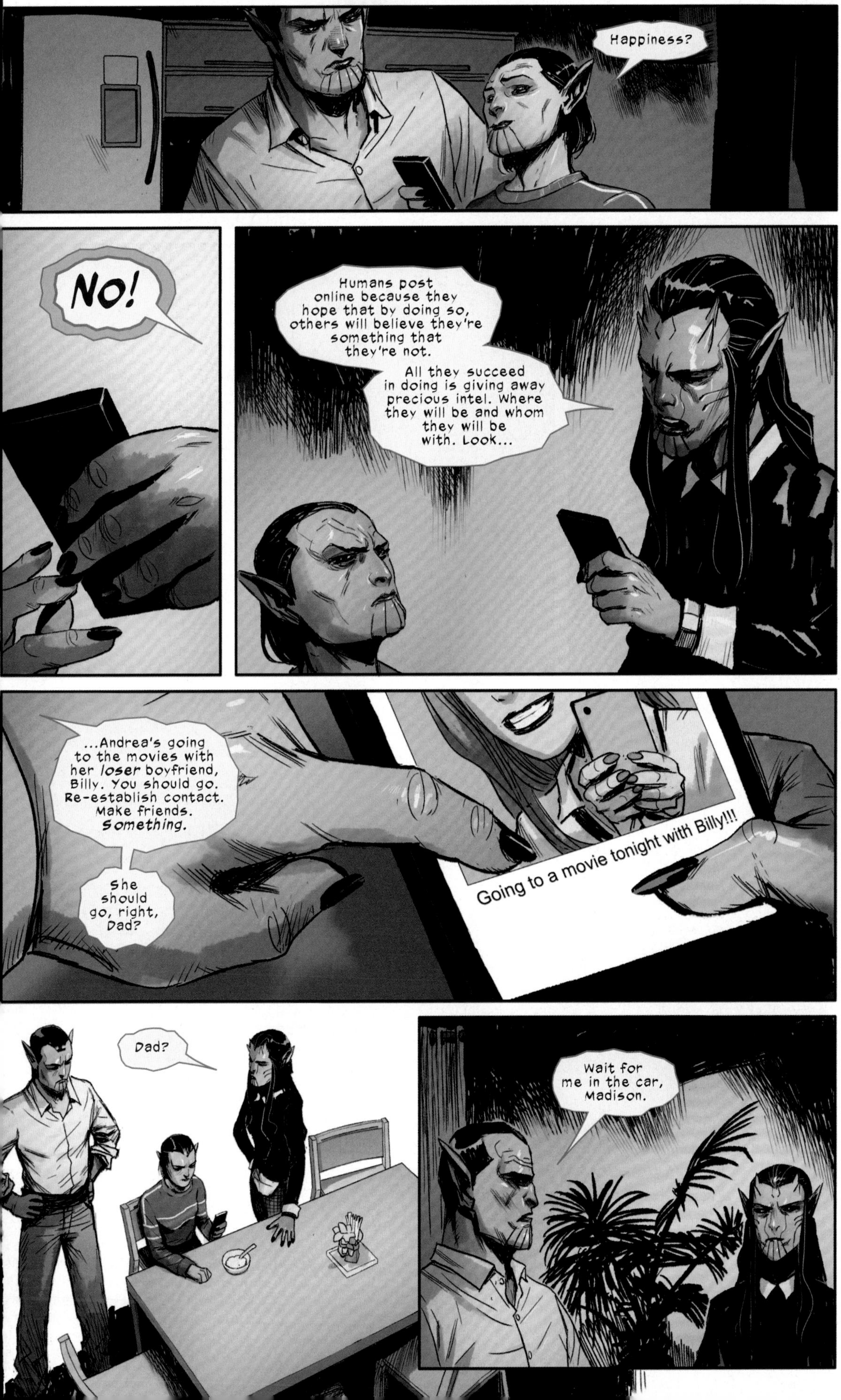
Happiness?
NO!
Humans post online because they hope that by doing so, others will believe they're something that they're not.
All they succeed in doing is giving away precious intel. Where they will be and whom they will be with. Look...
...Andrea's going to the movies with her *loser* boyfriend, Billy. You should go. Re-establish contact. Make friends. *Something.*
Going to a movie tonight with Billy!!!
She should go, right, Dad?
Dad?
Wait for me in the car, Madison.

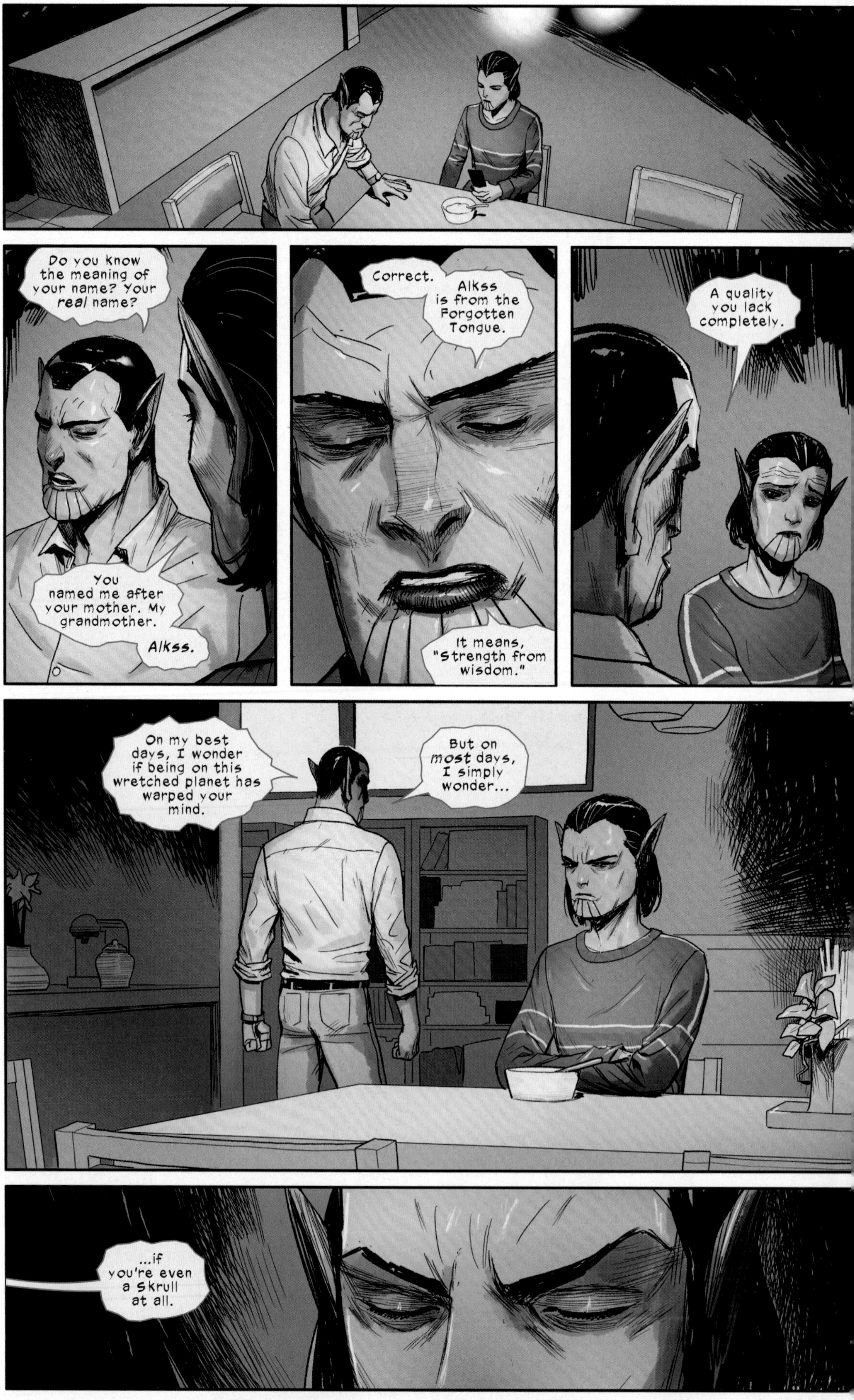

Do you know the meaning of your name? Your *real* name?
You named me after your mother. My grandmother.
Alkss.
Correct.
Alkss is from the Forgotten Tongue.
It means, "Strength from wisdom."
A quality you lack completely.
On my best days, I wonder if being on this wretched planet has warped your mind.
But on *most* days, I simply wonder...
...if you're even a Skrull at all.

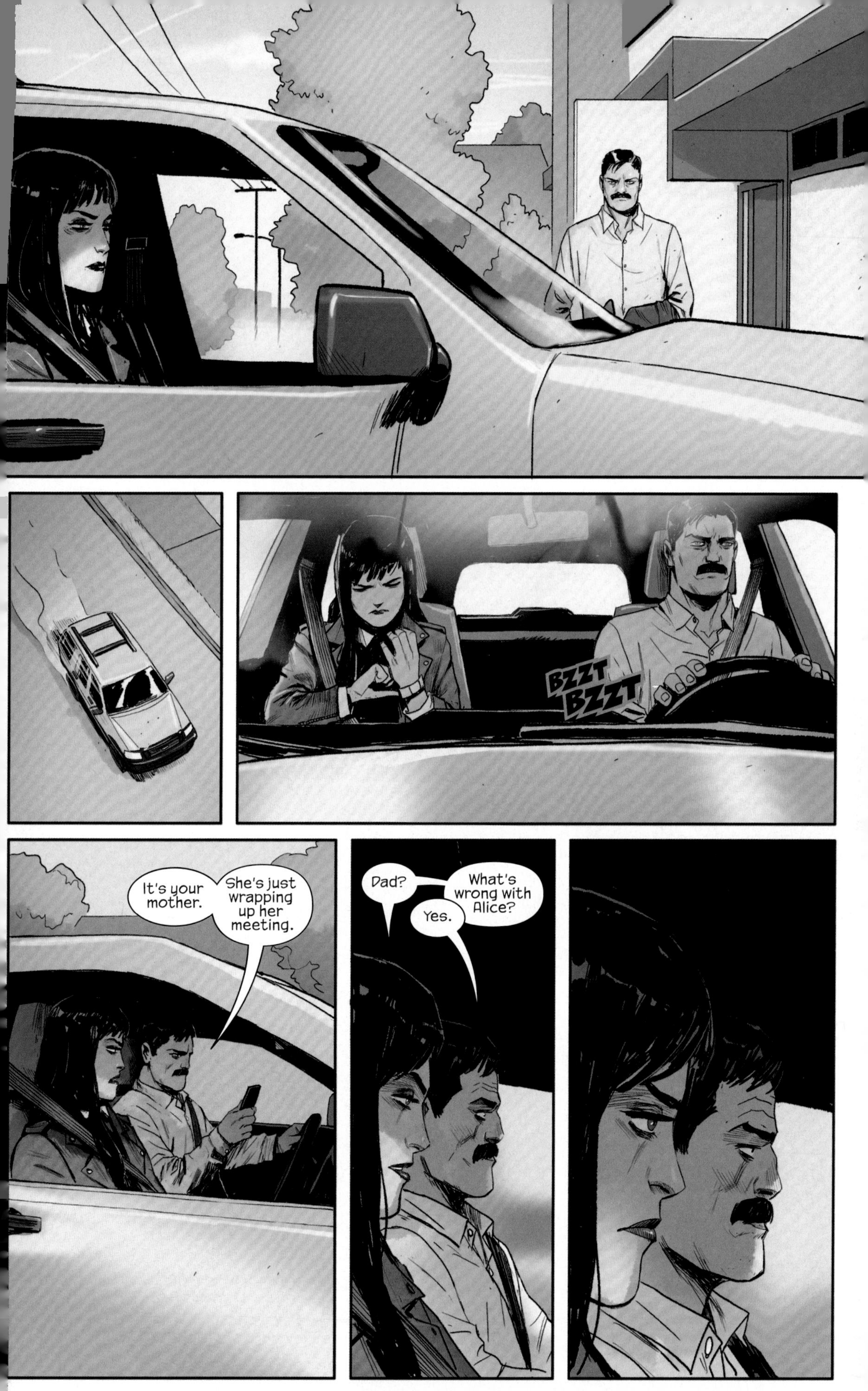
BZZT BZZT
It's your mother.
She's just wrapping up her meeting.
Dad?
What's wrong with Alice?
Yes.

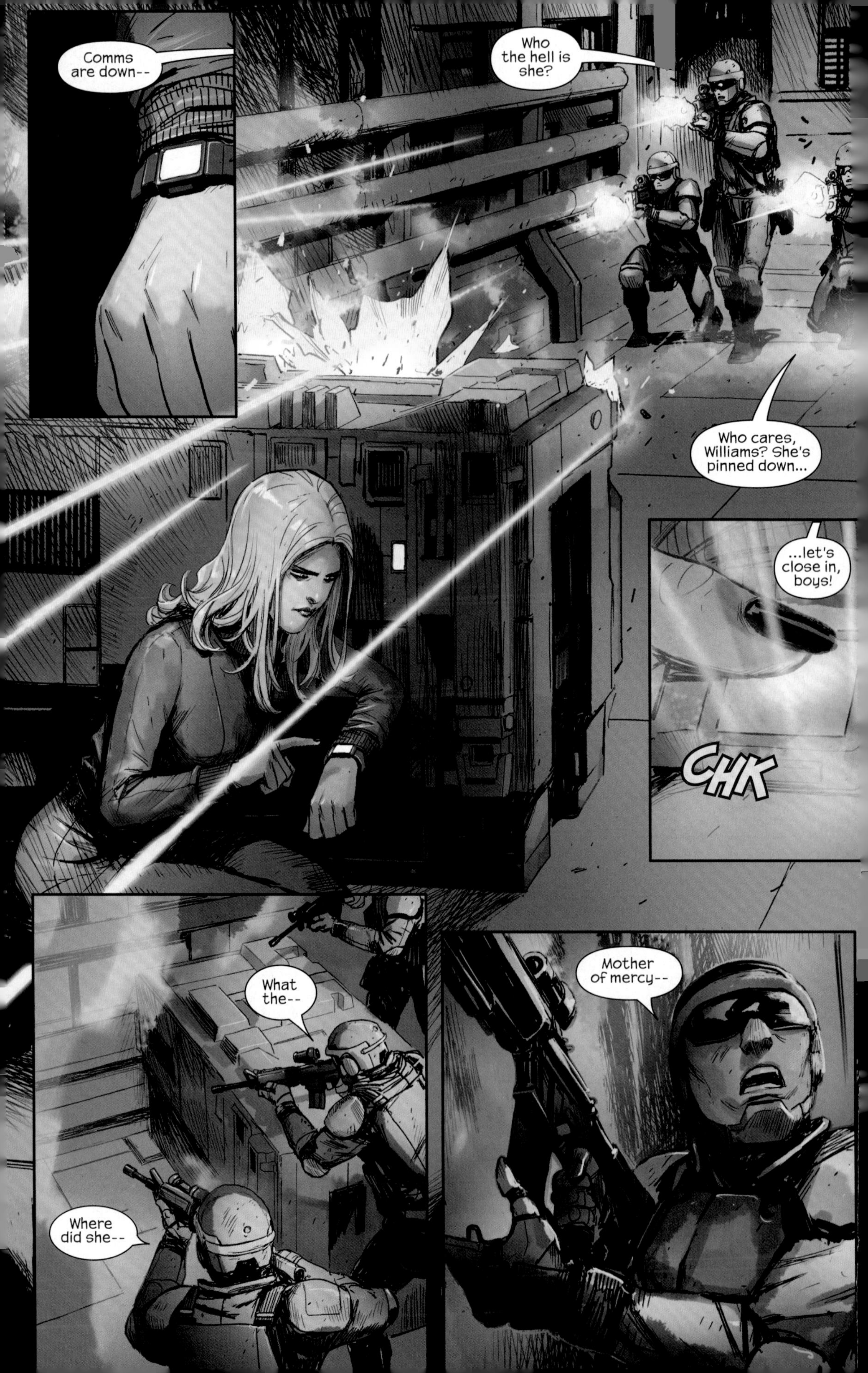
Comms are down--
Who the hell is she?
Who cares, Williams? She's pinned down...
...let's close in, boys!
CHK
What the--
Where did she--
Mother of mercy--

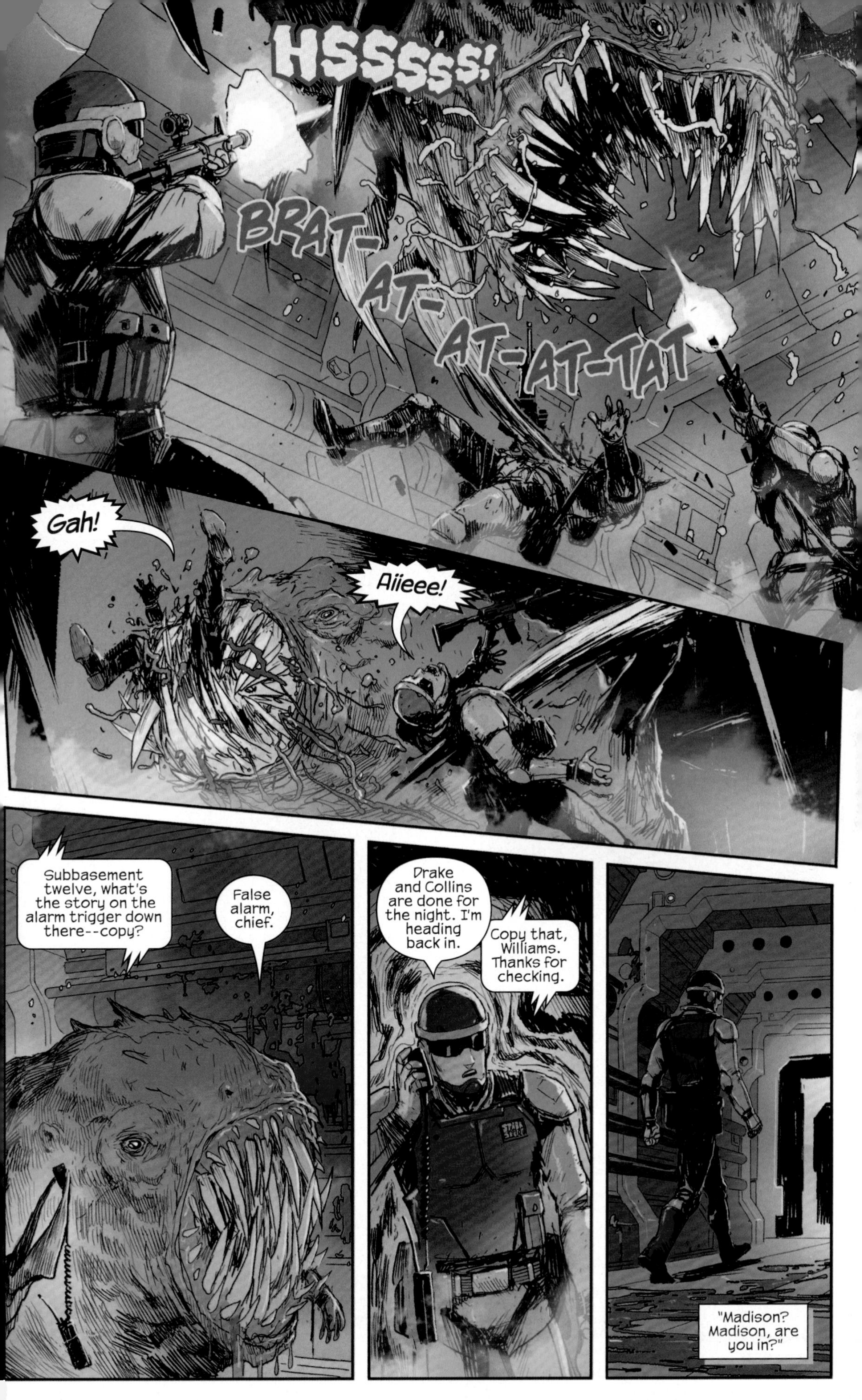
HSSSSSS!
BRAT-AT-AT-AT-TAT
Gah!
Aiieee!
Subbasement twelve, what's the story on the alarm trigger down there--copy?
False alarm, chief.
Drake and Collins are done for the night. I'm heading back in.
Copy that, Williams. Thanks for checking.
"Madison? Madison, are you in?"

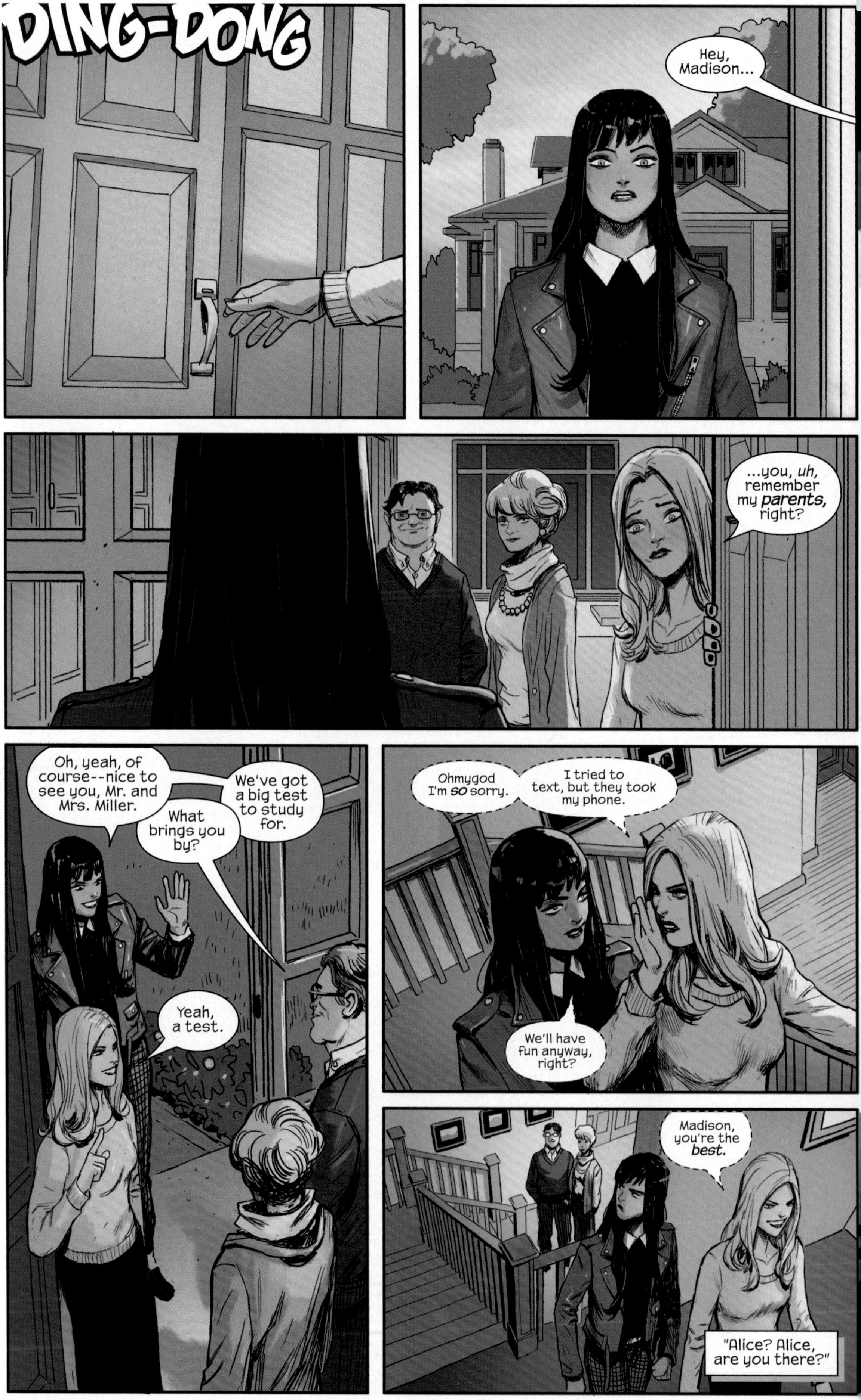
DING-DONG
Hey, Madison...
...you, uh, remember my parents, right?
Oh, yeah, of course--nice to see you, Mr. and Mrs. Miller.
What brings you by?
We've got a big test to study for.
Yeah, a test.
Ohmygod I'm SO sorry.
I tried to text, but they took my phone.
We'll have fun anyway, right?
Madison, you're the best.
"Alice? Alice, are you there?"

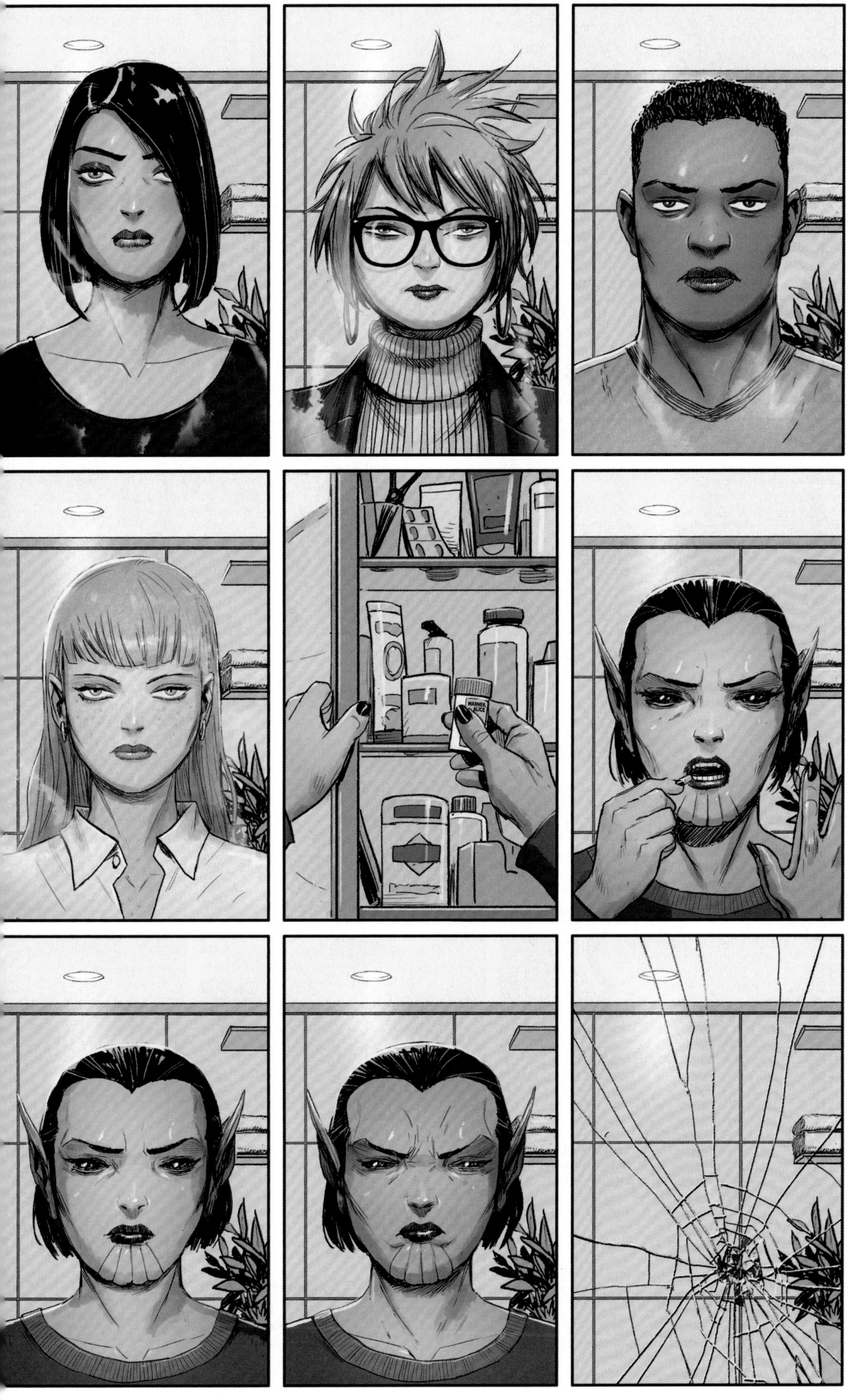
WARNER, ALICE

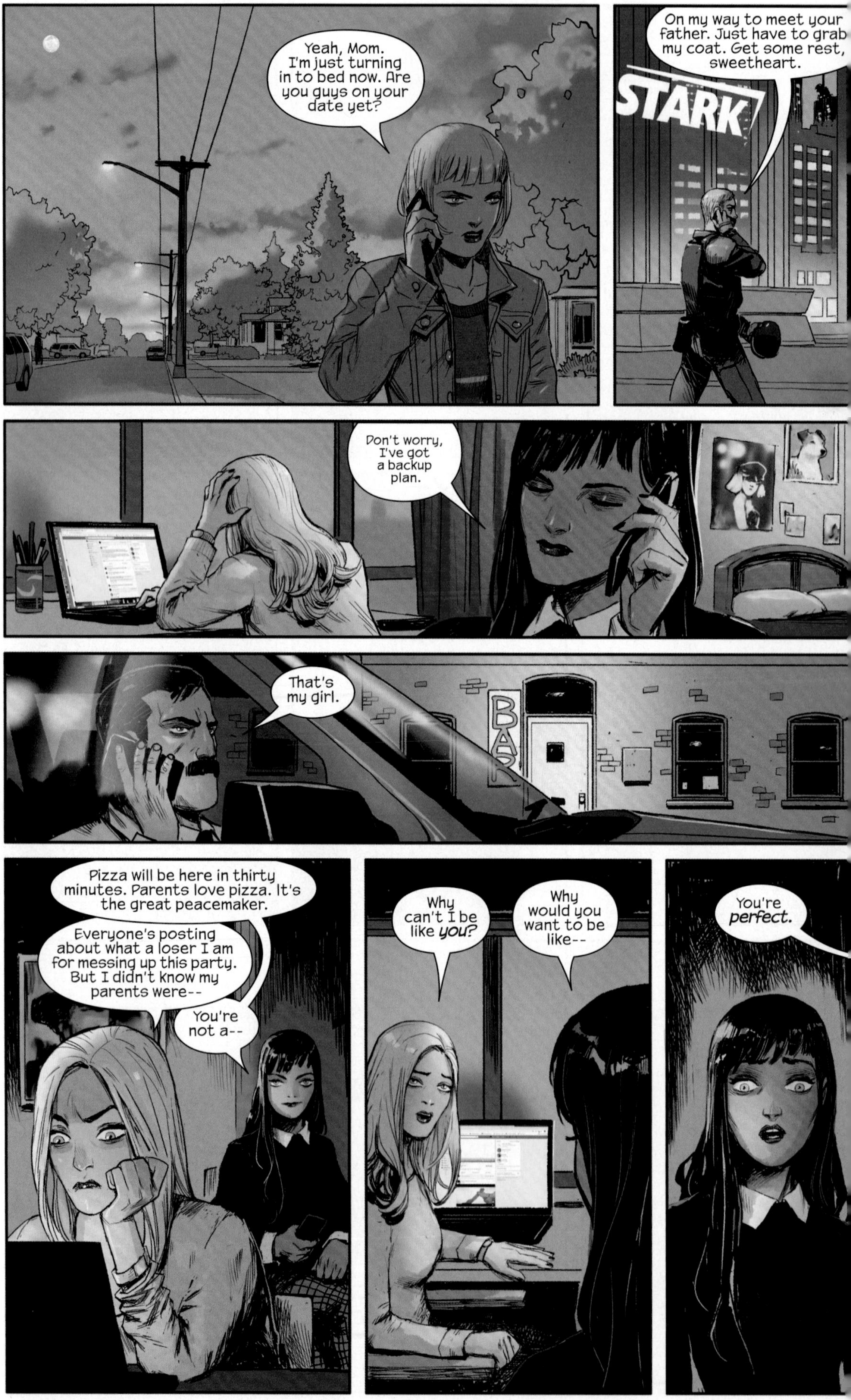
Yeah, Mom. I'm just turning in to bed now. Are you guys on your date yet?
On my way to meet your father. Just have to grab my coat. Get some rest, sweetheart.
STARK
Don't worry, I've got a backup plan.
That's my girl.
BAR
Pizza will be here in thirty minutes. Parents love pizza. It's the great peacemaker.
Everyone's posting about what a loser I am for messing up this party. But I didn't know my parents were--
You're not a--
Why can't I be like *you*?
Why would you want to be like--
You're *perfect.*

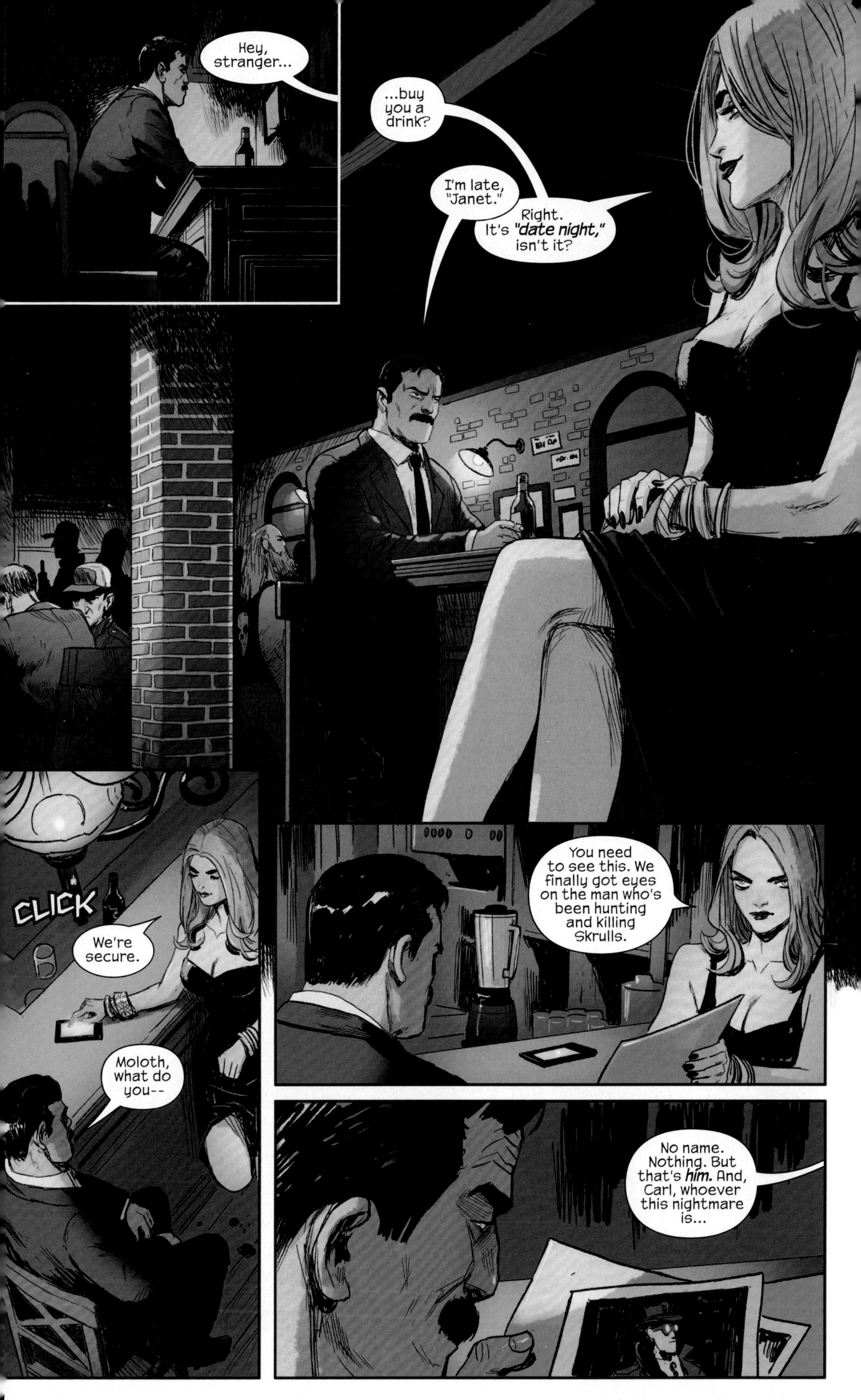

Hey, stranger...
...buy you a drink?
I'm late, "Janet."
Right. It's ***"date night,"*** isn't it?
CLICK
We're secure.
Moloth, what do you--
You need to see this. We finally got eyes on the man who's been hunting and killing Skrulls.
No name. Nothing. But that's ***him.*** And, Carl, whoever this nightmare is...

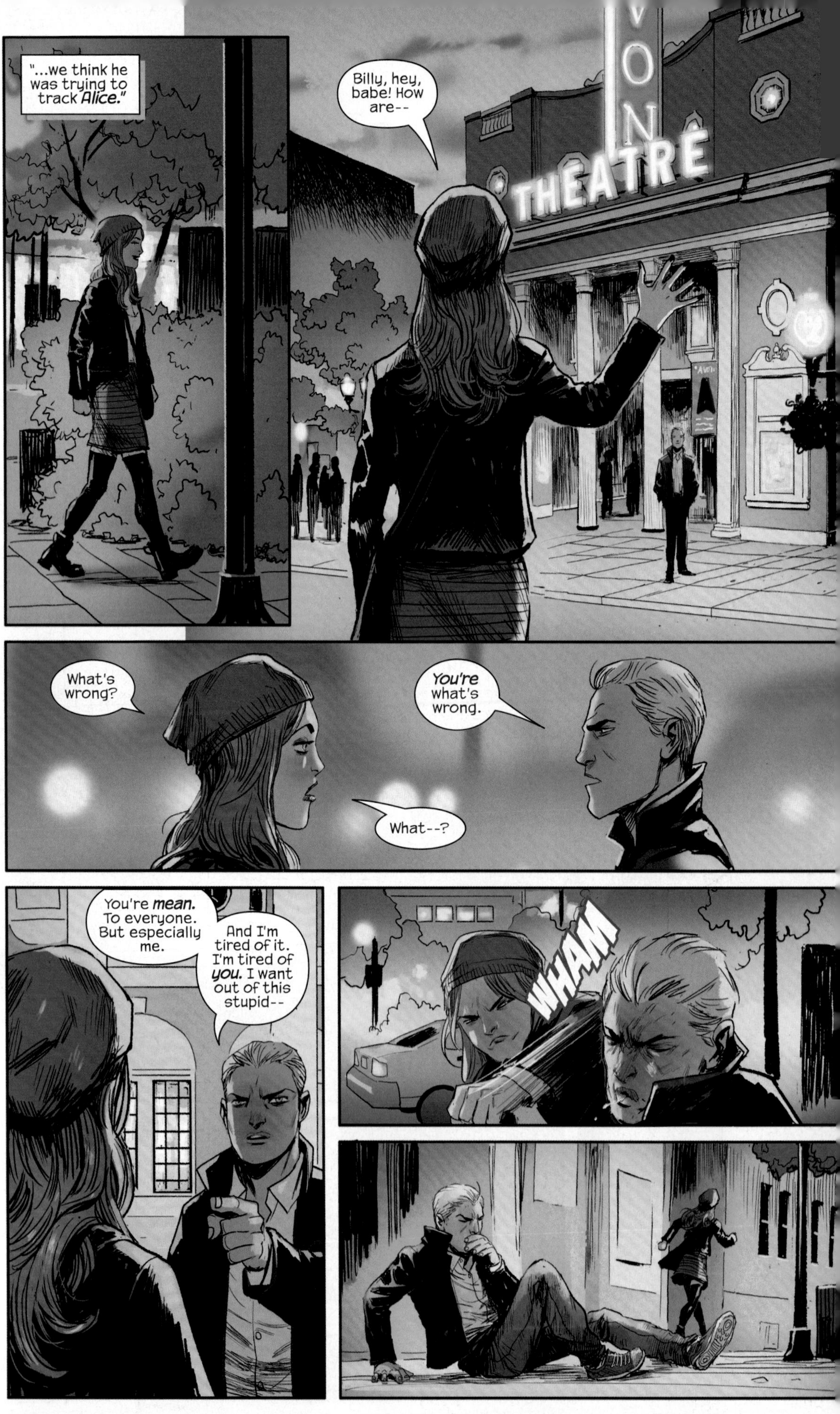
"...we think he was trying to track Alice."
Billy, hey, babe! How are--
VON
THEATRE
What's wrong?
You're what's wrong.
What--?
You're mean. To everyone. But especially me.
And I'm tired of it. I'm tired of you. I want out of this stupid--
WHAM

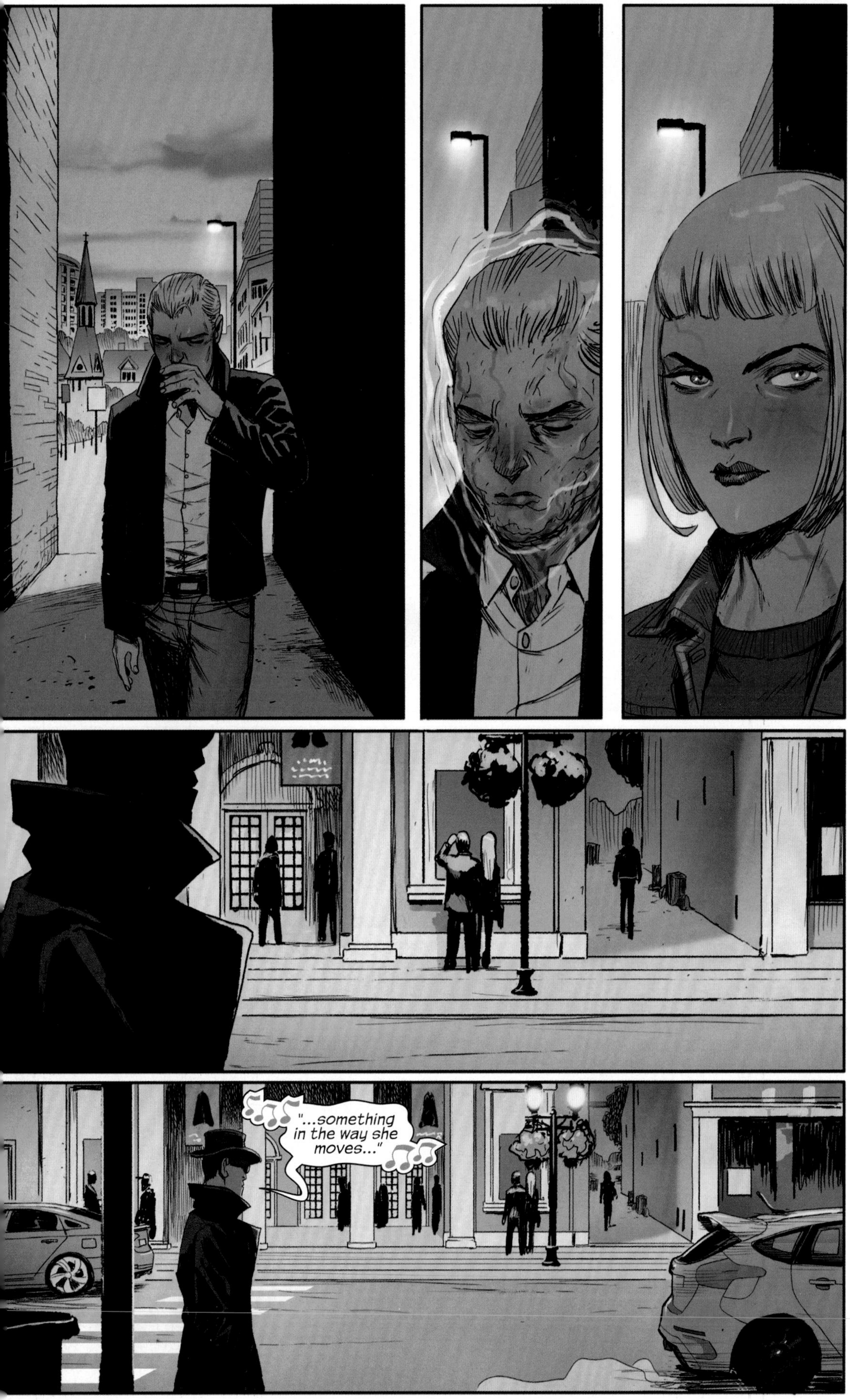
"...something in the way she moves..."

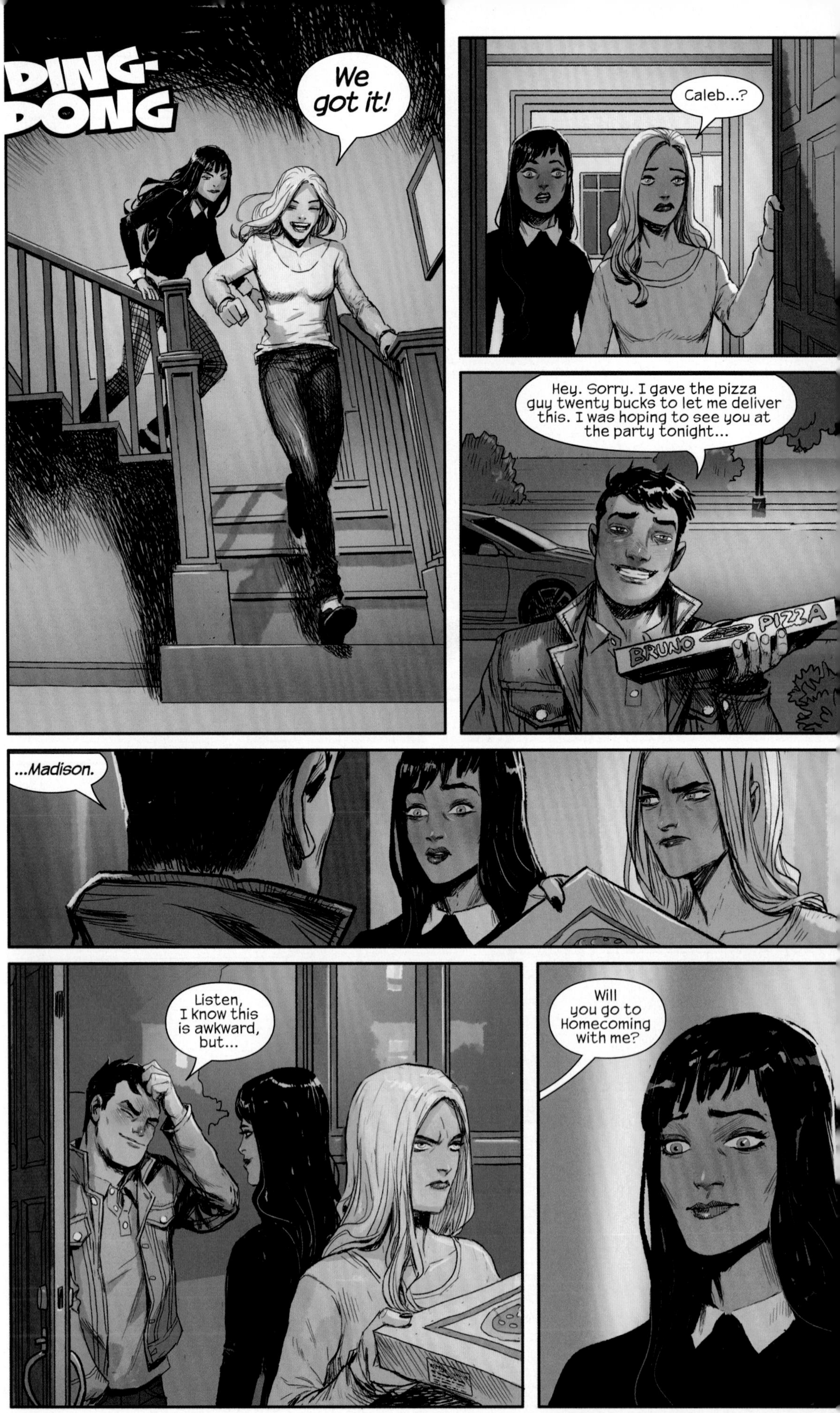
DING-DONG
We got it!
Caleb...?
Hey. Sorry. I gave the pizza guy twenty bucks to let me deliver this. I was hoping to see you at the party tonight...
BRUNO PIZZA
...Madison.
Listen, I know this is awkward, but...
Will you go to Homecoming with me?

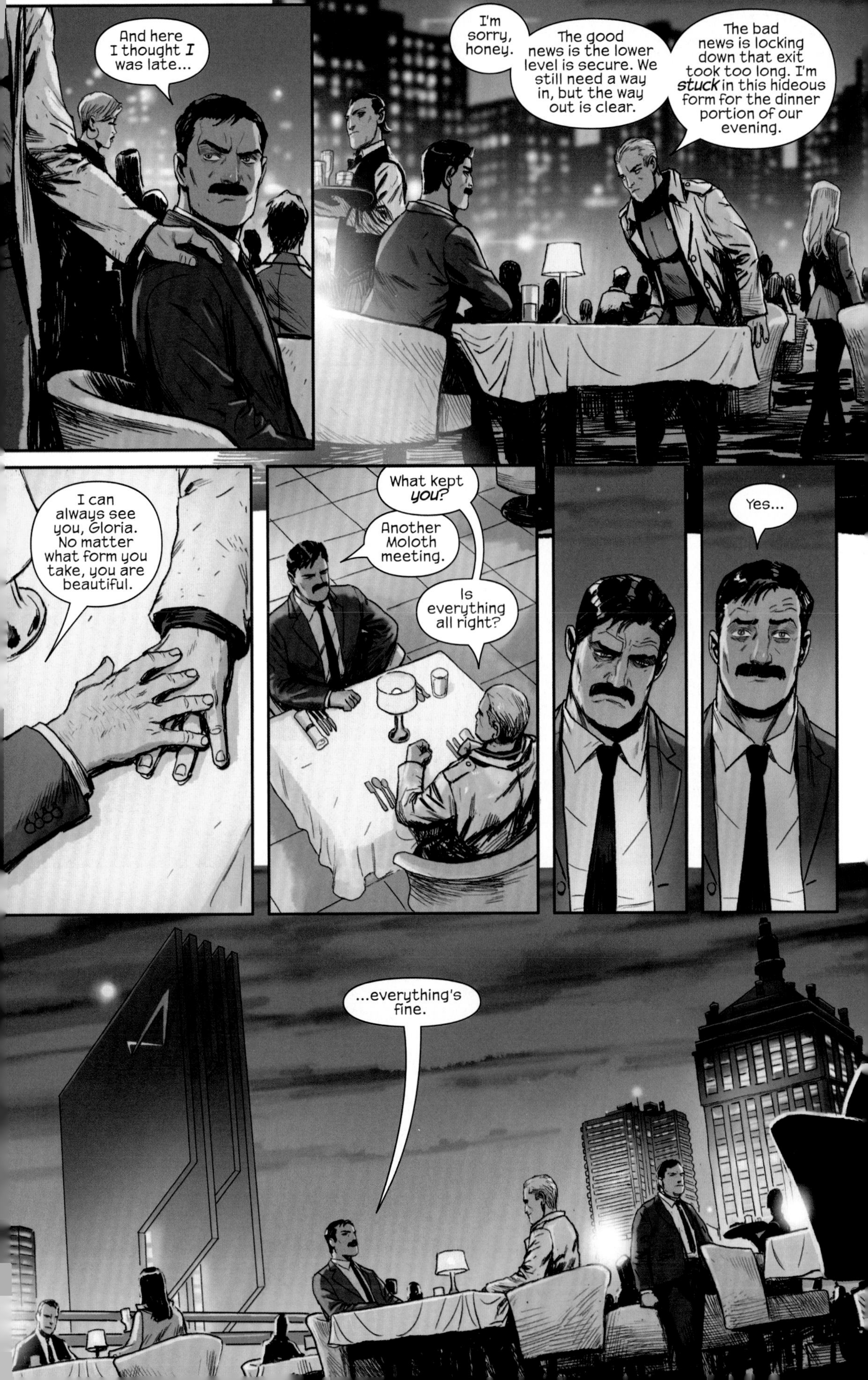
And here I thought I was late...
I'm sorry, honey.
The good news is the lower level is secure. We still need a way in, but the way out is clear.
The bad news is locking down that exit took too long. I'm stuck in this hideous form for the dinner portion of our evening.
I can always see you, Gloria. No matter what form you take, you are beautiful.
What kept you?
Another Moloth meeting.
Is everything all right?
Yes...
...everything's fine.

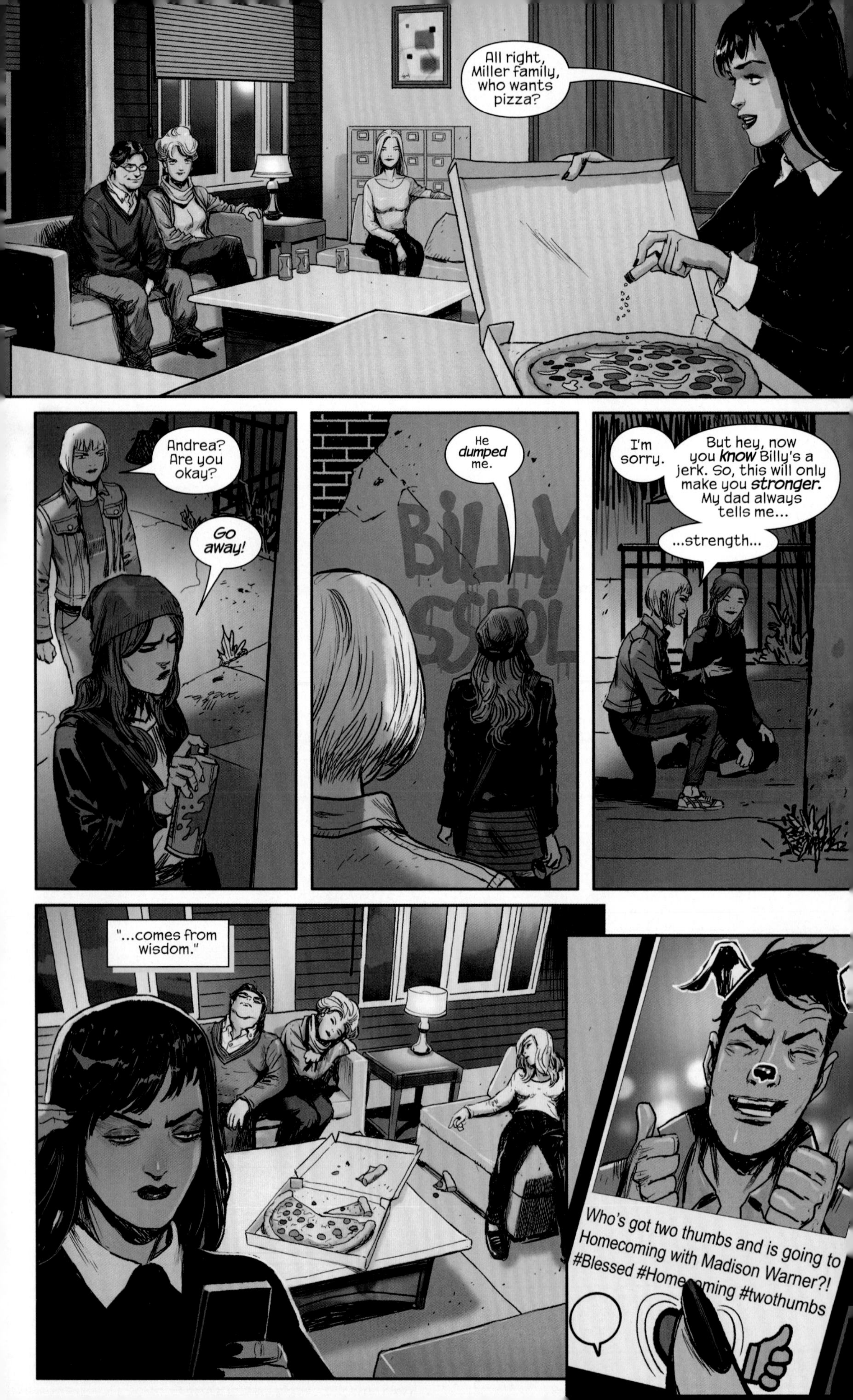
All right, Miller family, who wants pizza?
Andrea? Are you okay?
Go away!
He dumped me.
BILLY
SSHOL
I'm sorry.
But hey, now you know Billy's a jerk. So, this will only make you stronger. My dad always tells me...
...strength...
"...comes from wisdom."
Who's got two thumbs and is going to Homecoming with Madison Warner?! #Blessed #Homecoming #twothumbs

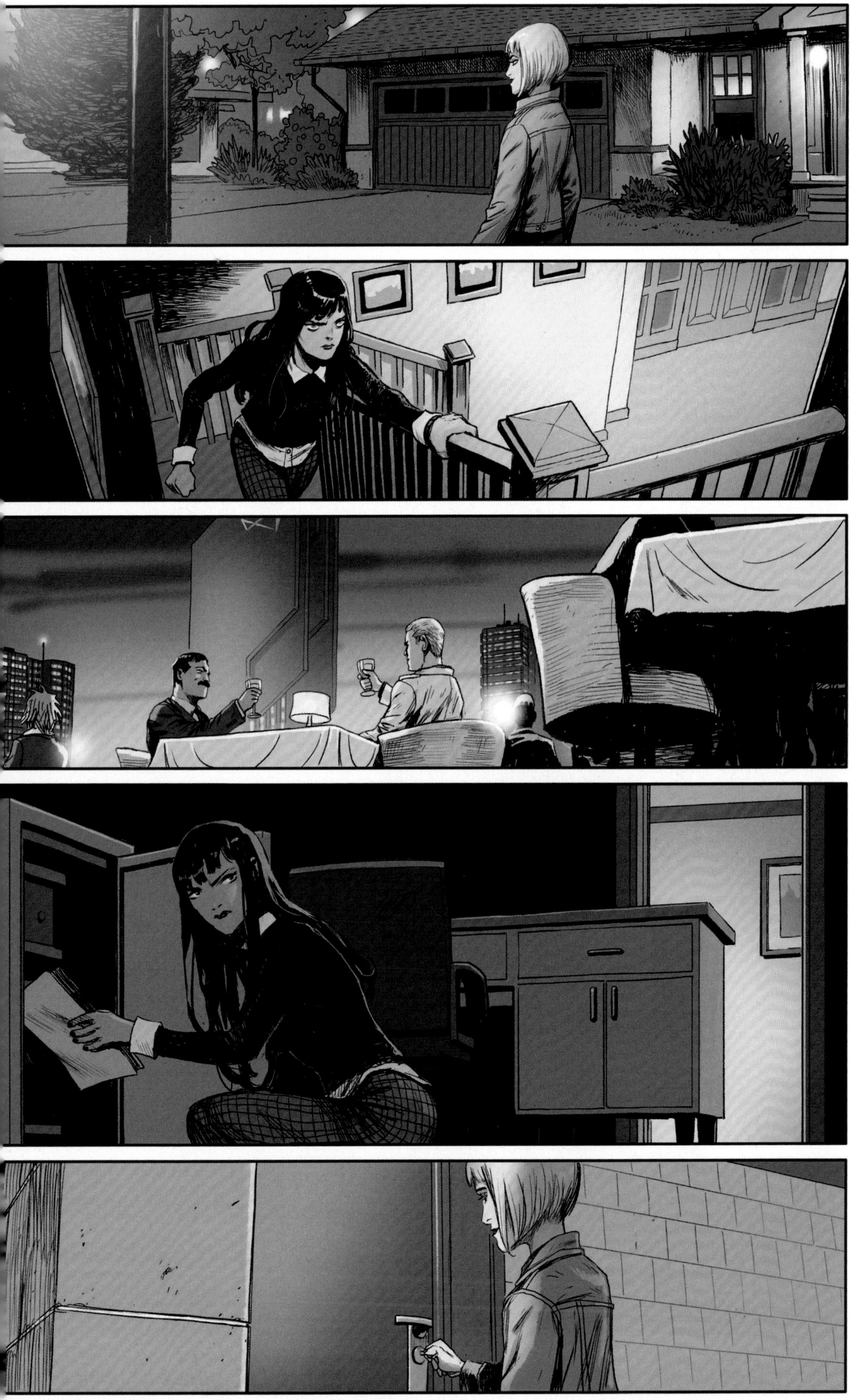

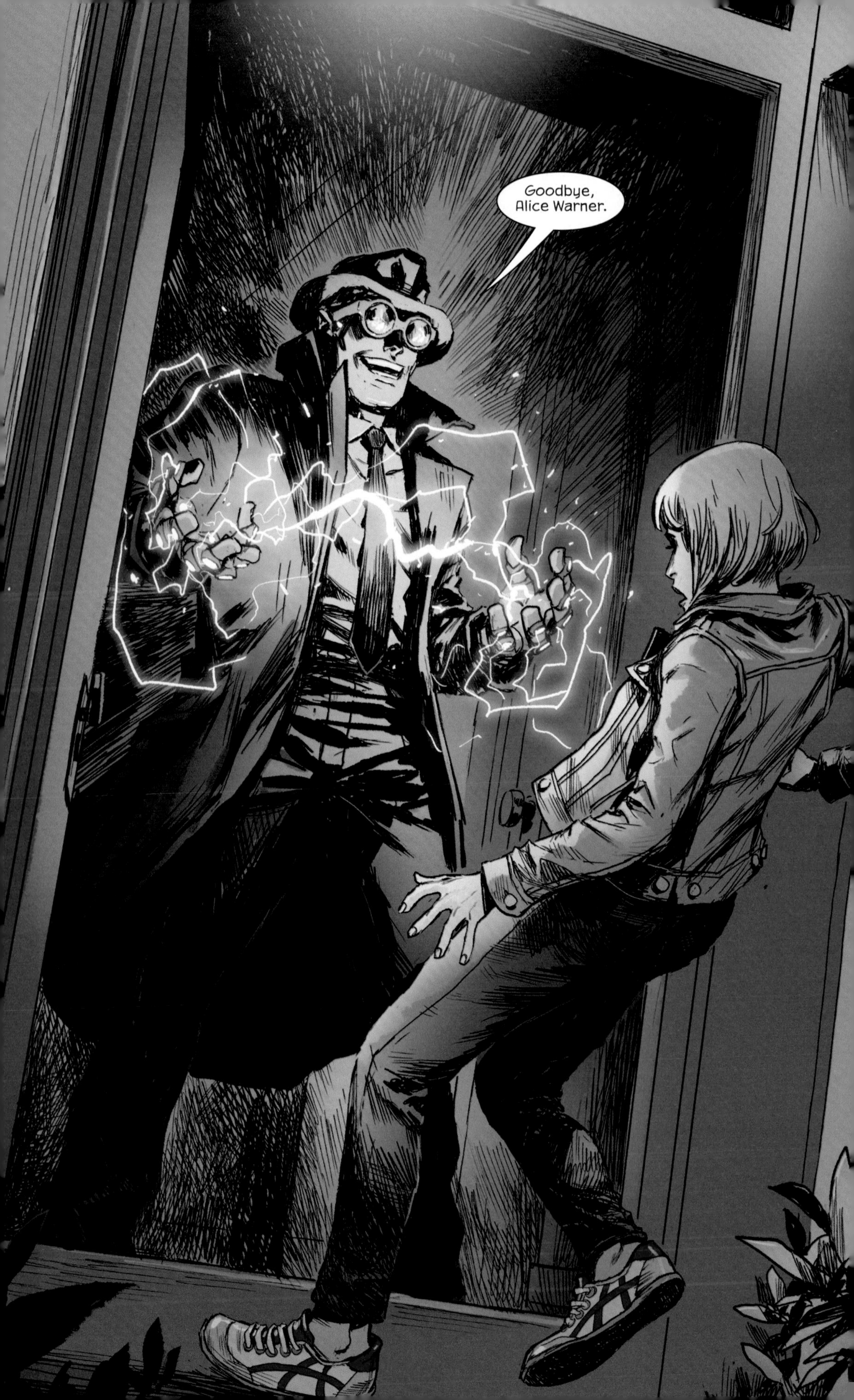
Goodbye, Alice Warner.

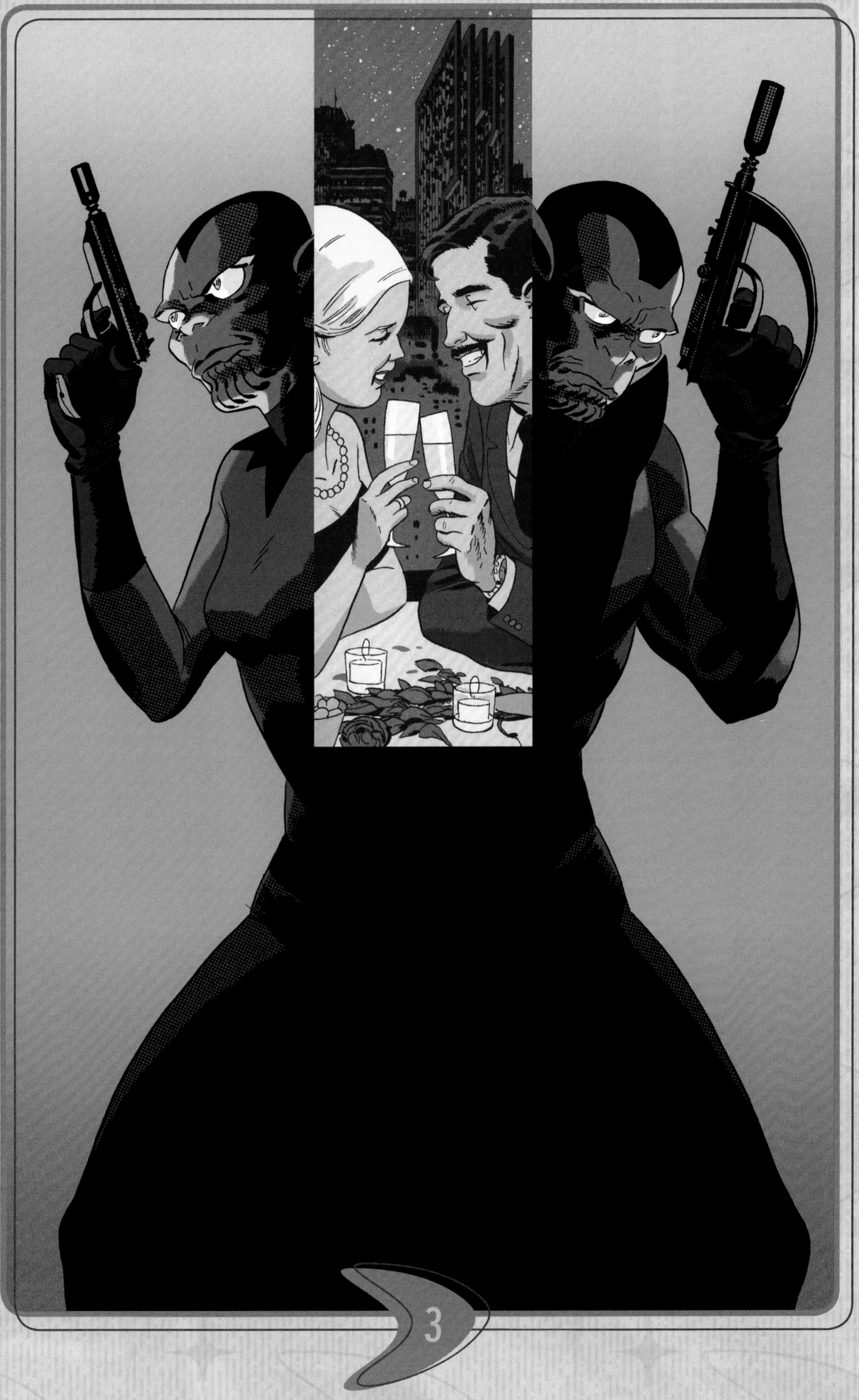

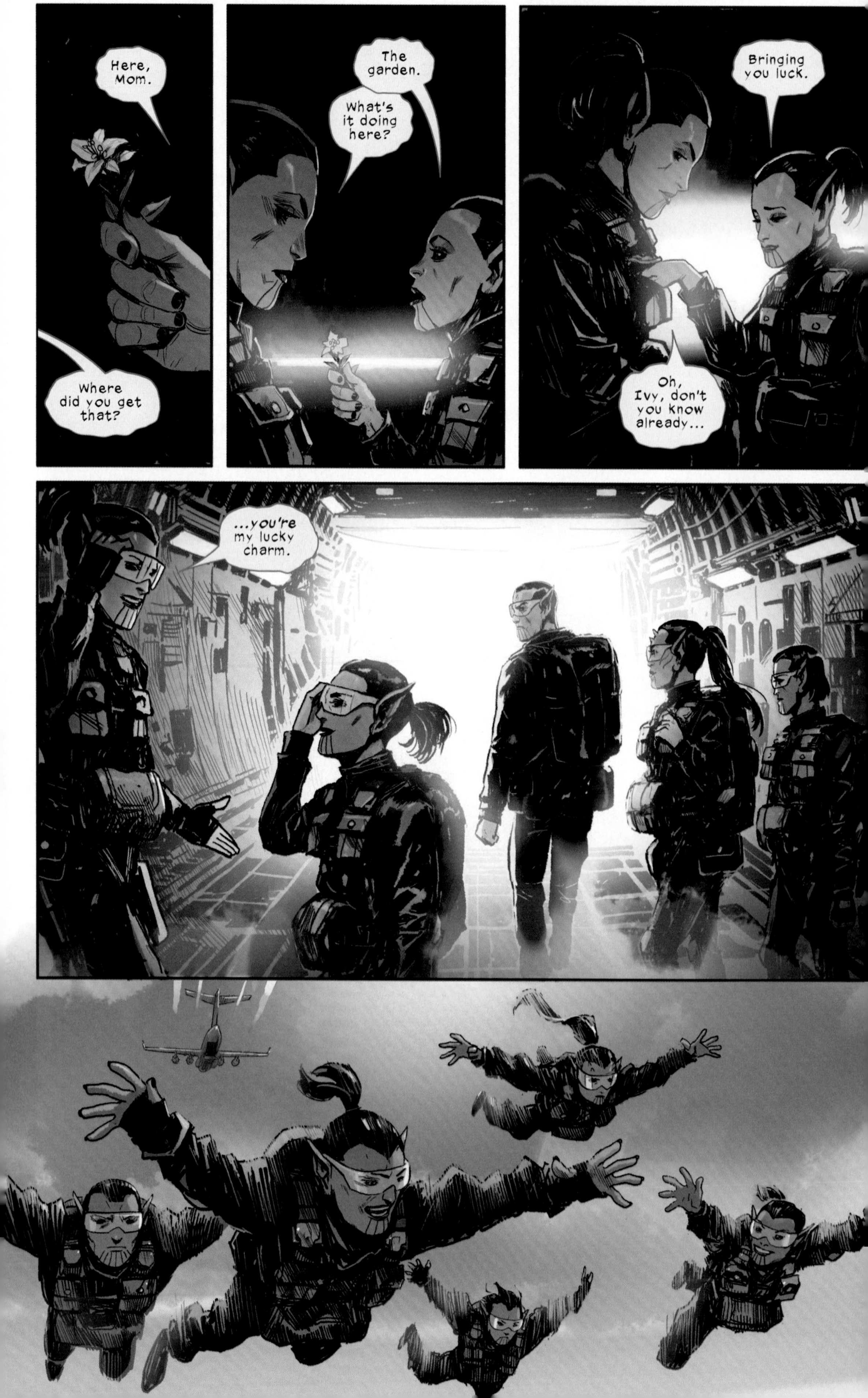
Here, Mom.
Where did you get that?
The garden.
What's it doing here?
Bringing you luck.
Oh, Ivy, don't you know already...
...you're my lucky charm.

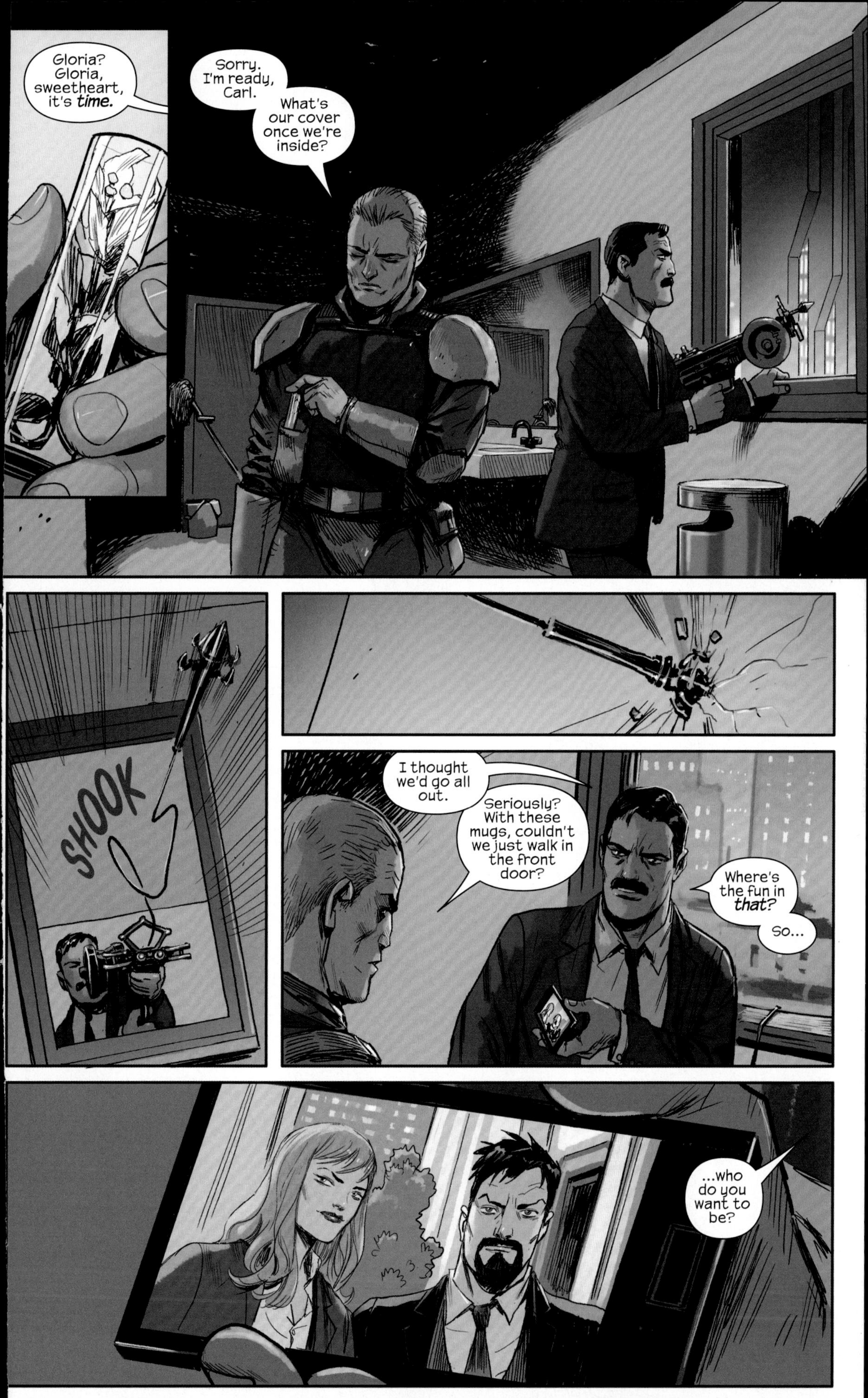
Gloria? Gloria, sweetheart, it's *time.*
Sorry. I'm ready, Carl.
What's our cover once we're inside?
SHOOK
I thought we'd go all out.
Seriously? With these mugs, couldn't we just walk in the front door?
Where's the fun in *that?*
So...
...who do you want to be?

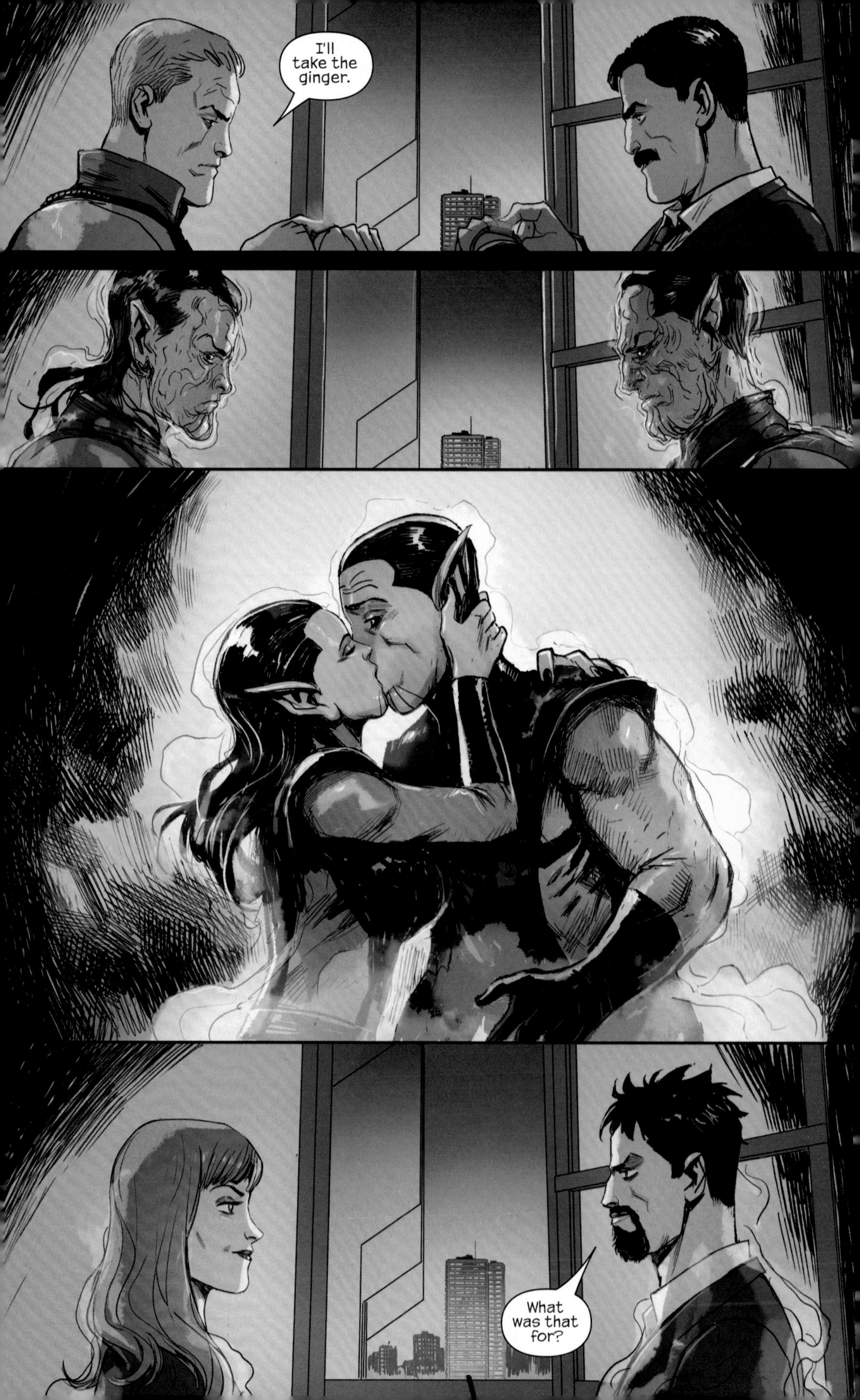
I'll take the ginger.
What was that for?

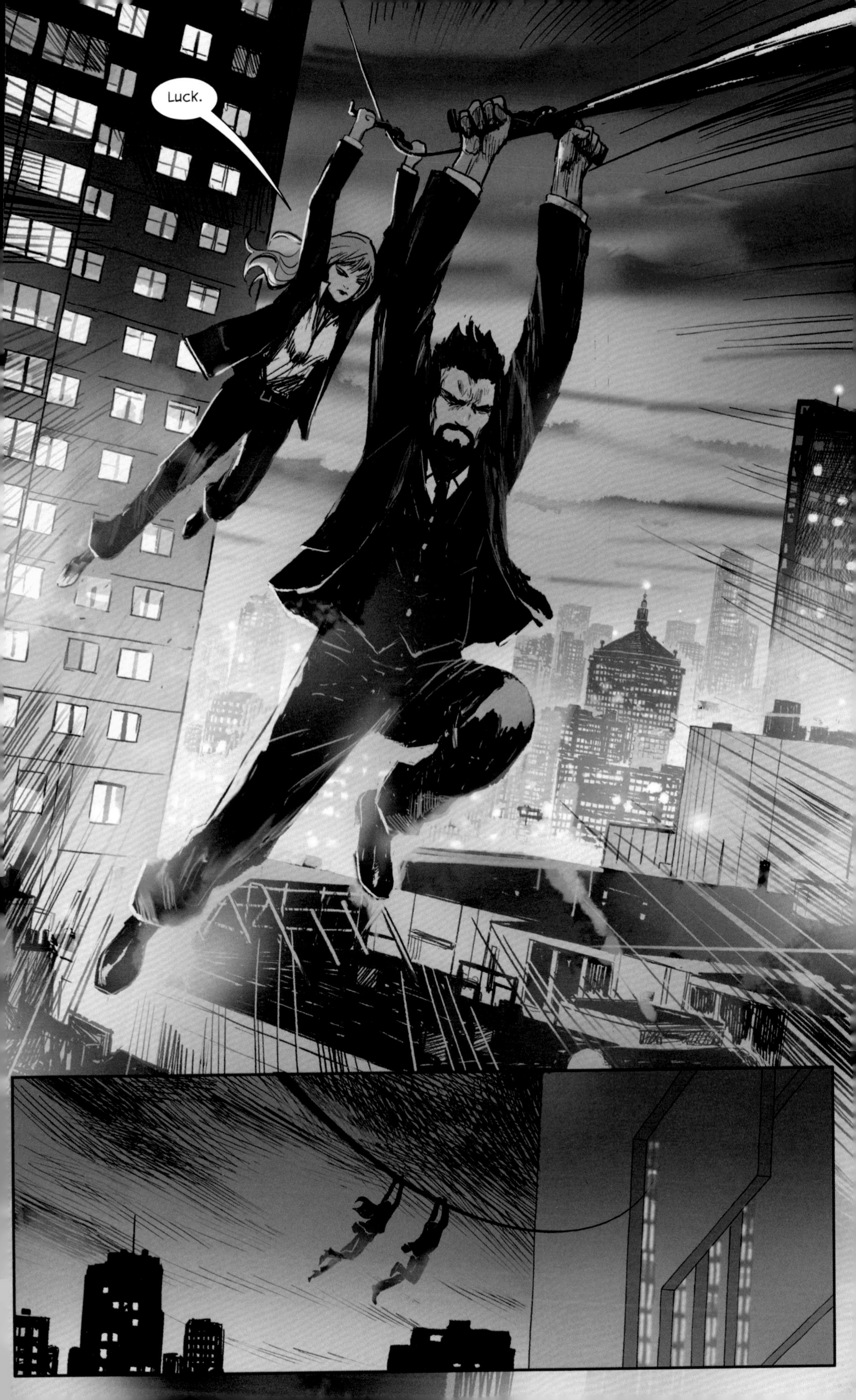
Luck.

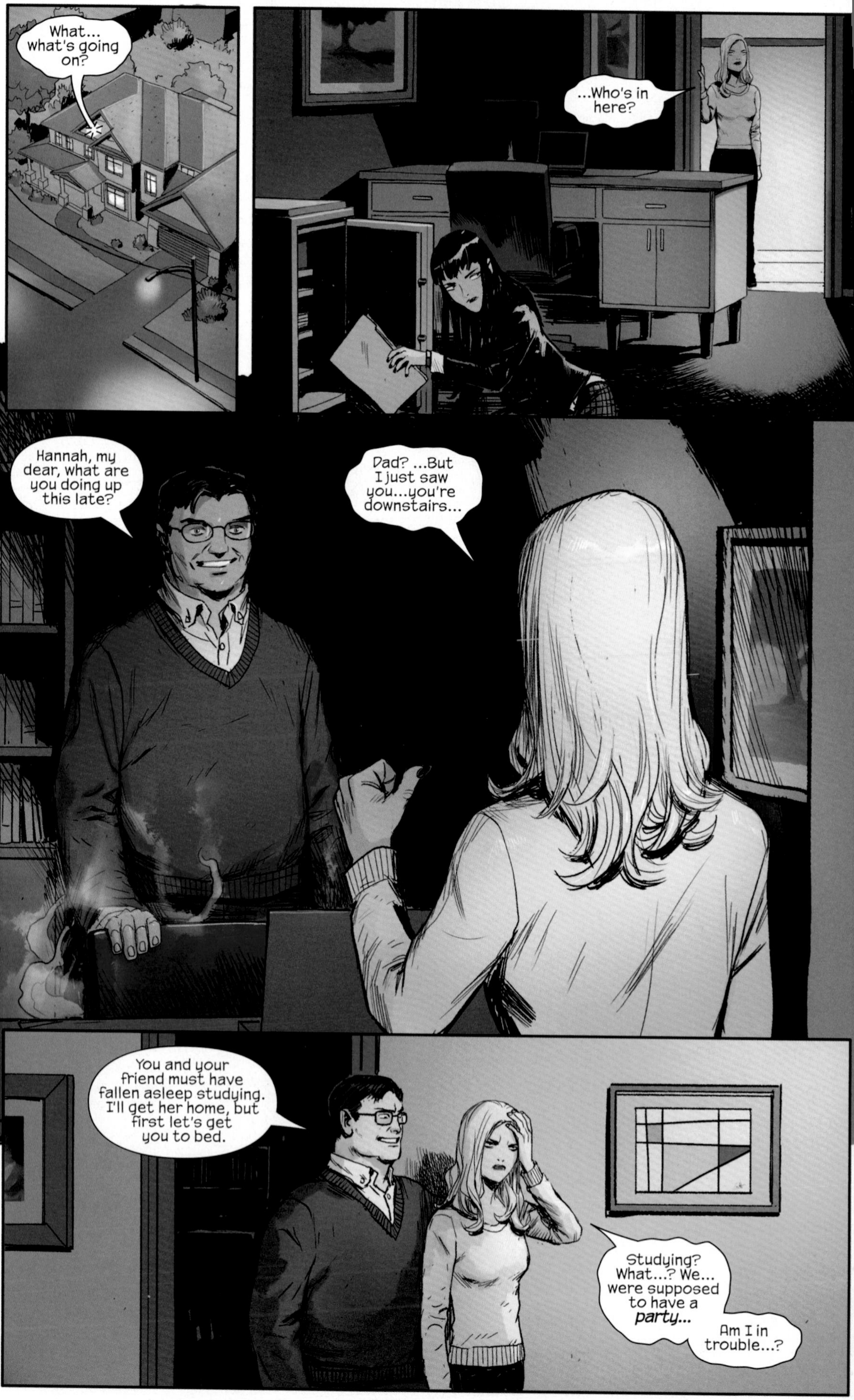

What... what's going on?
...Who's in here?
Hannah, my dear, what are you doing up this late?
Dad? ...But I just saw you...you're downstairs...
You and your friend must have fallen asleep studying. I'll get her home, but first let's get you to bed.
Studying? What...? We... were supposed to have a *party...*
Am I in trouble...?

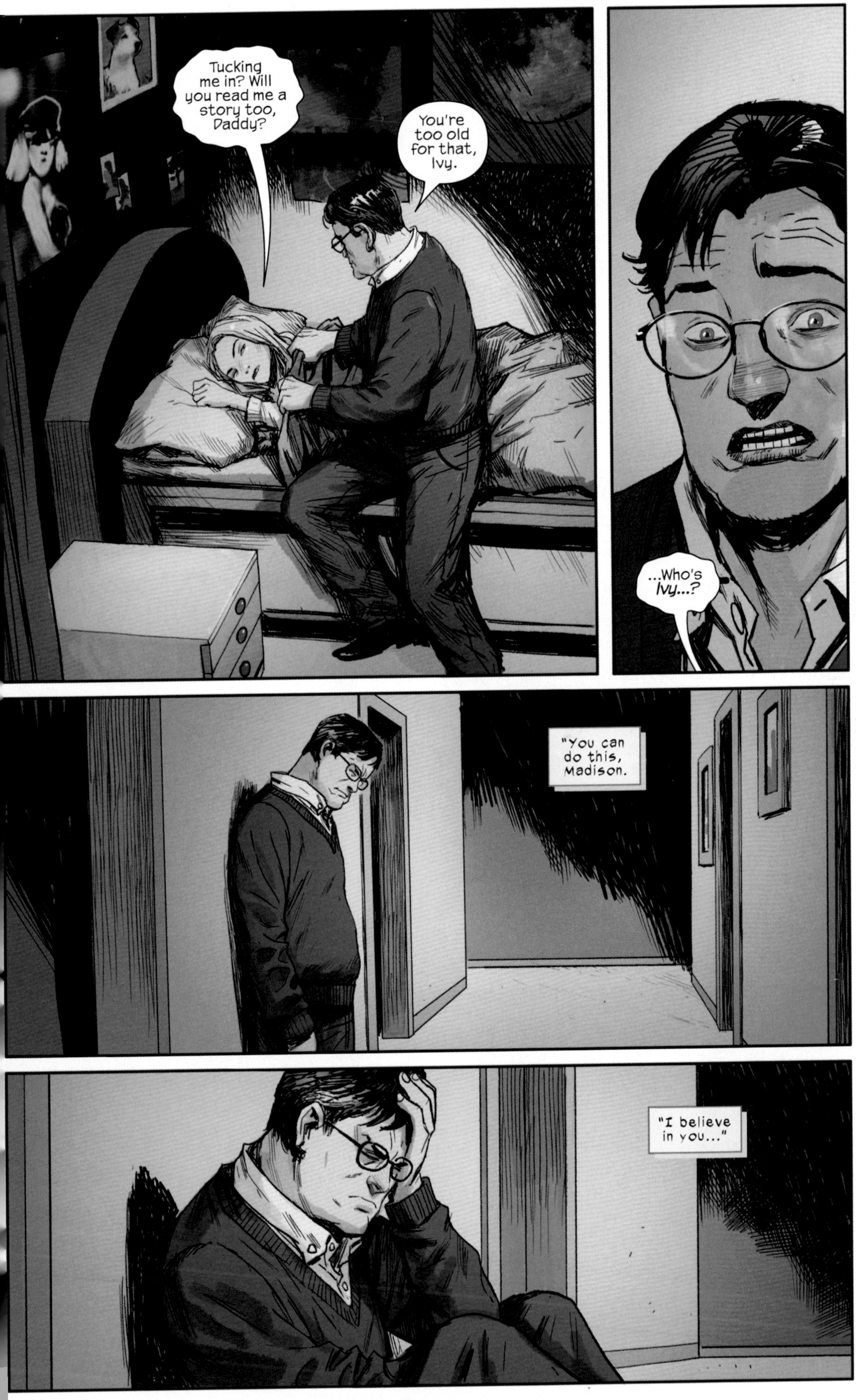
Tucking me in? Will you read me a story too, Daddy?
You're too old for that, Ivy.
...Who's Ivy...?
"You can do this, Madison.
"I believe in you..."

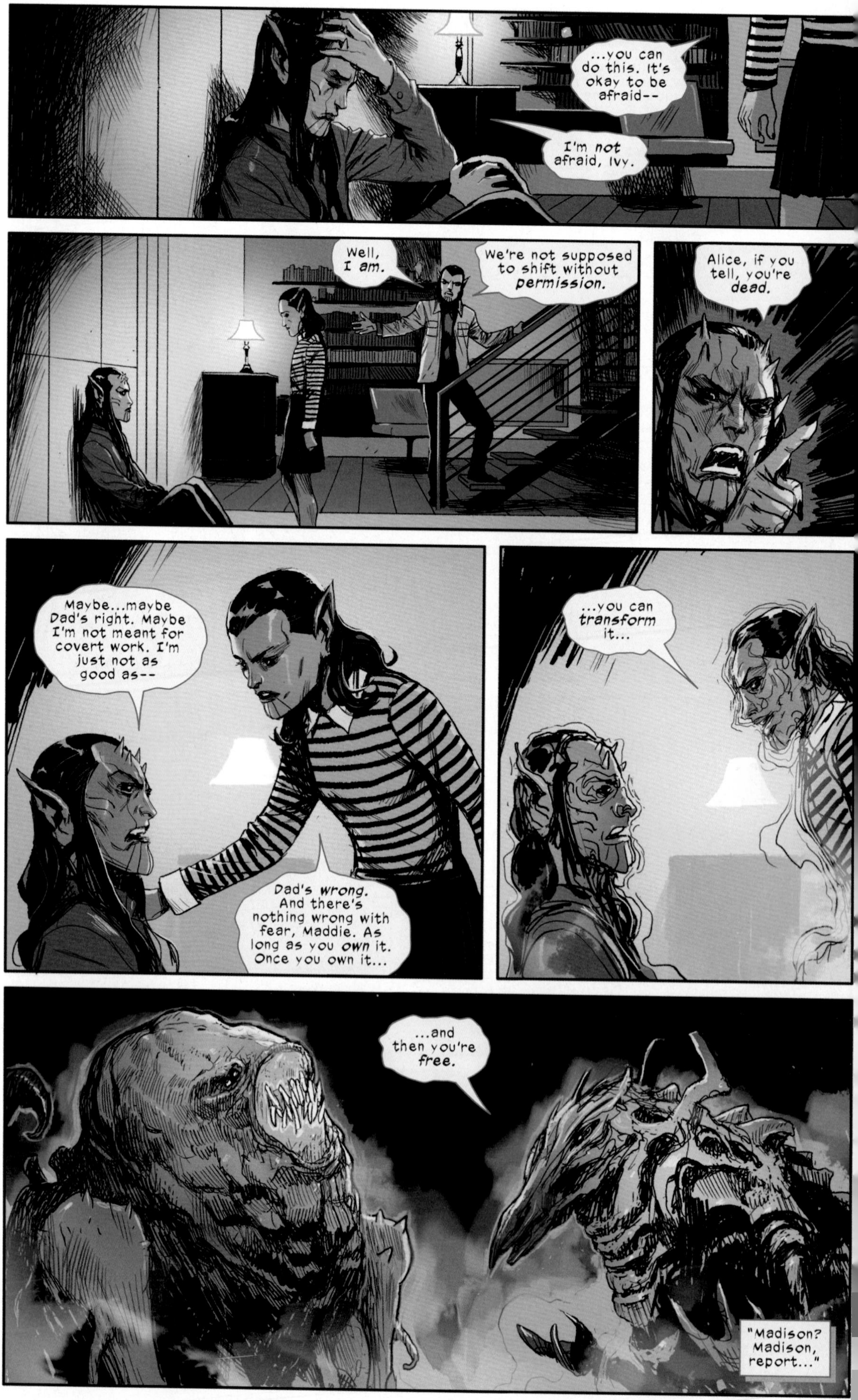
...you can do this. It's okay to be afraid--
I'm not afraid, Ivy.
Well, I am.
We're not supposed to shift without permission.
Alice, if you tell, you're dead.
Maybe...maybe Dad's right. Maybe I'm not meant for covert work. I'm just not as good as--
Dad's wrong. And there's nothing wrong with fear, Maddie. As long as you own it. Once you own it...
...you can transform it...
...and then you're free.
"Madison? Madison, report..."

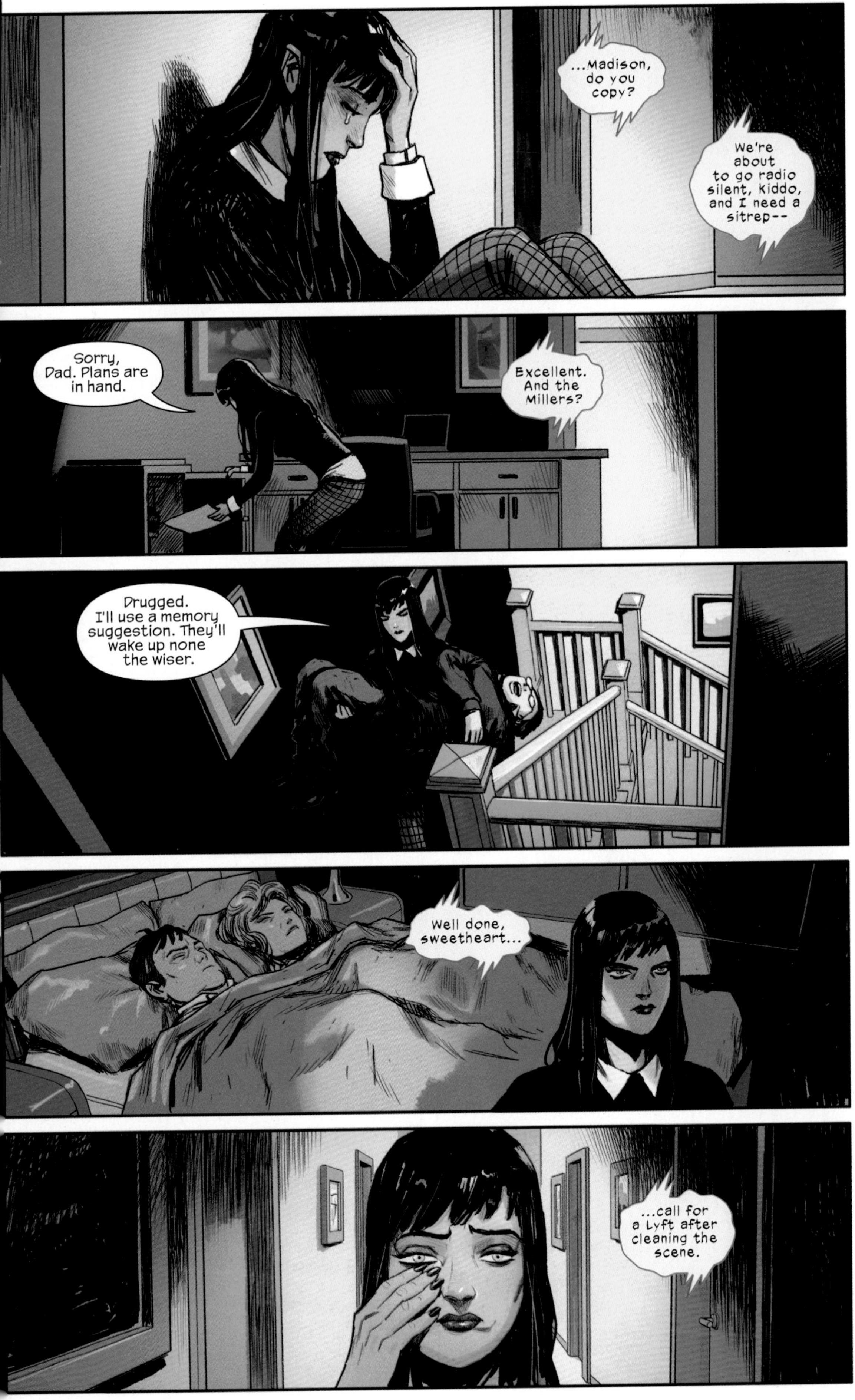
...Madison, do you copy?
We're about to go radio silent, kiddo, and I need a sitrep--
Sorry, Dad. Plans are in hand.
Excellent. And the Millers?
Drugged. I'll use a memory suggestion. They'll wake up none the wiser.
Well done, sweetheart...
...call for a Lyft after cleaning the scene.

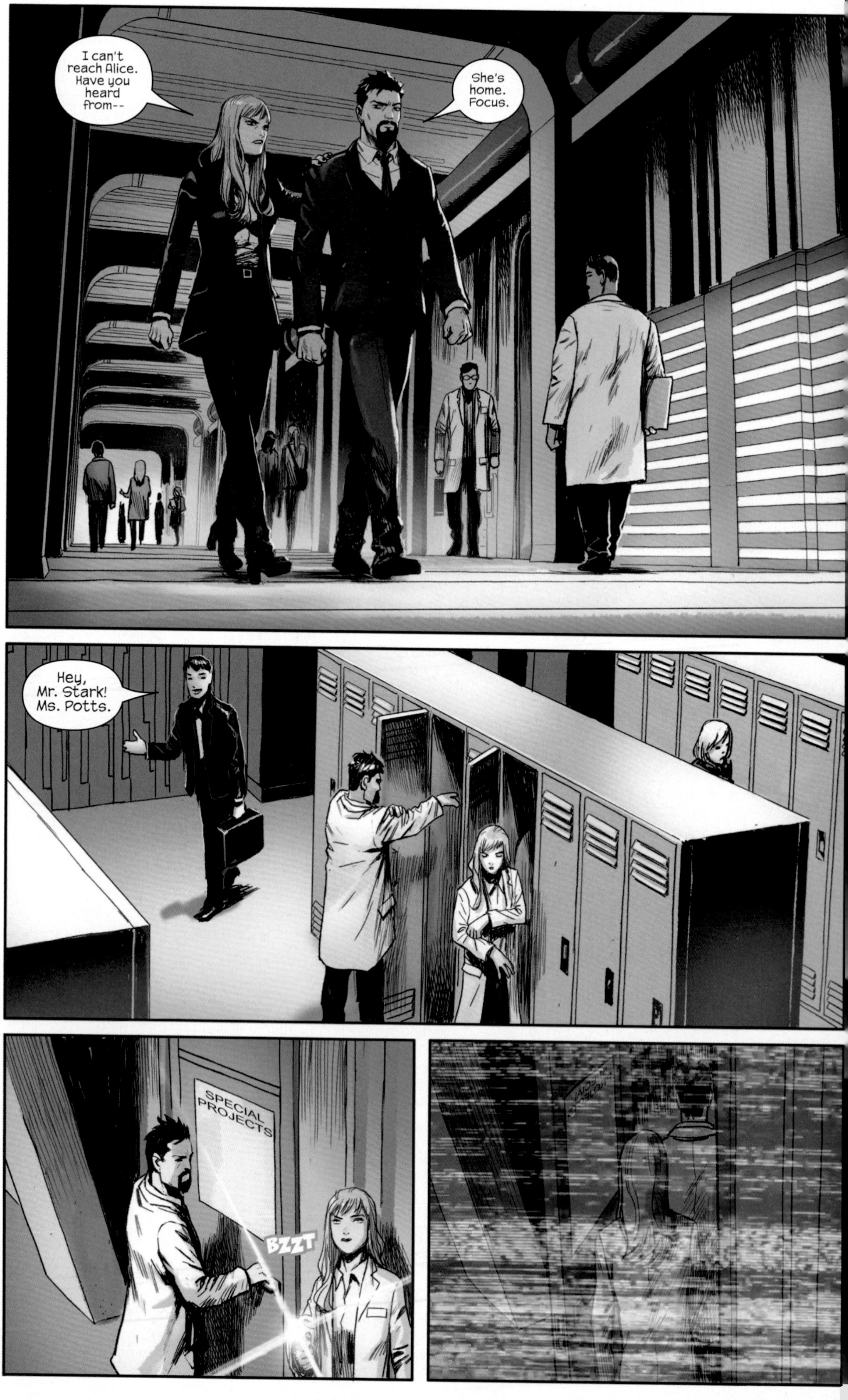
I can't reach Alice. Have you heard from--
She's home. Focus.
Hey, Mr. Stark! Ms. Potts.
SPECIAL PROJECTS
BZZT

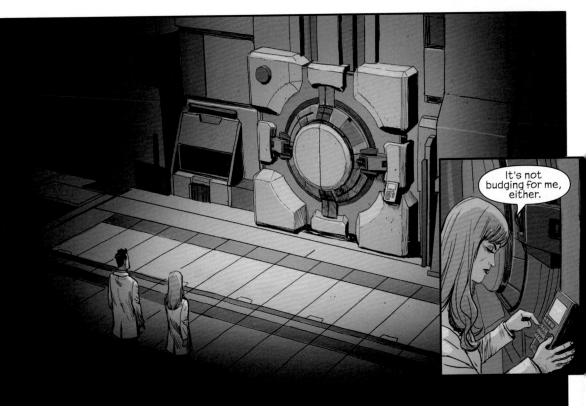

It's not budging for me, either.

Not even *Stark* can get in here?

How is that possible?

Who *knows* with him.

Fortunately, we have alternate ways in.

I'll be right back.

"Be right back, Daddy."

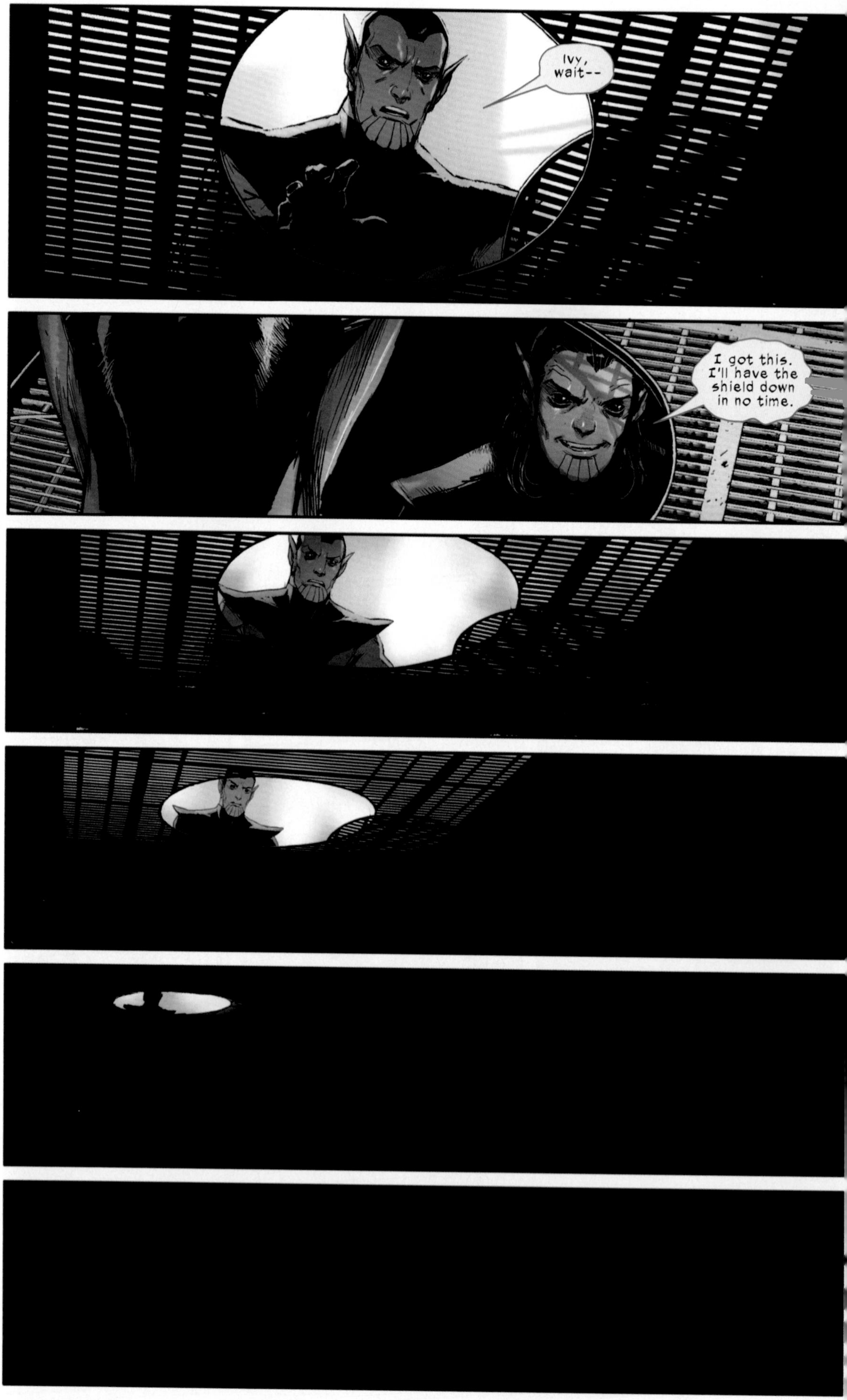
Ivy, wait--
I got this. I'll have the shield down in no time.

C'mon, open, you sonova--

Carl?

What the--

Skrulls?!

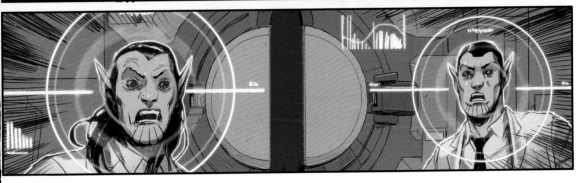

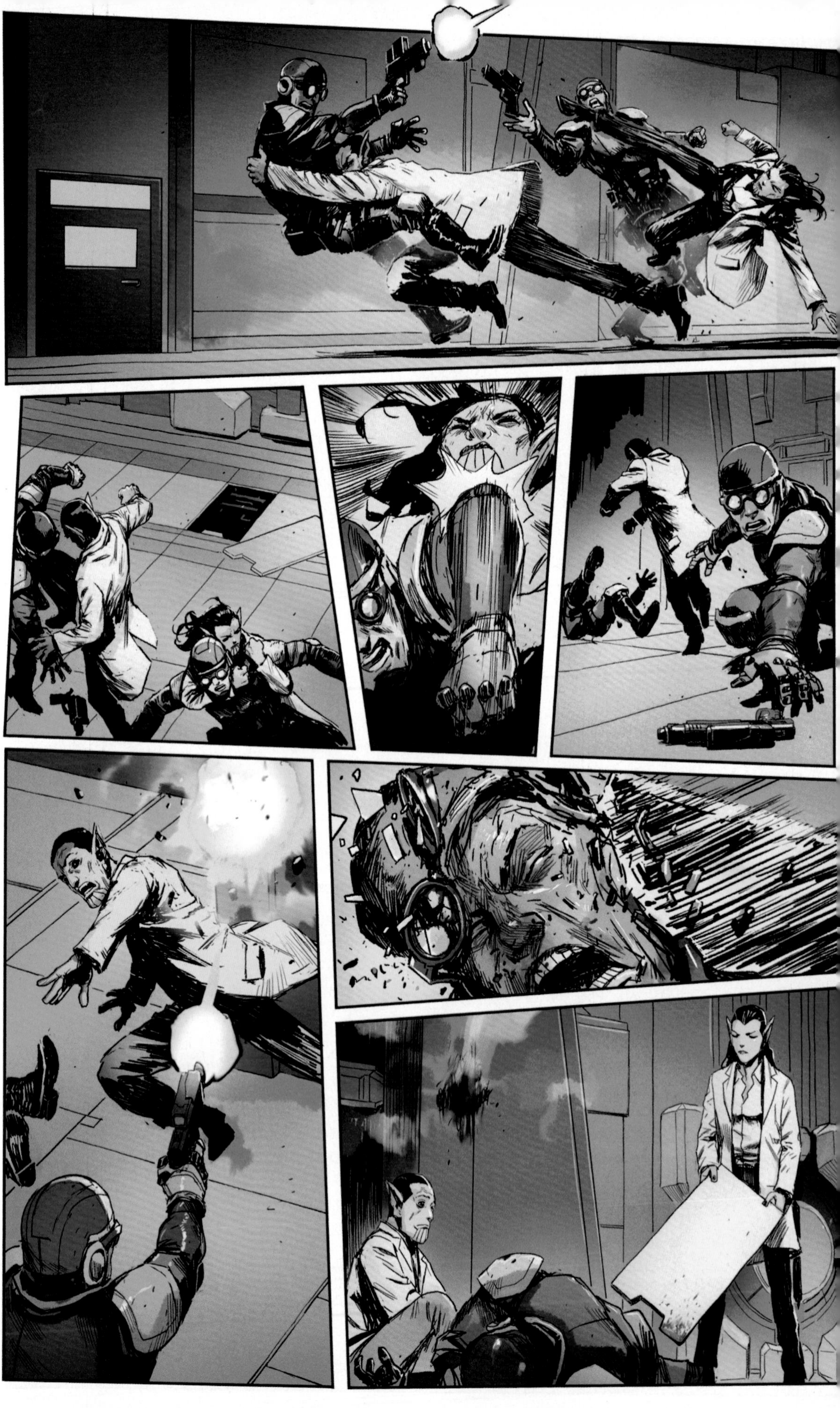

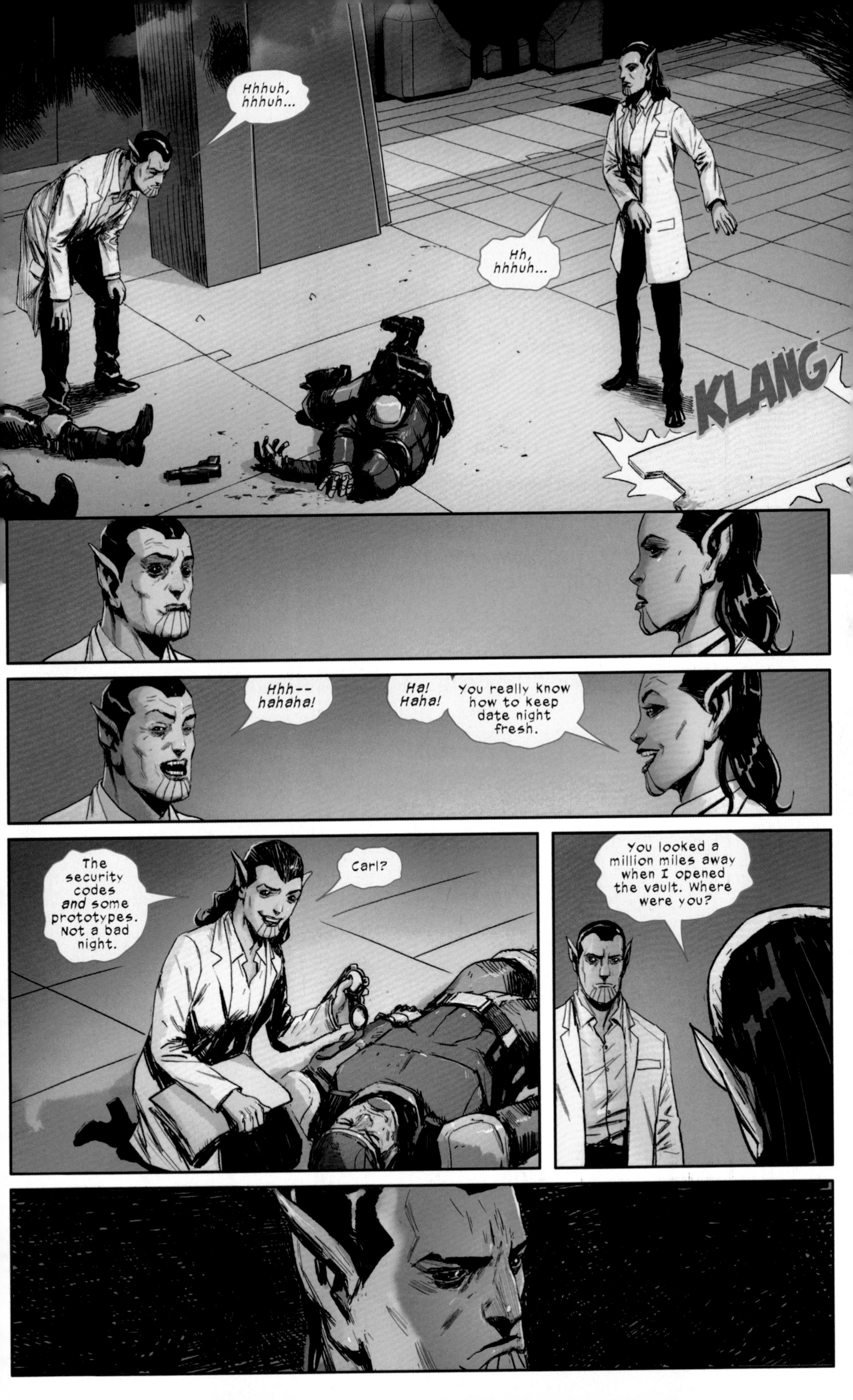
Hhhuh,
hhhuh...
Hh,
hhhuh...
KLANG
Hhh--
hahaha!
Ha!
Haha!
You really know how to keep date night fresh.
The security codes and some prototypes. Not a bad night.
Carl?
You looked a million miles away when I opened the vault. Where were you?

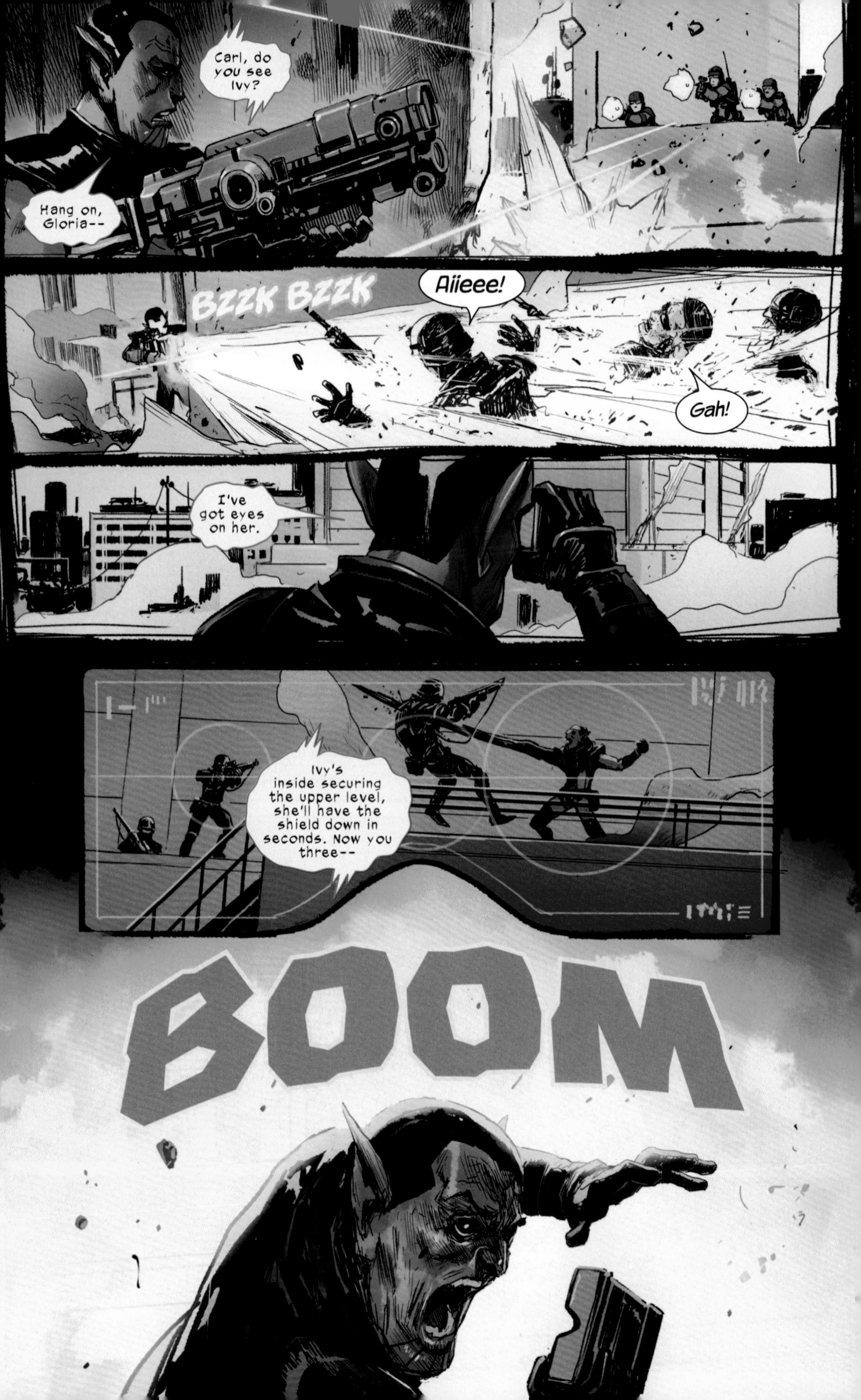

Carl, do you see Ivy?
Hang on, Gloria--
BZZK BZZK
Aiieee!
Gah!
I've got eyes on her.
Ivy's inside securing the upper level, she'll have the shield down in seconds. Now you three--
BOOM

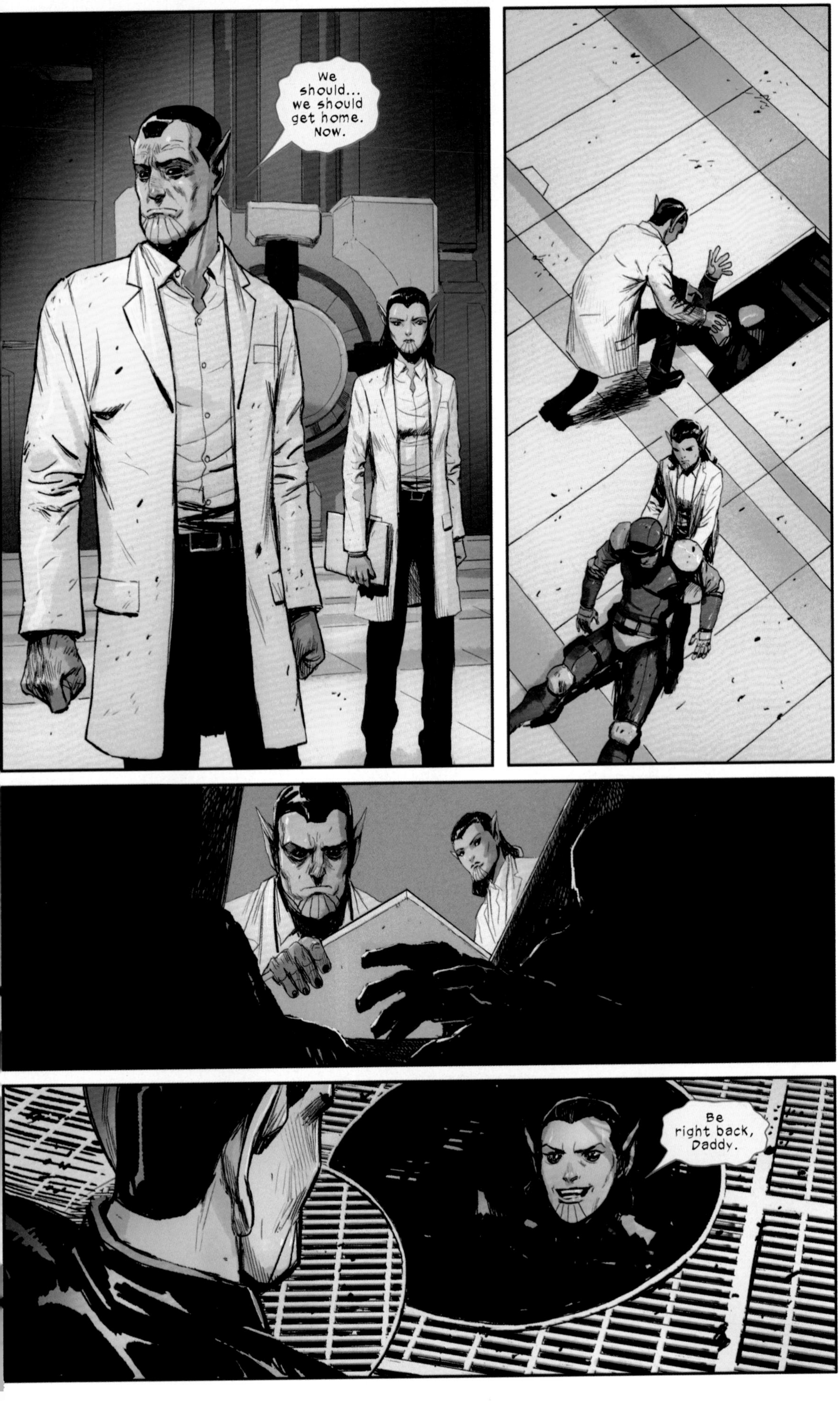
We should... we should get home. Now.
Be right back, Daddy.

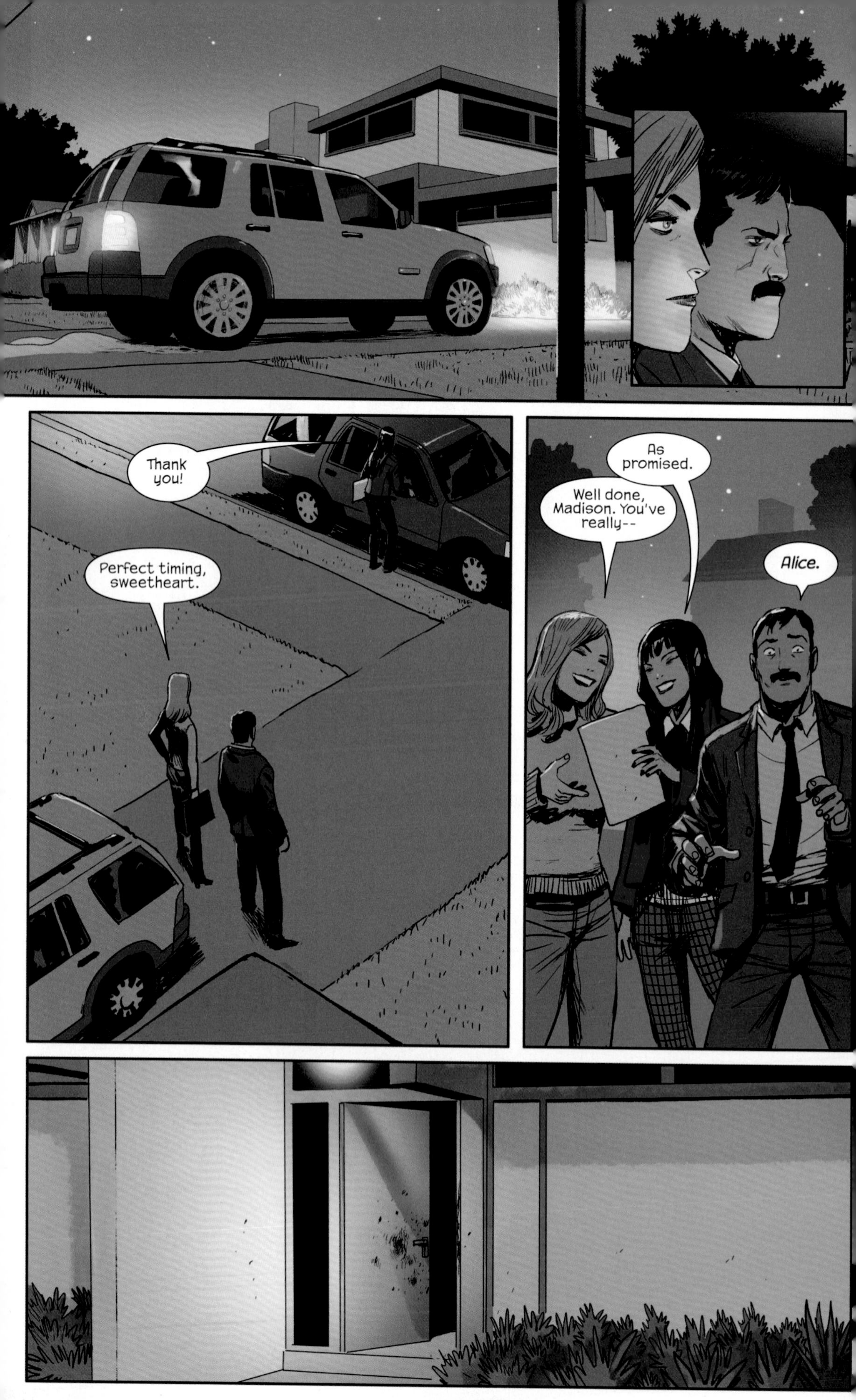

Thank you!
Perfect timing, sweetheart.
Well done, Madison. You've really--
As promised.
Alice.

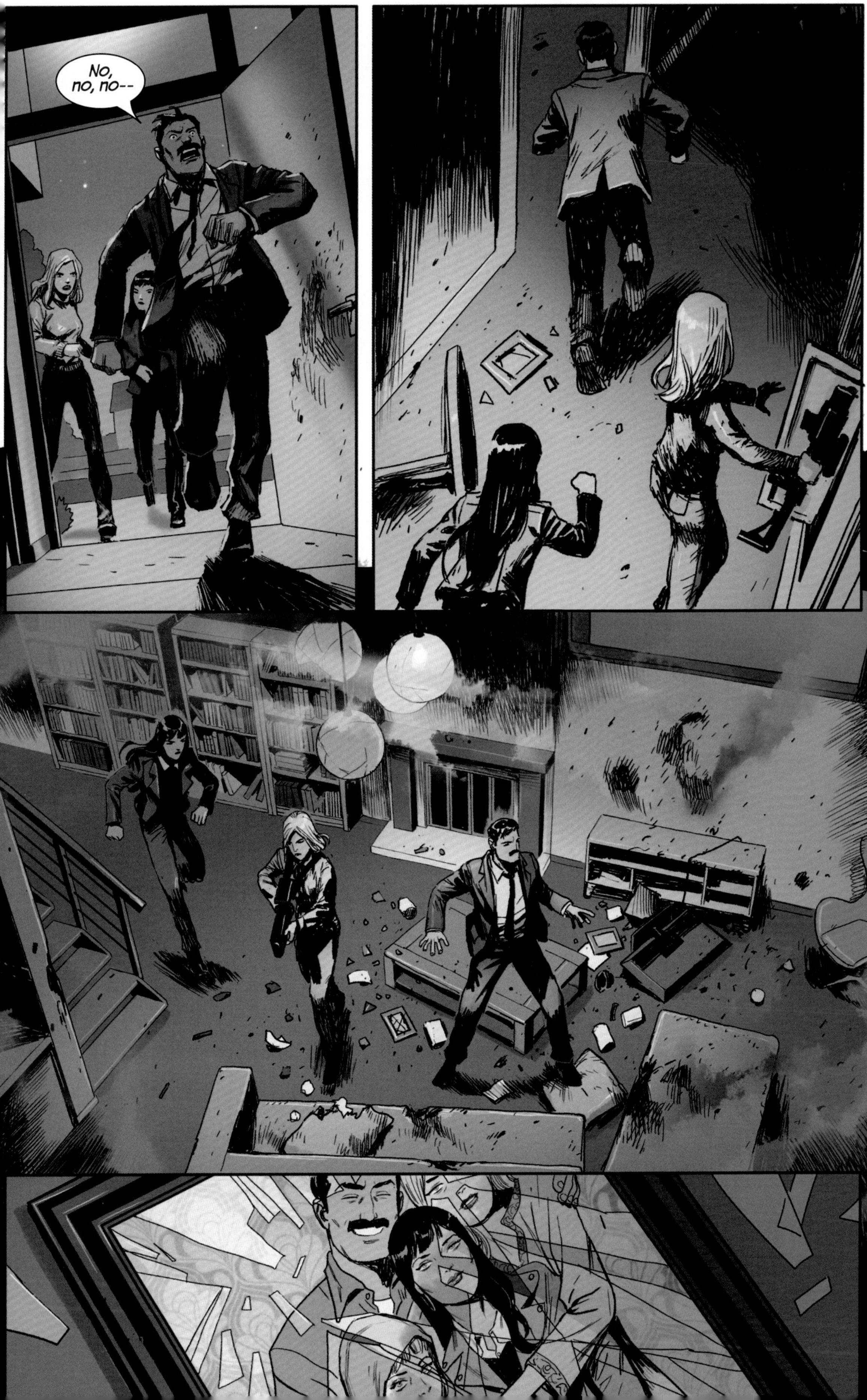
No, no, no--

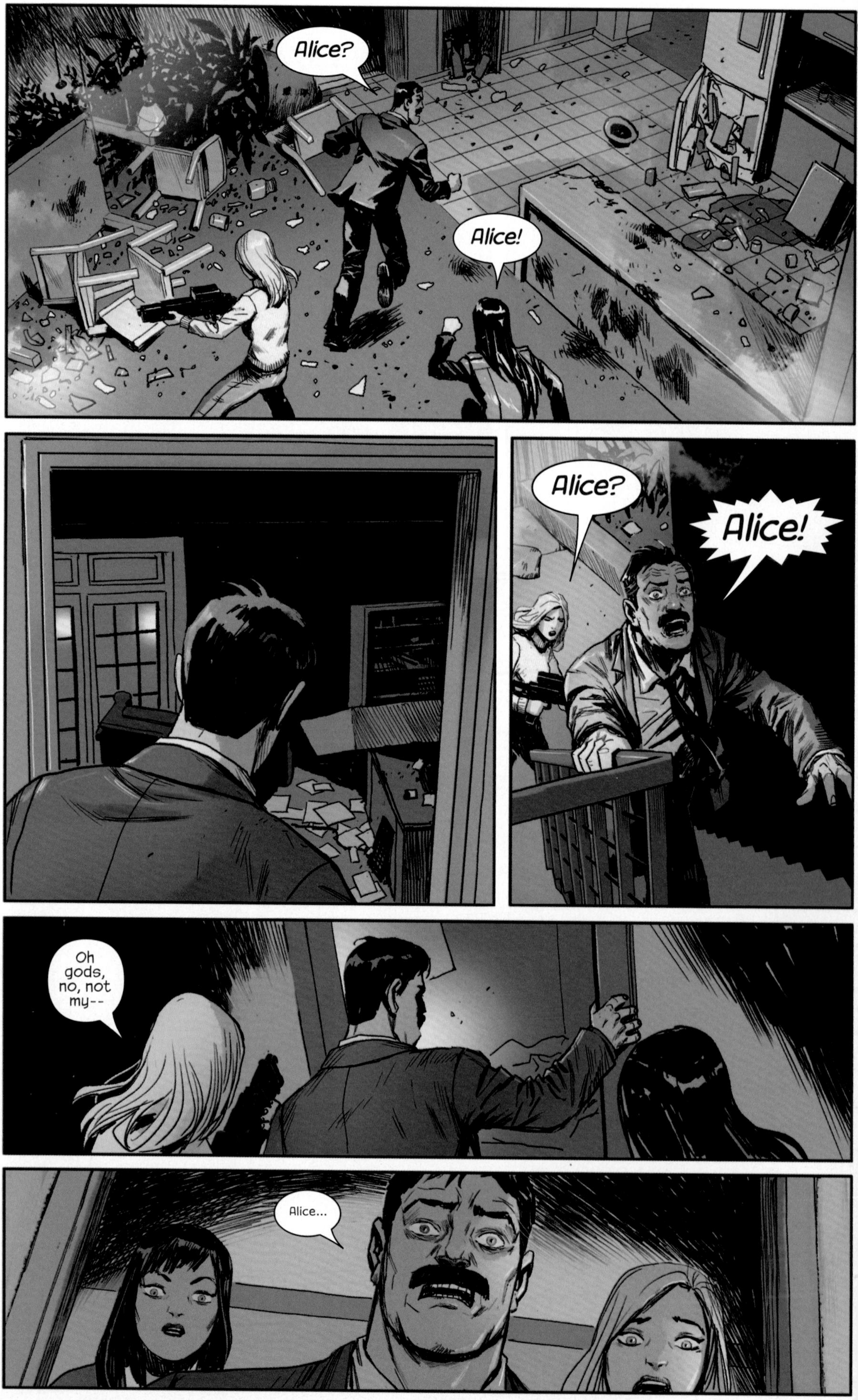
Alice?
Alice!
Alice?
Alice!
Oh gods, no, not my--
Alice...

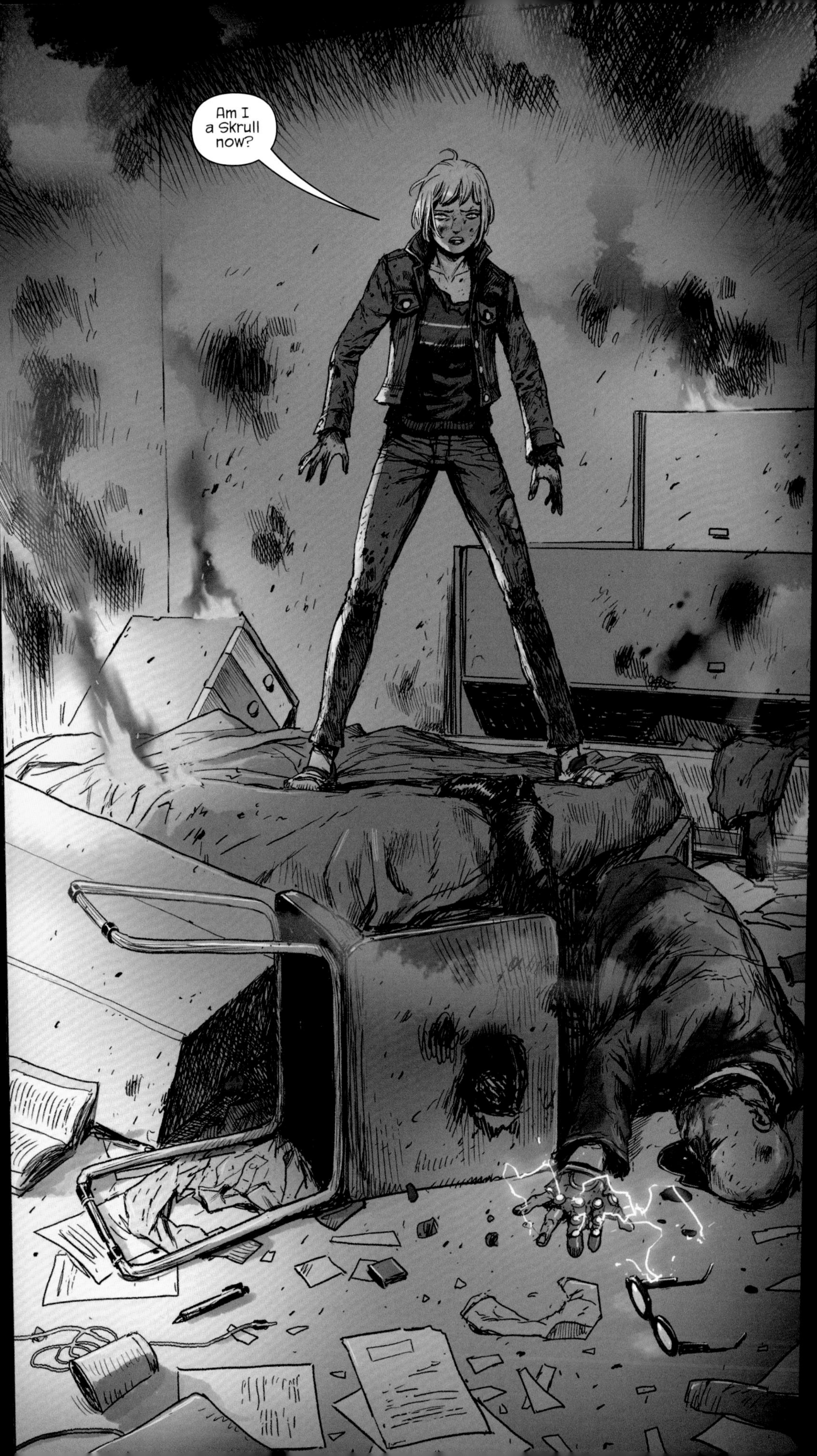
Am I a Skrull now?

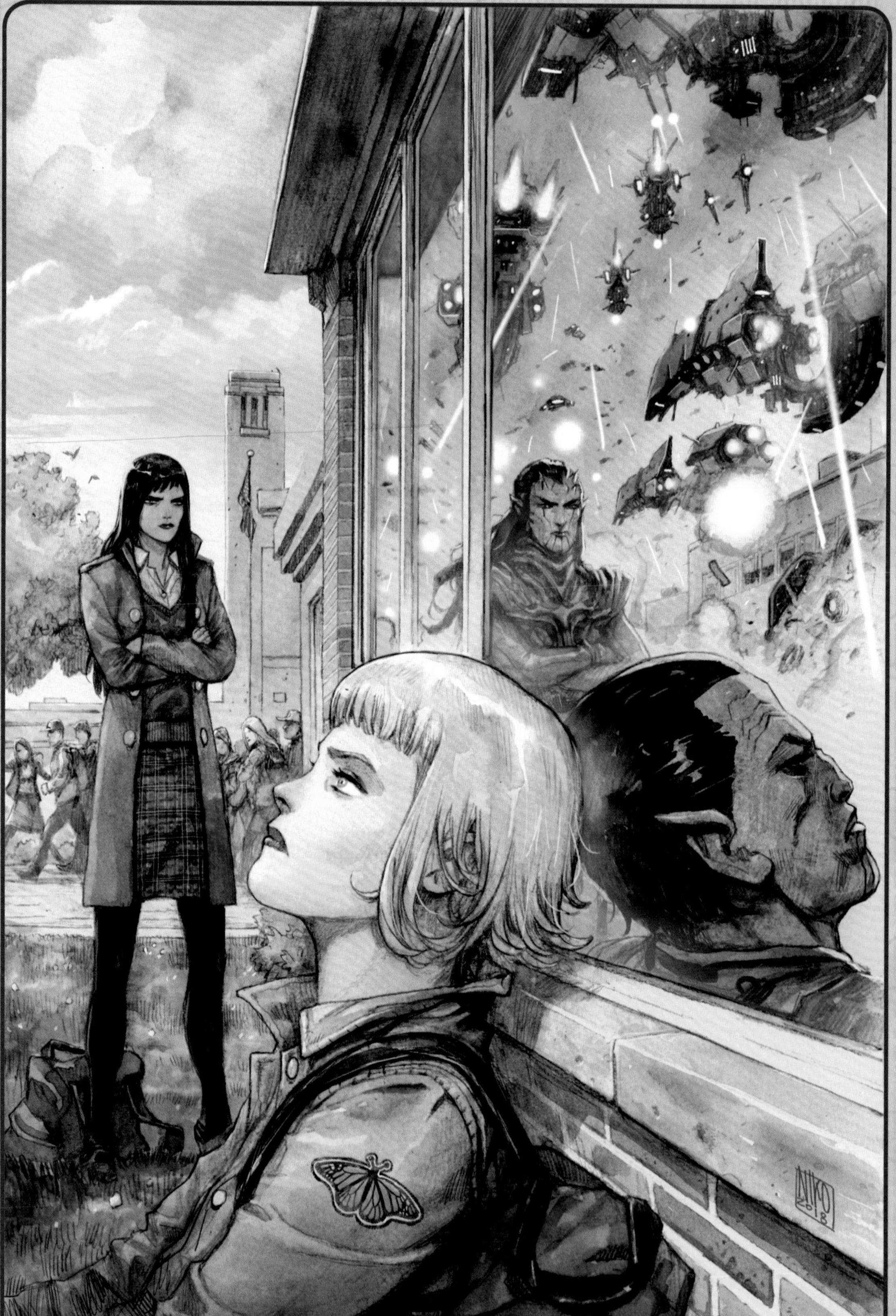
NIKO
2018

NIKO HENRICHON
#1 Variant

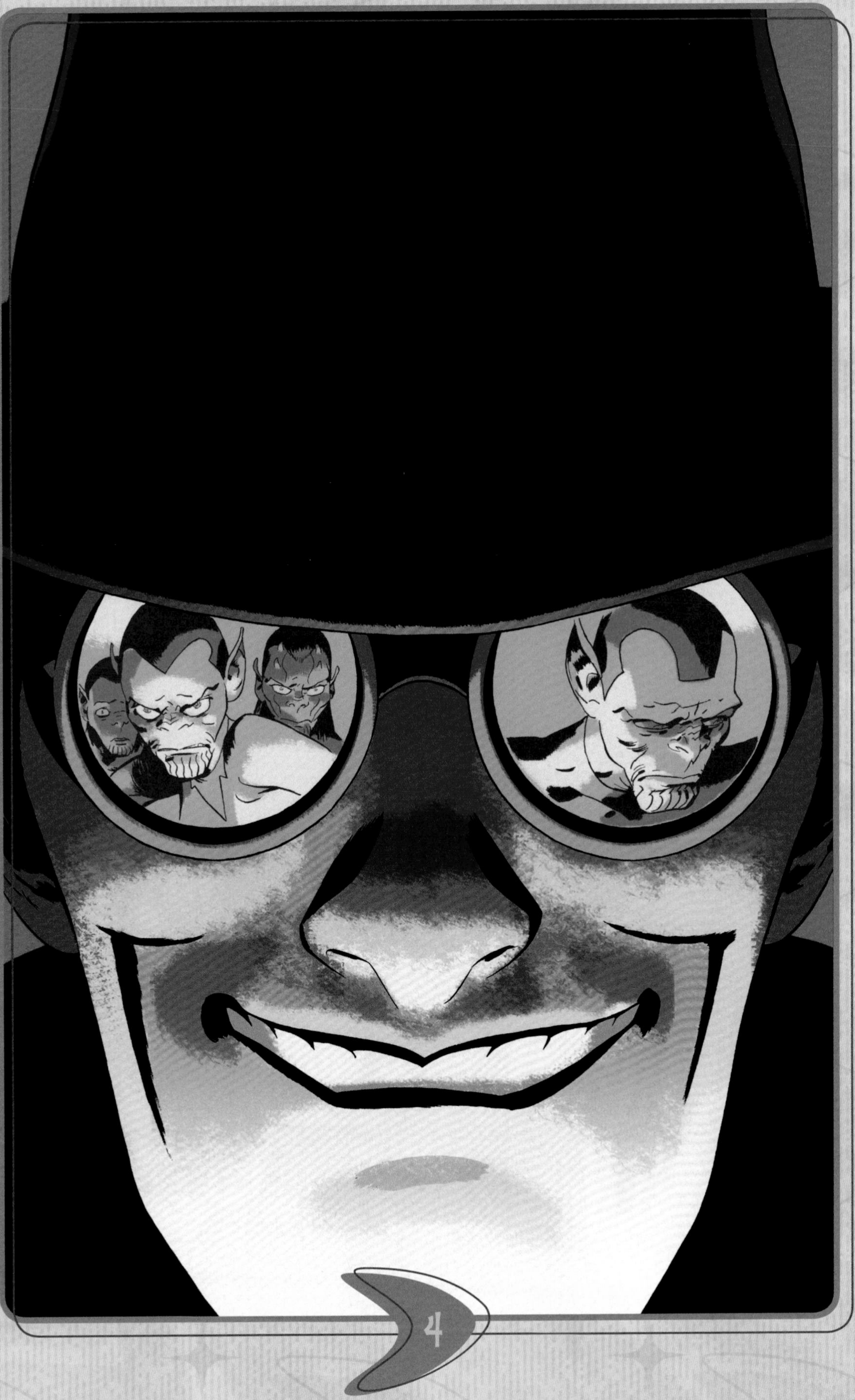

4

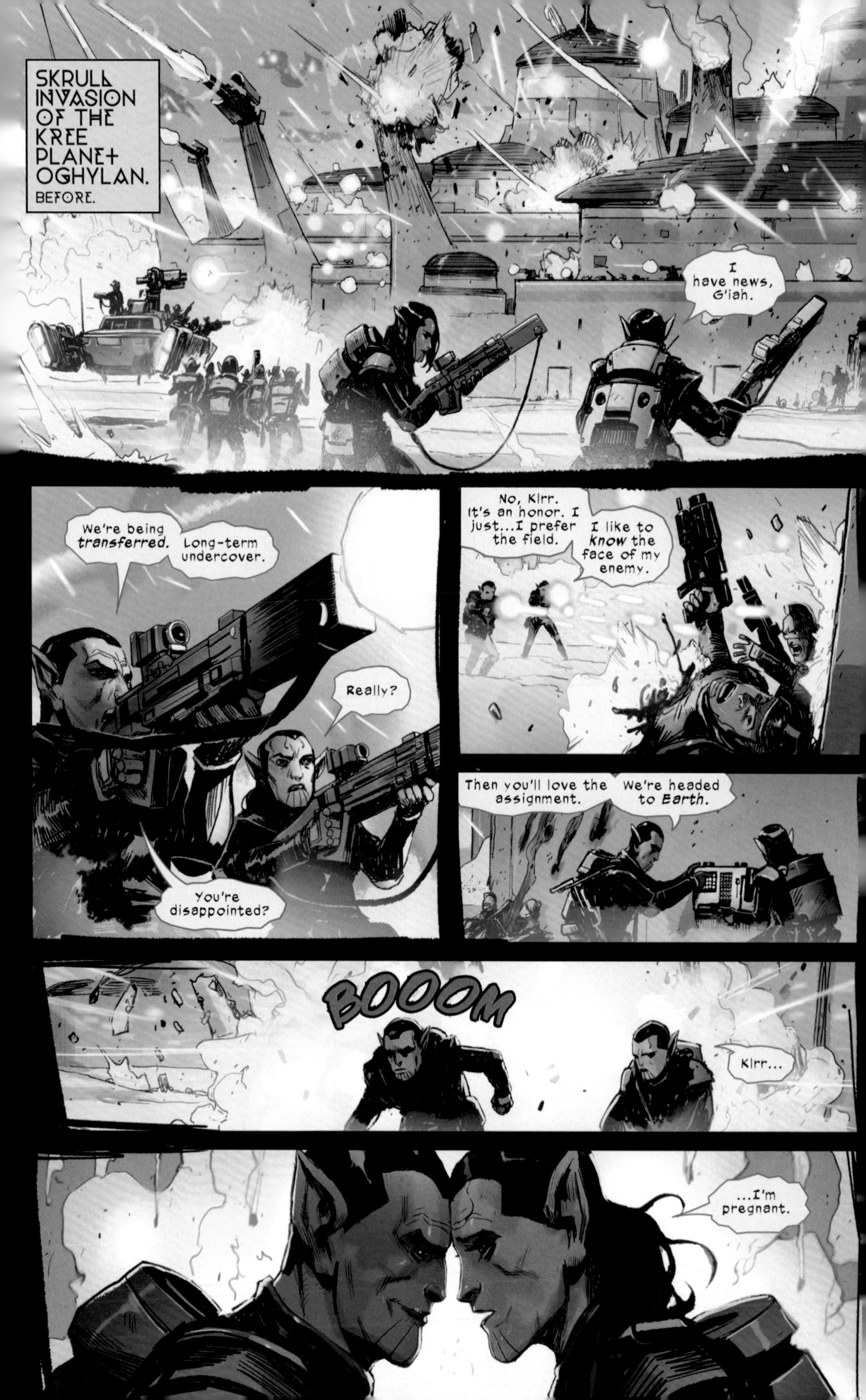
SKRULL INVASION OF THE KREE PLANET OGHYLAN.
BEFORE.
I have news, G'iah.
We're being *transferred.*
Long-term undercover.
Really?
You're disappointed?
No, Klrr. It's an honor. I just...I prefer the field.
I like to *know* the face of my enemy.
Then you'll love the assignment.
We're headed to *Earth.*
BOOOM
Klrr...
...I'm pregnant.

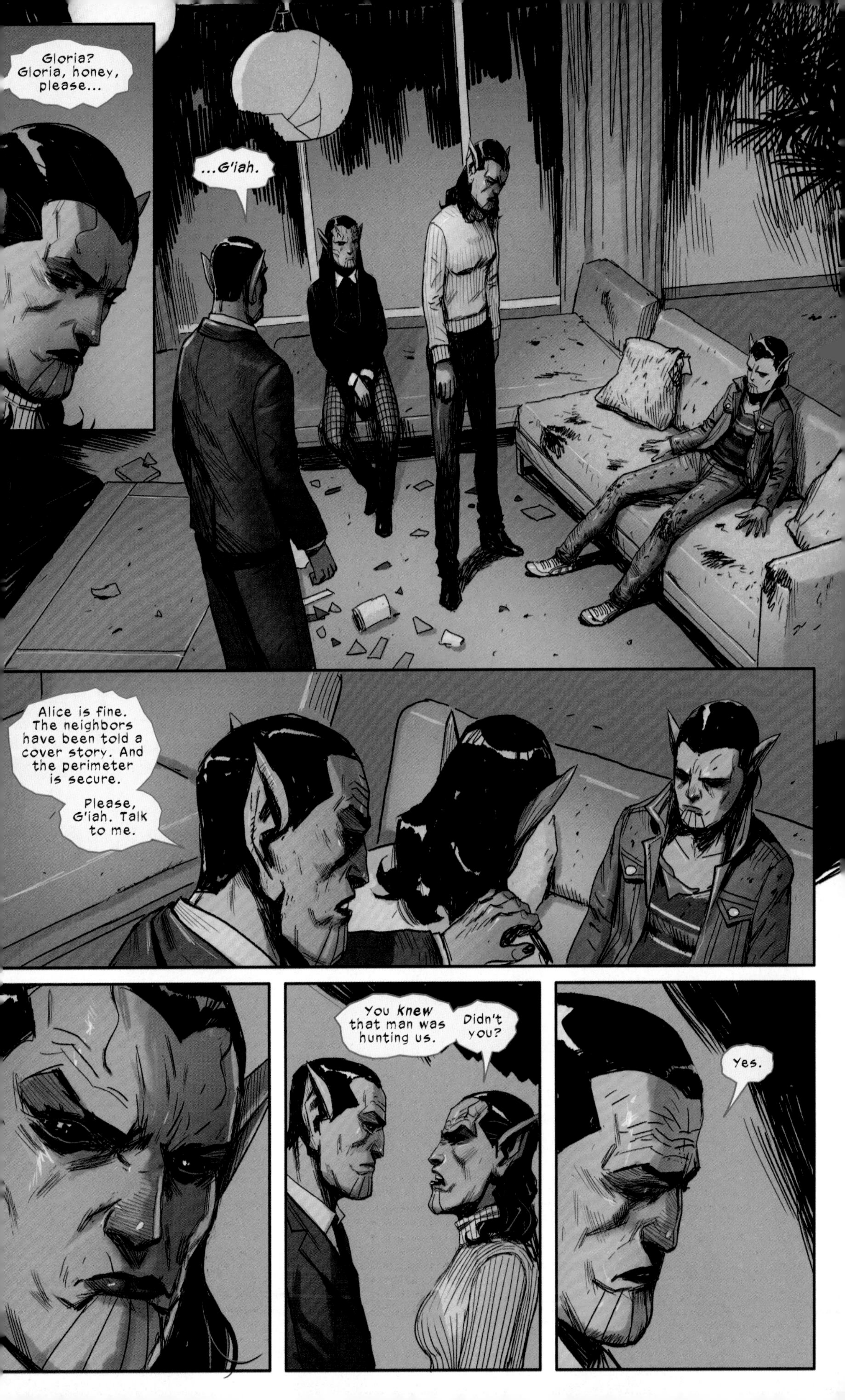
Gloria? Gloria, honey, please...
...G'iah.
Alice is fine. The neighbors have been told a cover story. And the perimeter is secure.
Please, G'iah. Talk to me.
You *knew* that man was hunting us.
Didn't you?
Yes.

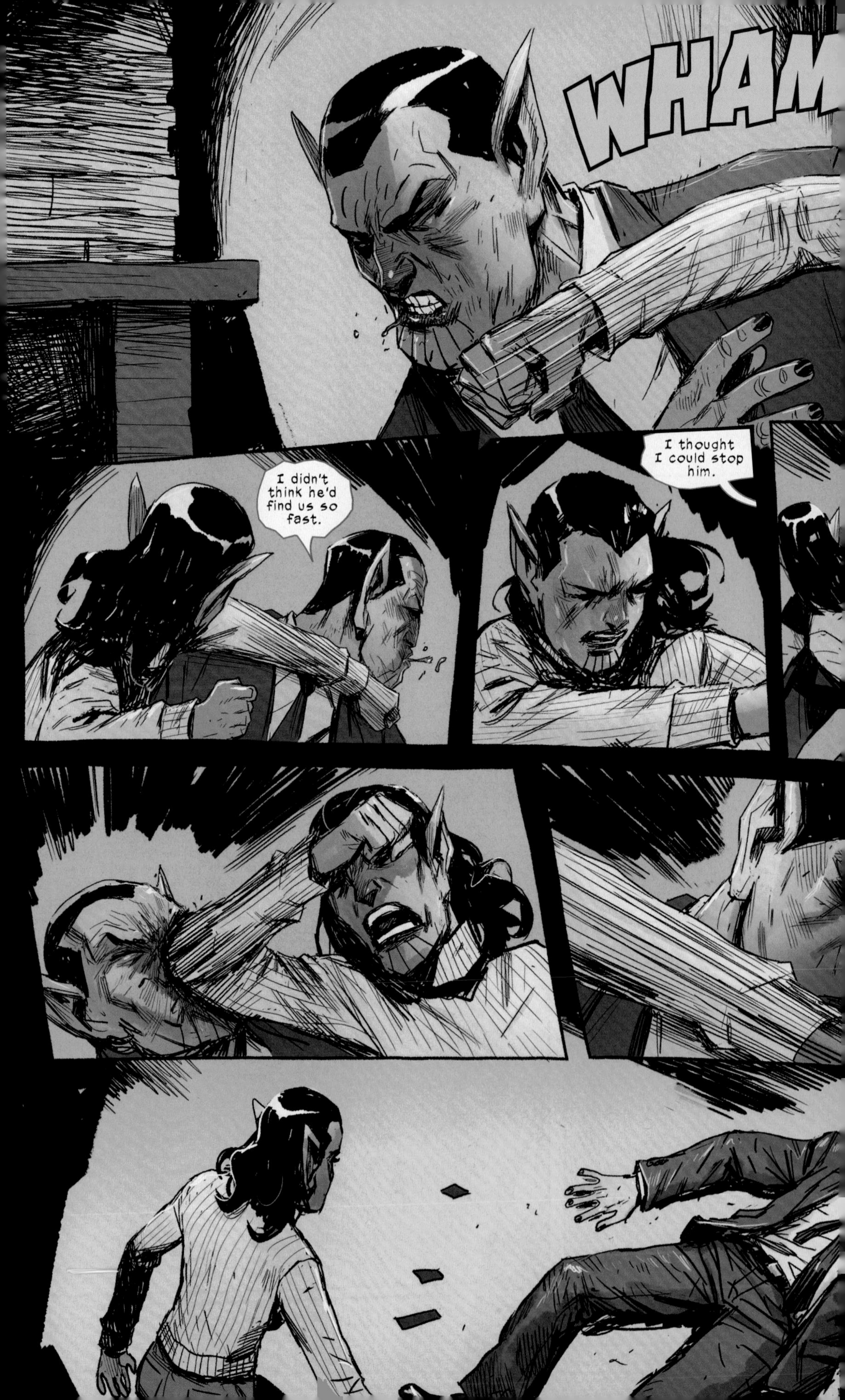
WHAM
I didn't think he'd find us so fast.
I thought I could stop him.

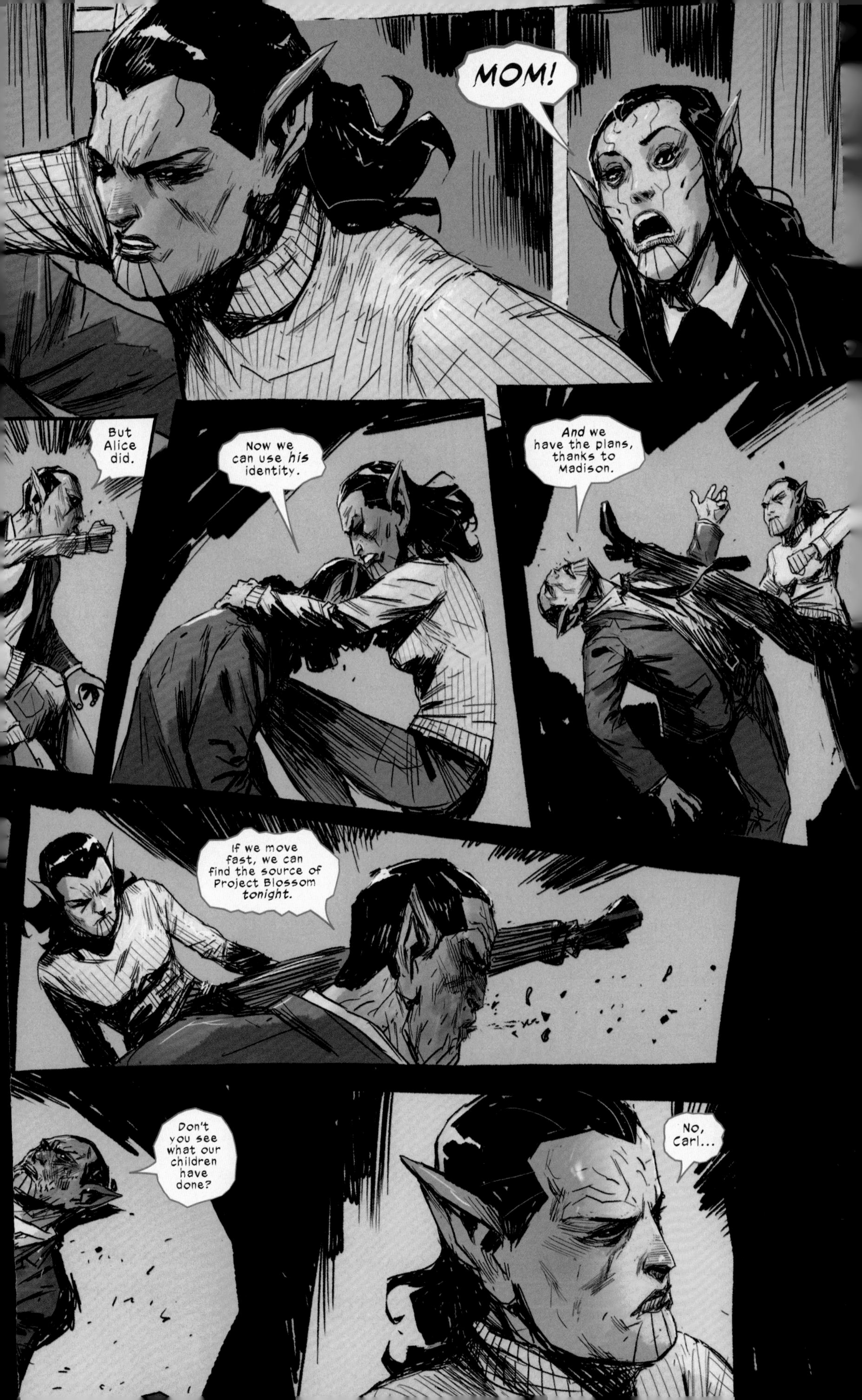
MOM!
But Alice did.
Now we can use *his* identity.
And we have the plans, thanks to Madison.
If we move fast, we can find the source of Project Blossom *tonight*.
Don't you see what our children have done?
No, Carl...

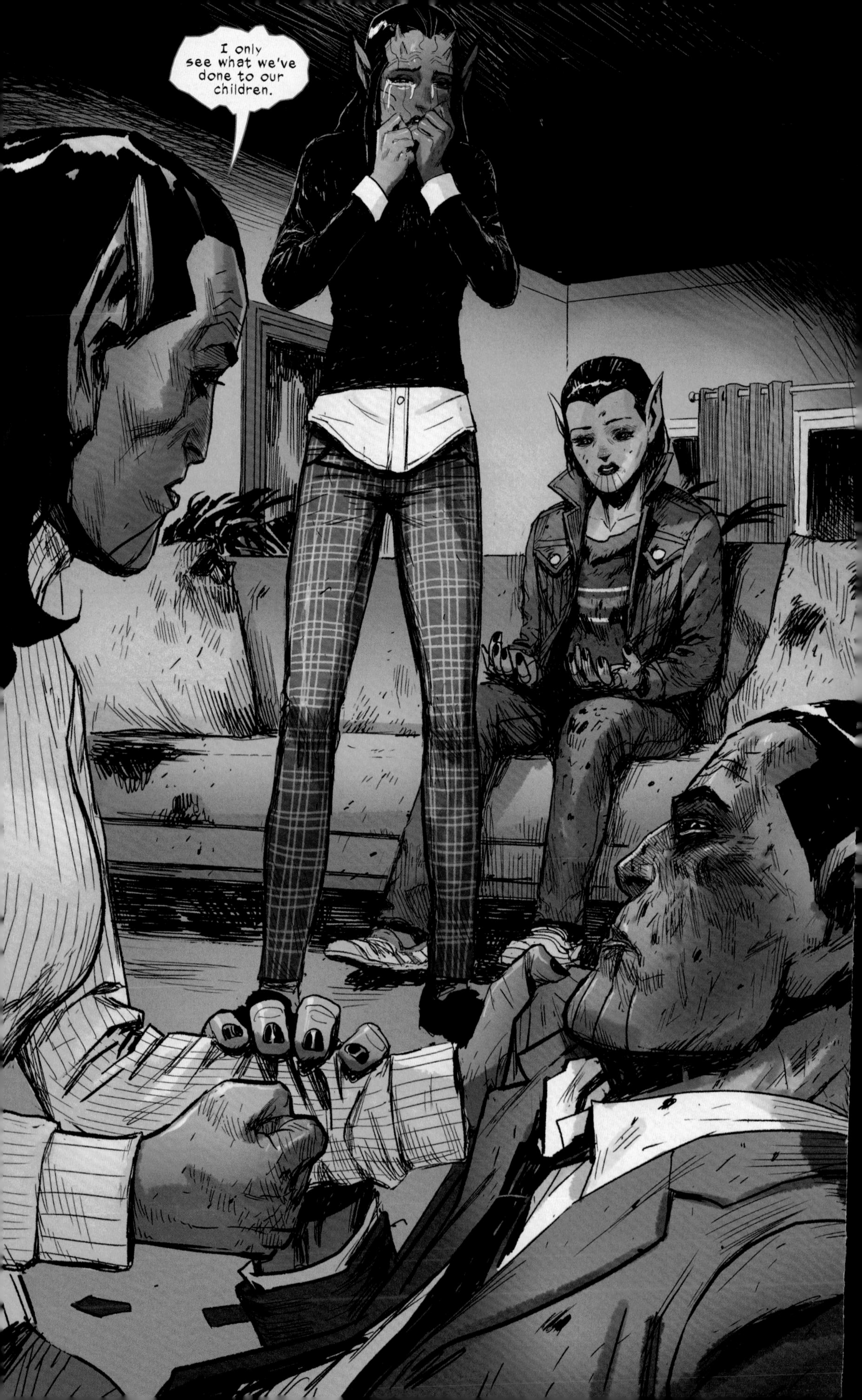
I only see what we've done to our children.

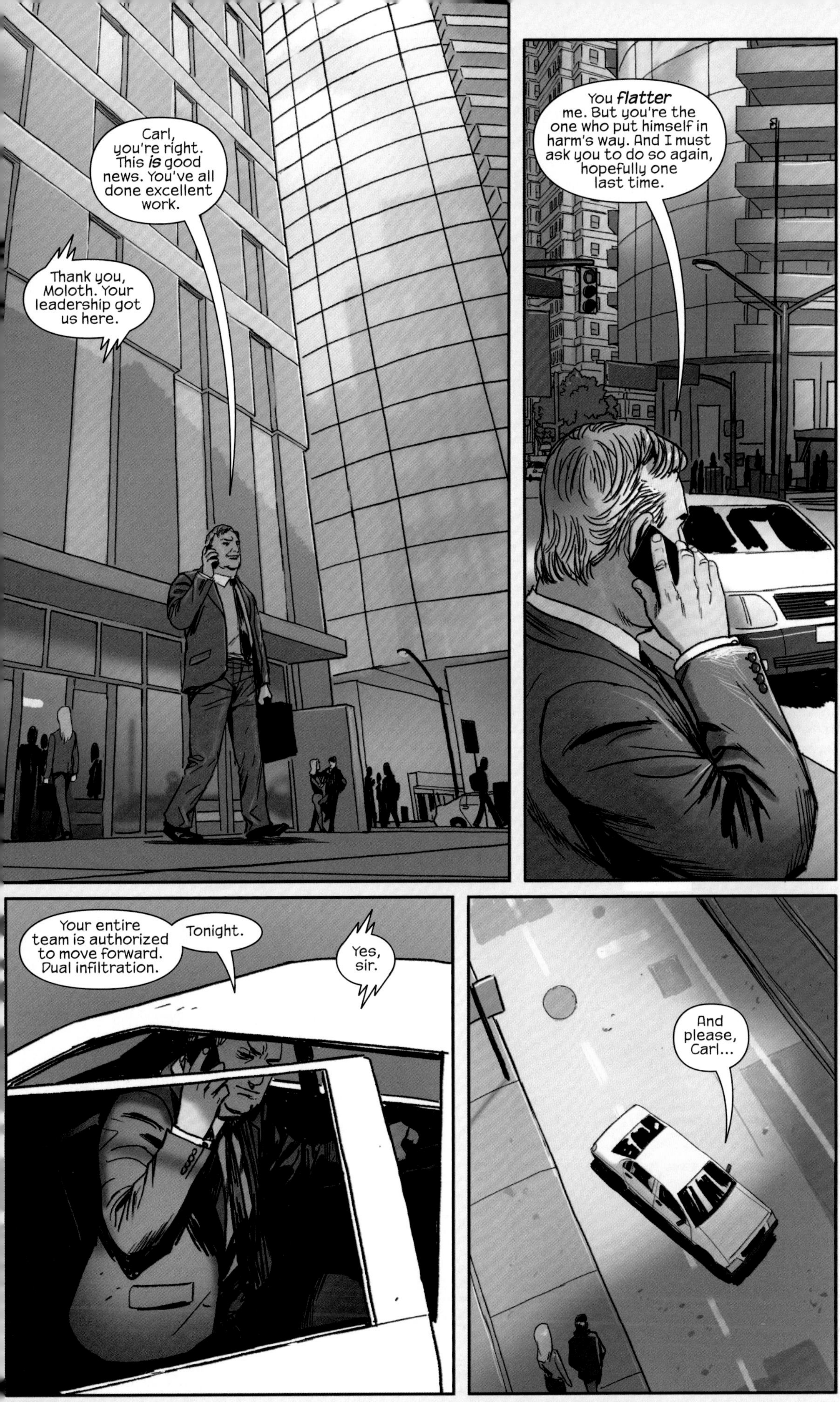

Carl, you're right. This *is* good news. You've all done excellent work.
Thank you, Moloth. Your leadership got us here.
You *flatter* me. But you're the one who put himself in harm's way. And I must ask you to do so again, hopefully one last time.
Your entire team is authorized to move forward. Dual infiltration.
Tonight.
Yes, sir.
And please, Carl...

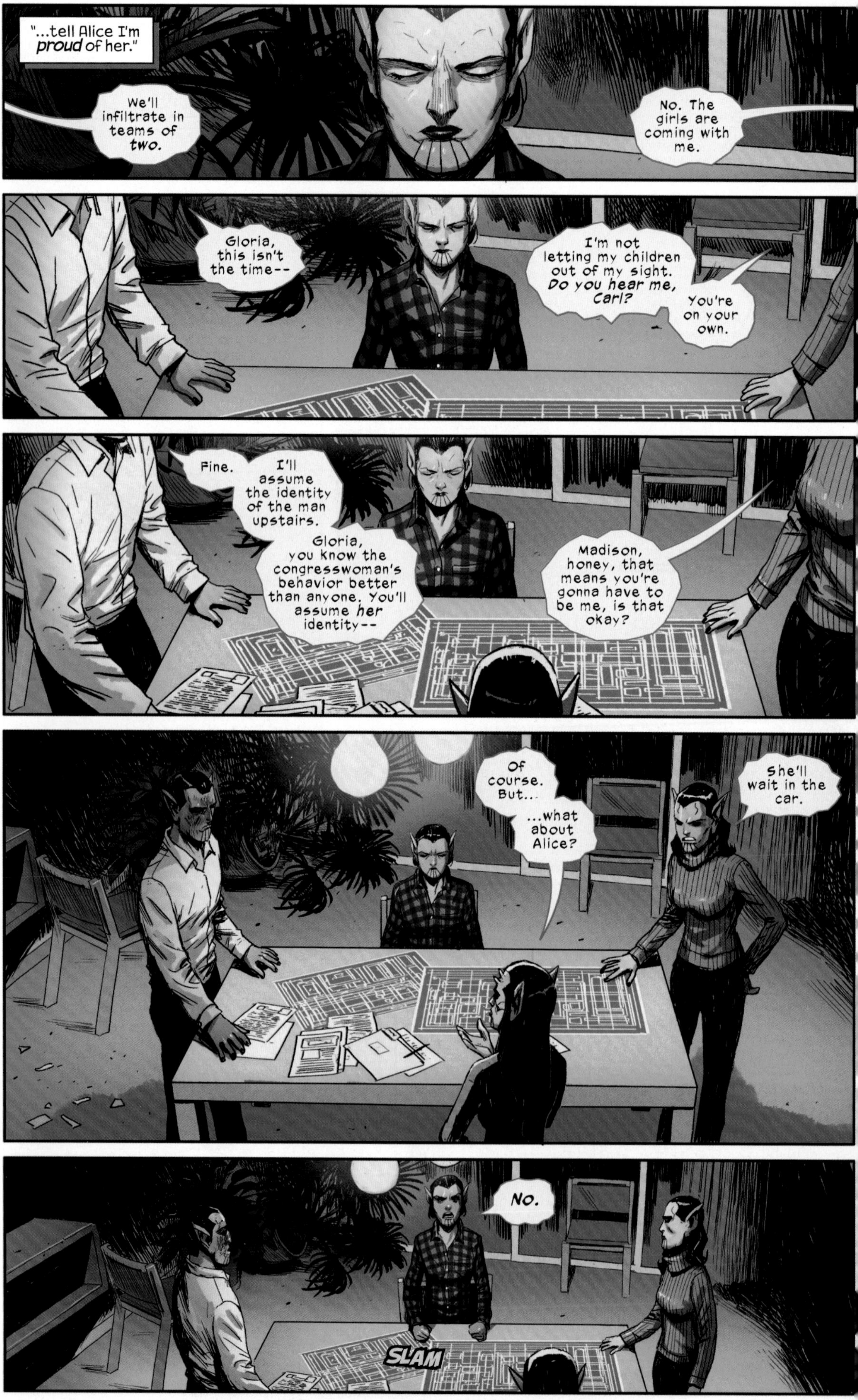
"...tell Alice I'm *proud* of her."
We'll infiltrate in teams of *two.*
No. The girls are coming with me.
Gloria, this isn't the time--
I'm not letting my children out of my sight. *Do you hear me, Carl?*
You're on your own.
Fine.
I'll assume the identity of the man upstairs.
Gloria, you know the congresswoman's behavior better than anyone. You'll assume *her* identity--
Madison, honey, that means you're gonna have to be me, is that okay?
Of course. But...
...what about Alice?
She'll wait in the car.
No.
SLAM

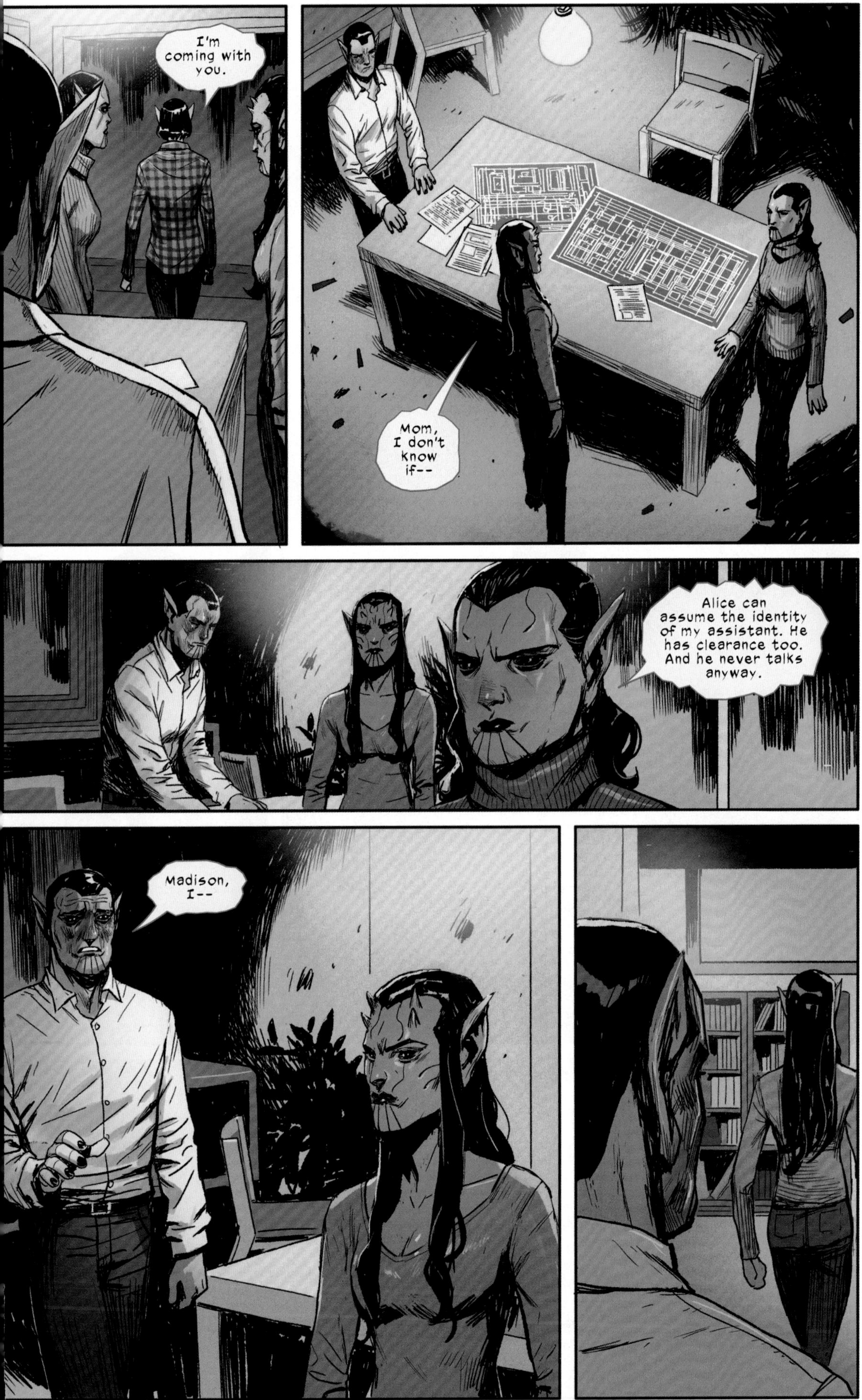
I'm coming with you.
Mom, I don't know if--
Alice can assume the identity of my assistant. He has clearance too. And he never talks anyway.
Madison, I--

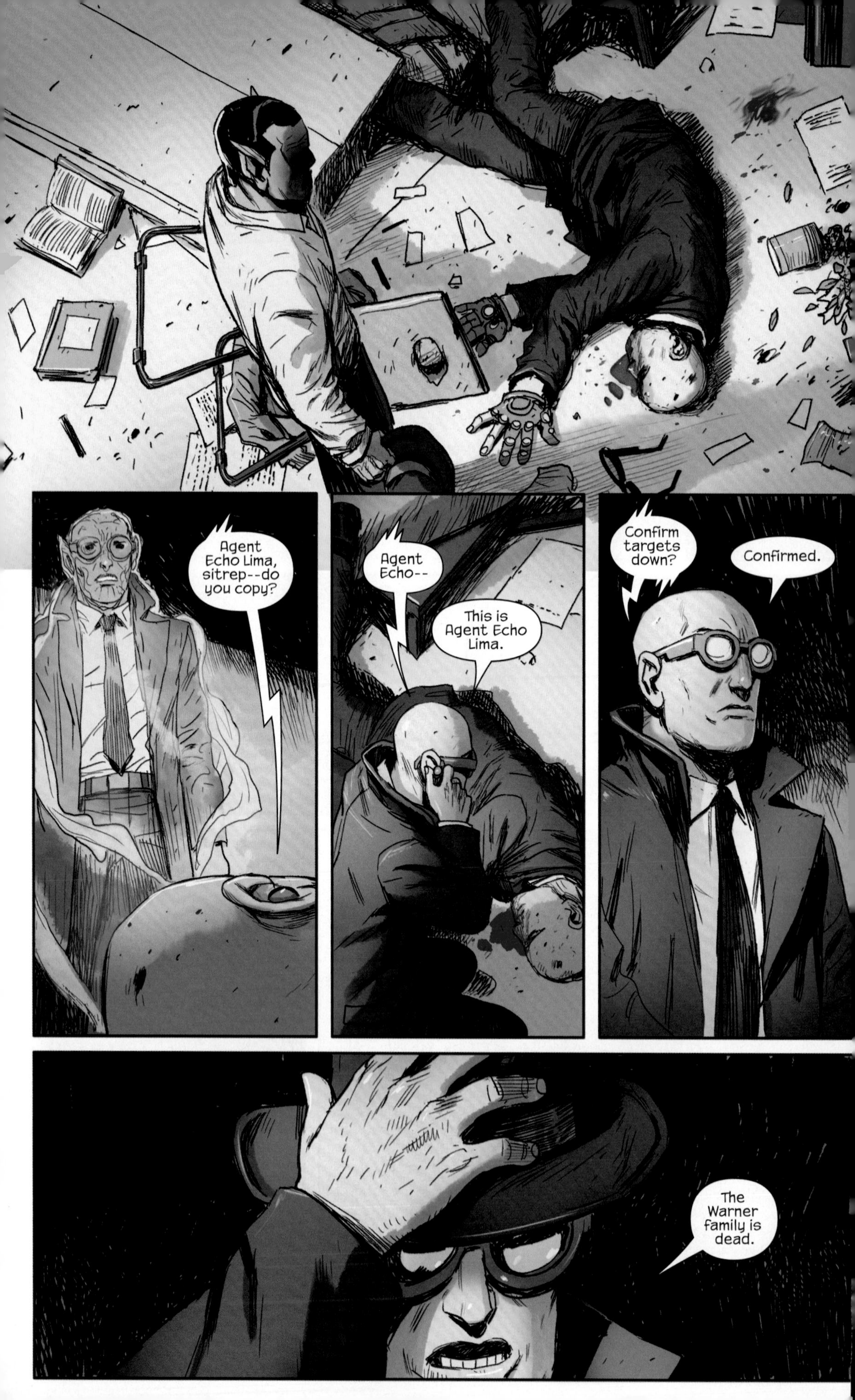
Agent Echo Lima, sitrep--do you copy?
Agent Echo--
This is Agent Echo Lima.
Confirm targets down?
Confirmed.
The Warner family is dead.

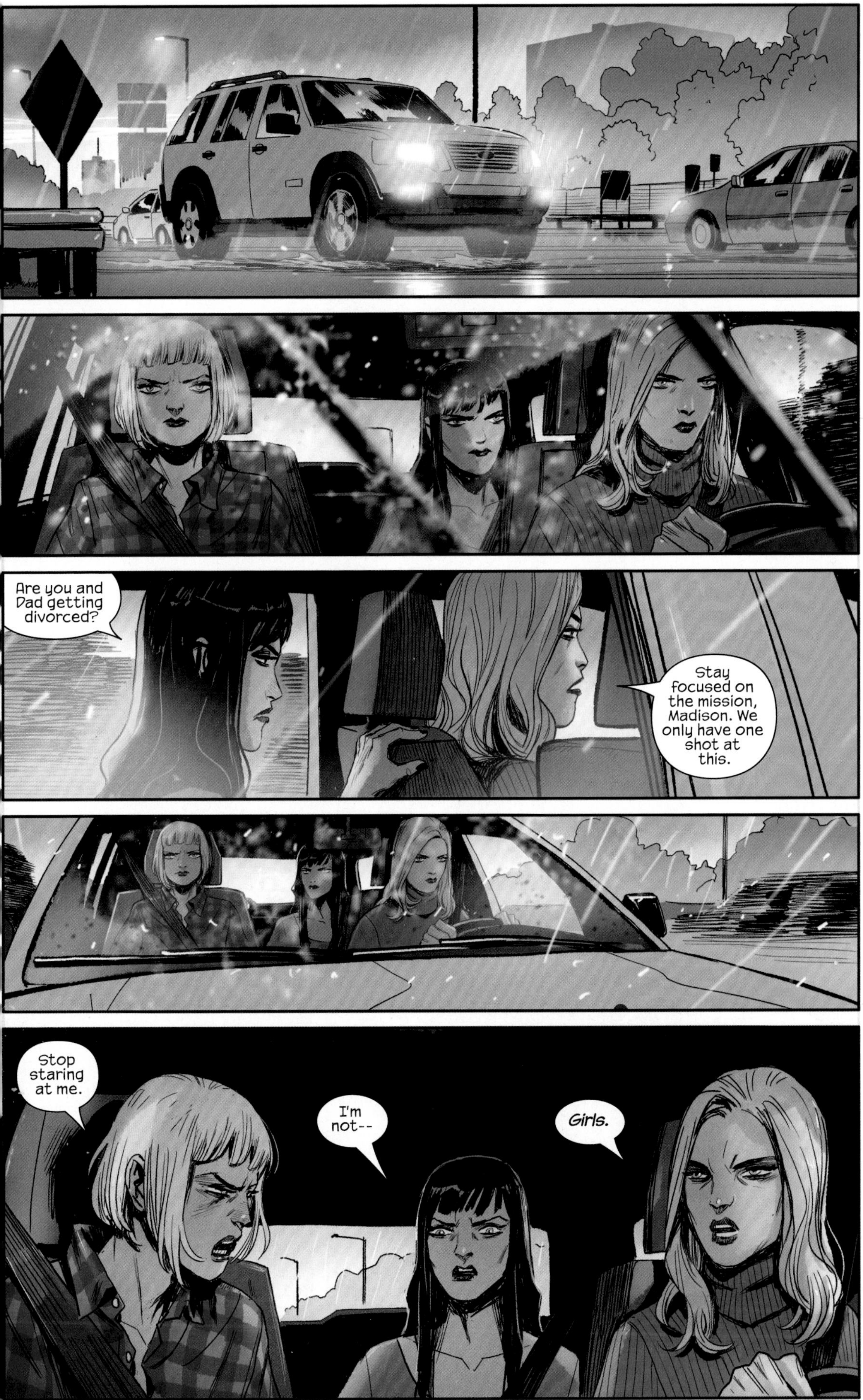
Are you and Dad getting divorced?
Stay focused on the mission, Madison. We only have one shot at this.
Stop staring at me.
I'm not--
Girls.

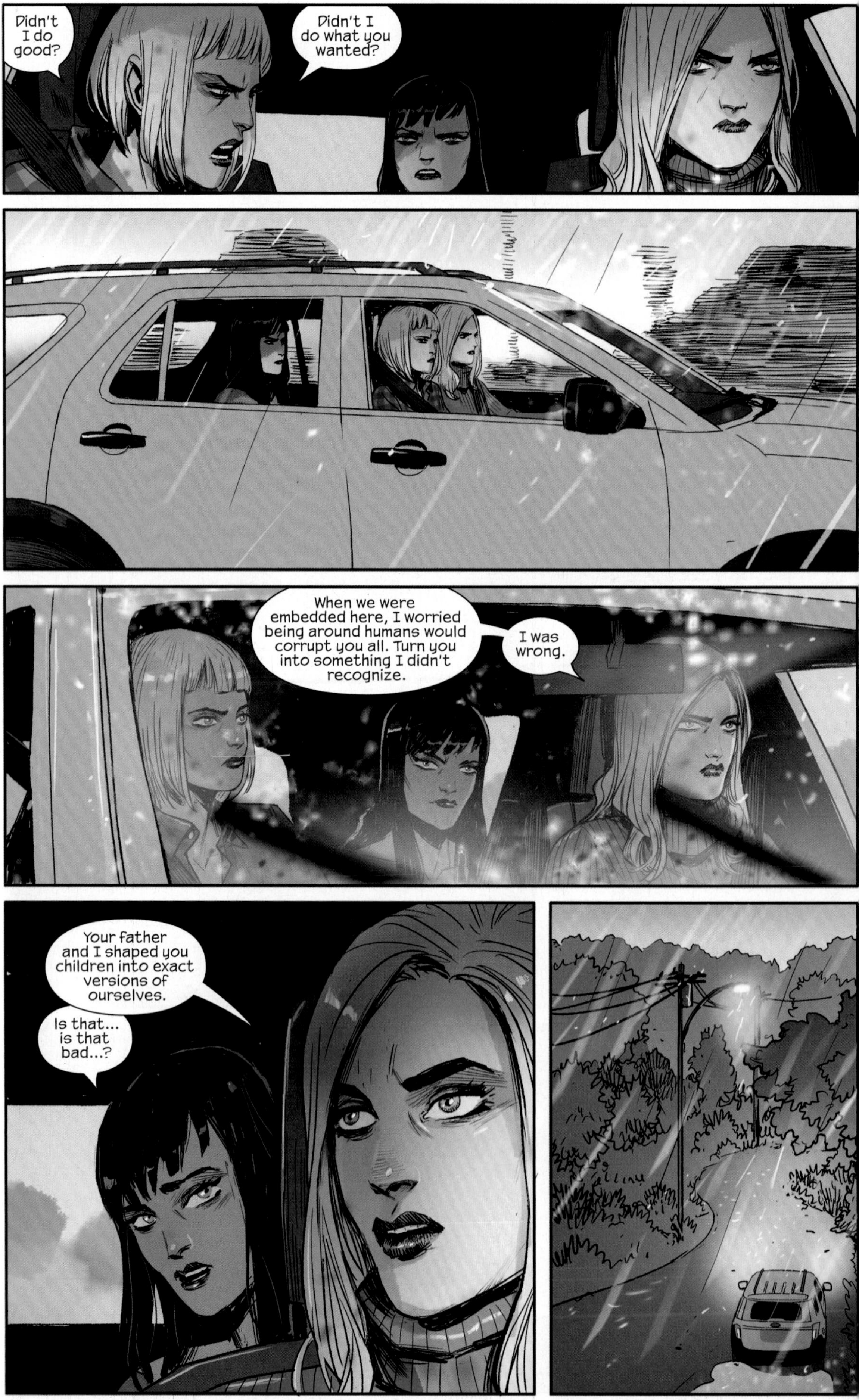
Didn't I do good?
Didn't I do what you wanted?
When we were embedded here, I worried being around humans would corrupt you all. Turn you into something I didn't recognize.
I was wrong.
Your father and I shaped you children into exact versions of ourselves.
Is that... is that bad...?

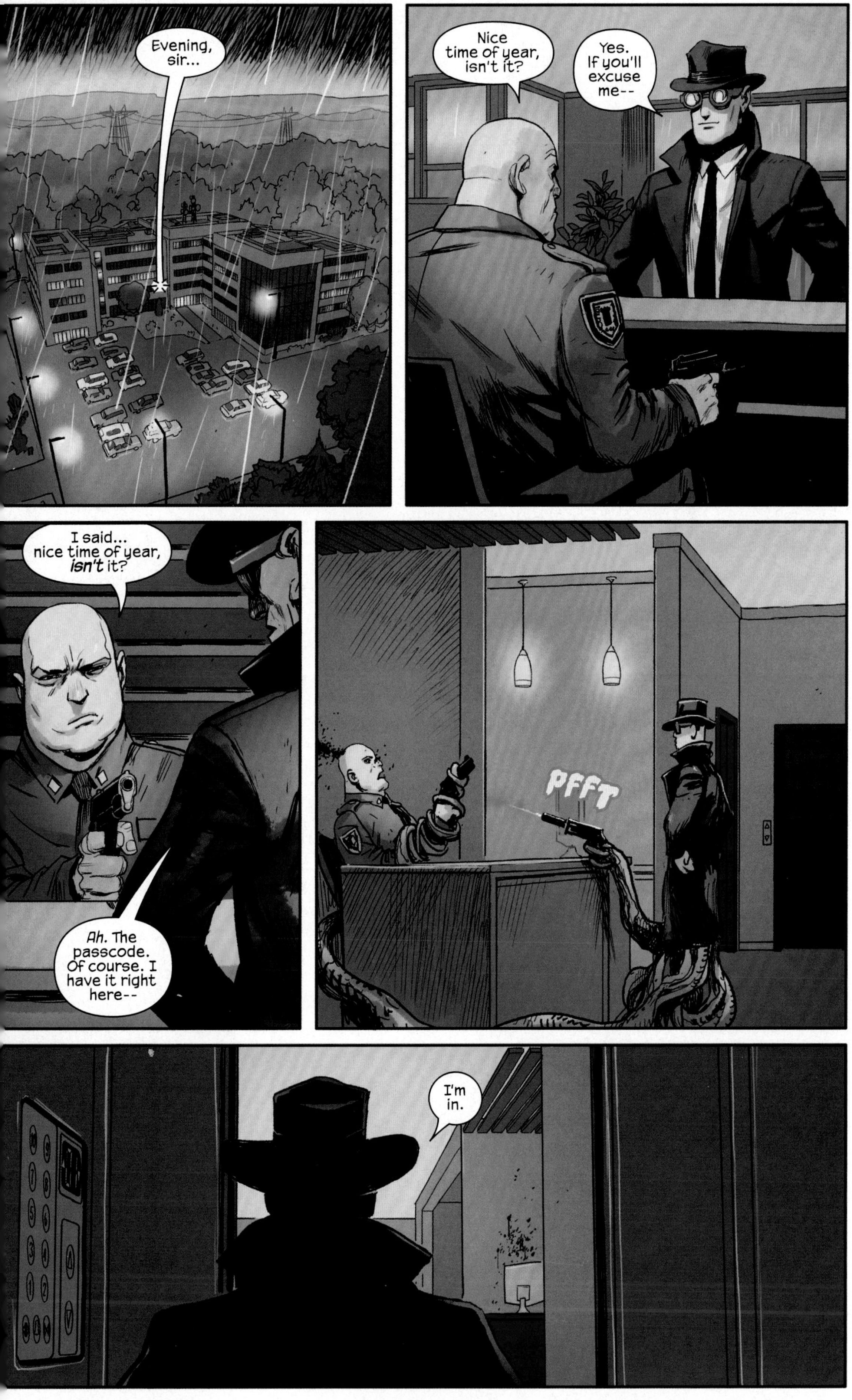
Evening, sir...
Nice time of year, isn't it?
Yes. If you'll excuse me--
I said... nice time of year, *isn't* it?
Ah. The passcode. Of course. I have it right here--
PFFT
I'm in.

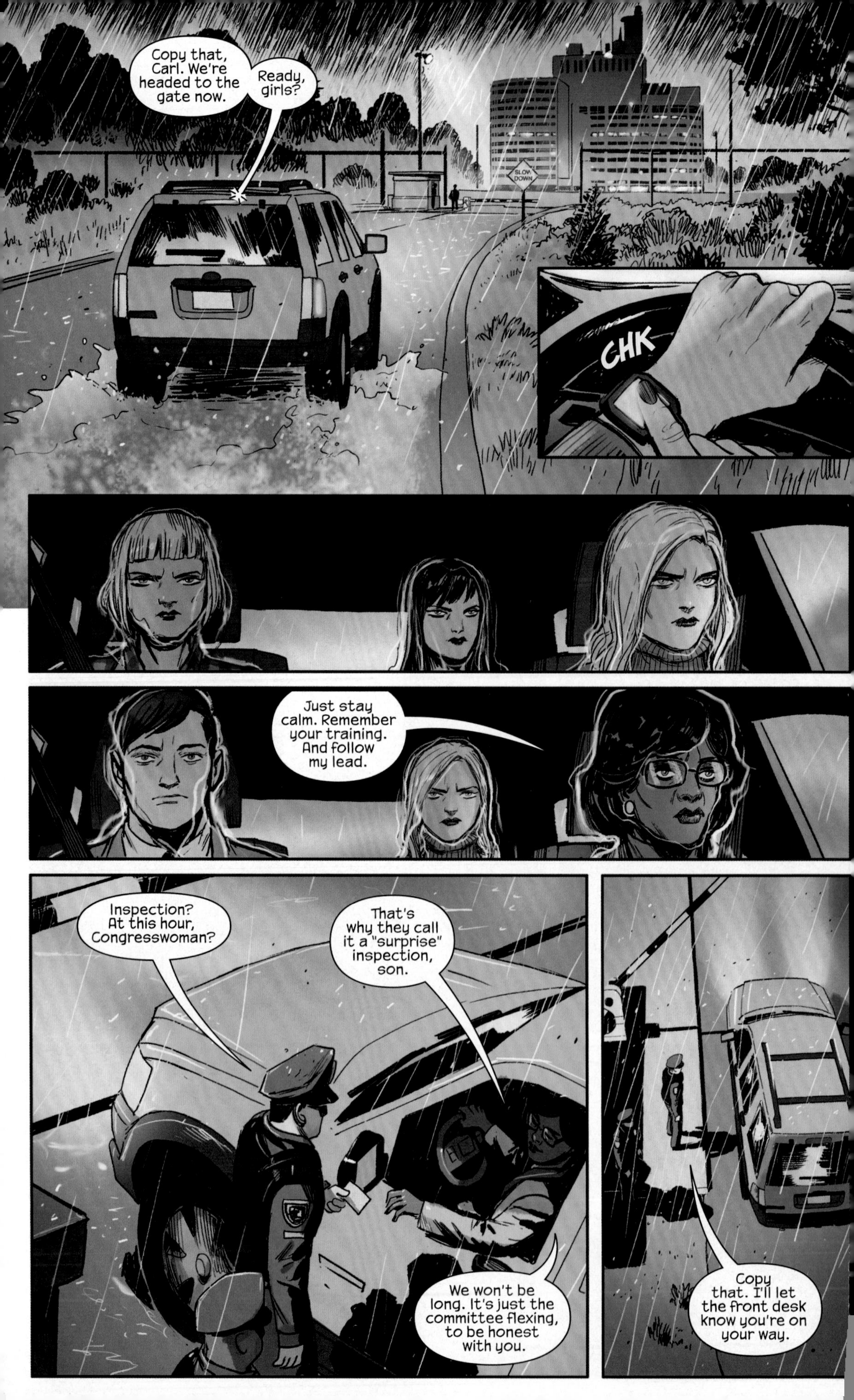
Copy that, Carl. We're headed to the gate now.
Ready, girls?
SLOW DOWN
CHK
Just stay calm. Remember your training. And follow my lead.
Inspection? At this hour, Congresswoman?
That's why they call it a "surprise" inspection, son.
We won't be long. It's just the committee flexing, to be honest with you.
Copy that. I'll let the front desk know you're on your way.

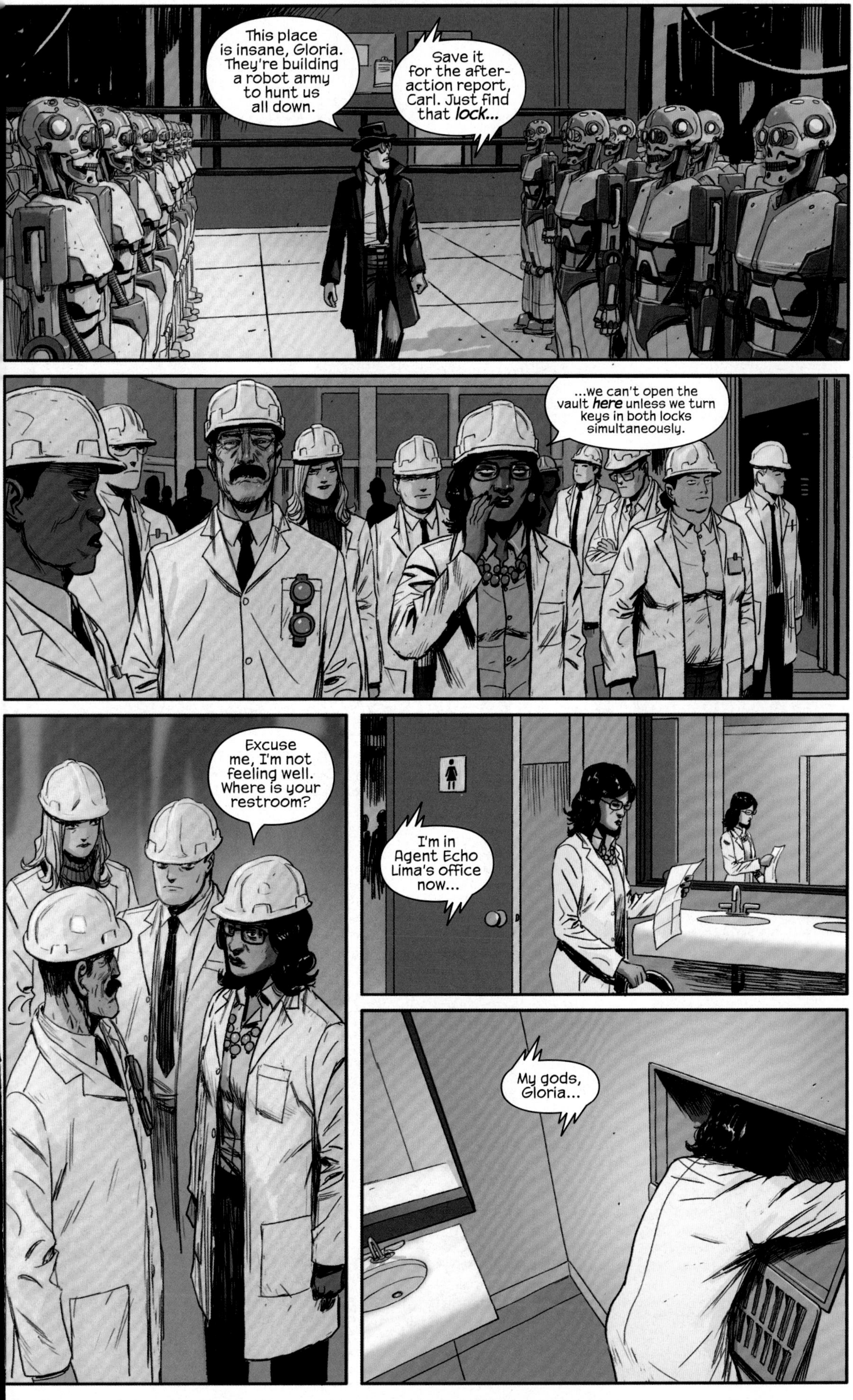
This place is insane, Gloria. They're building a robot army to hunt us all down.
Save it for the after-action report, Carl. Just find that *lock*...
...we can't open the vault *here* unless we turn keys in both locks simultaneously.
Excuse me, I'm not feeling well. Where is your restroom?
I'm in Agent Echo Lima's office now...
My gods, Gloria...

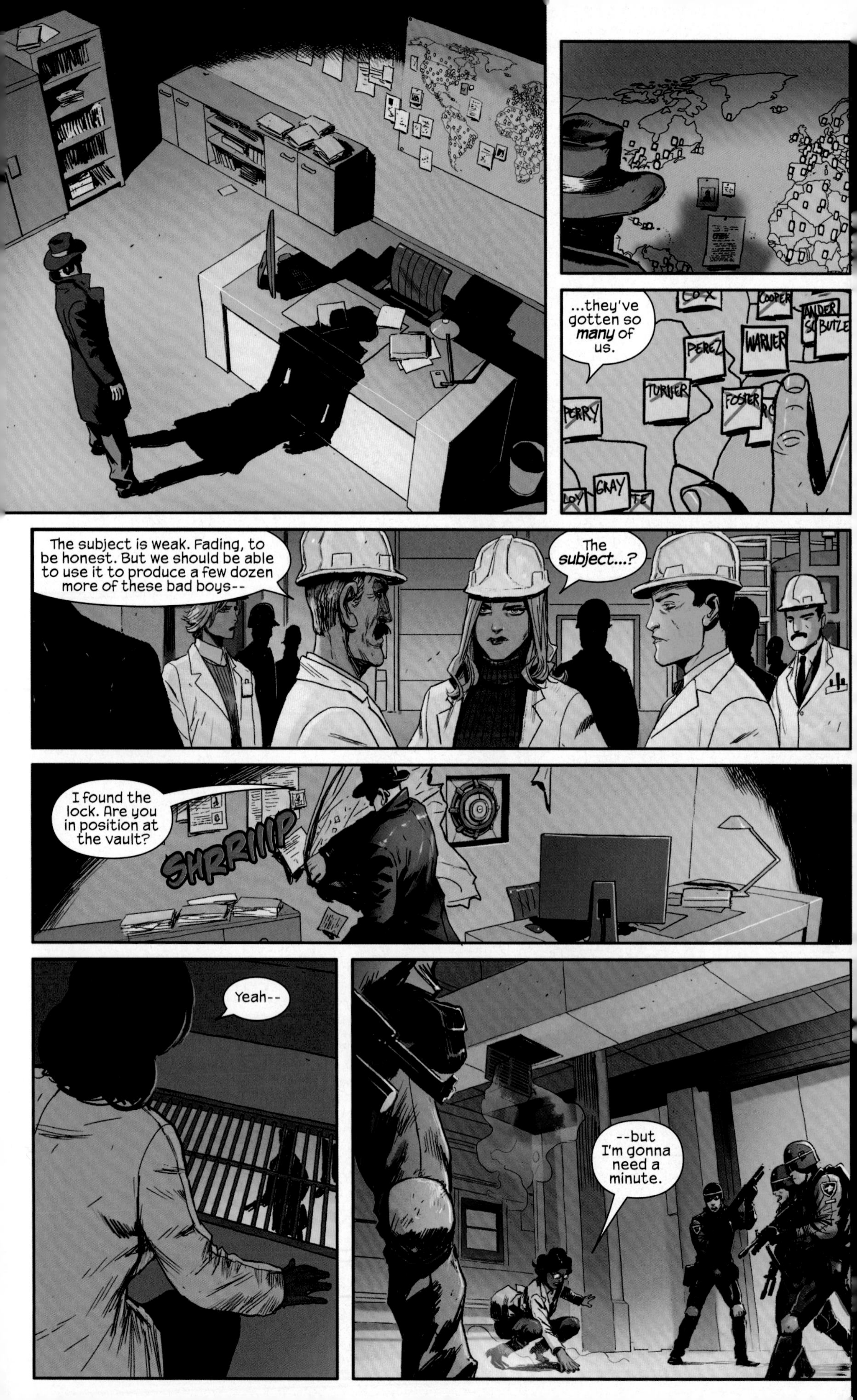
...they've gotten so *many* of us.
The subject is weak. Fading, to be honest. But we should be able to use it to produce a few dozen more of these bad boys--
The *subject...?*
I found the lock. Are you in position at the vault?
SHRRIIIP
Yeah--
--but I'm gonna need a minute.

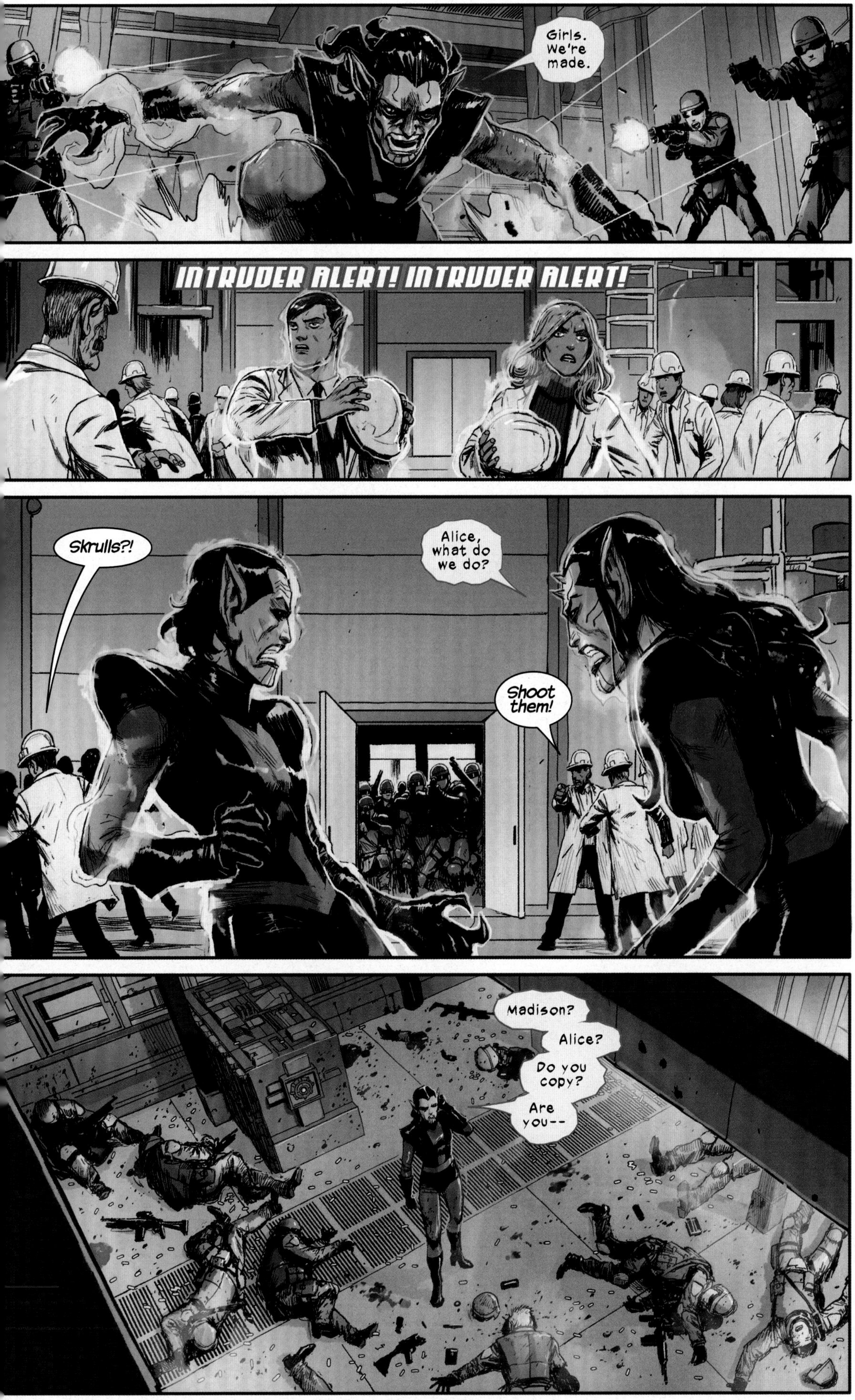
Girls. We're made.
INTRUDER ALERT! INTRUDER ALERT!
Skrulls?!
Alice, what do we do?
Shoot them!
Madison?
Alice?
Do you copy?
Are you--

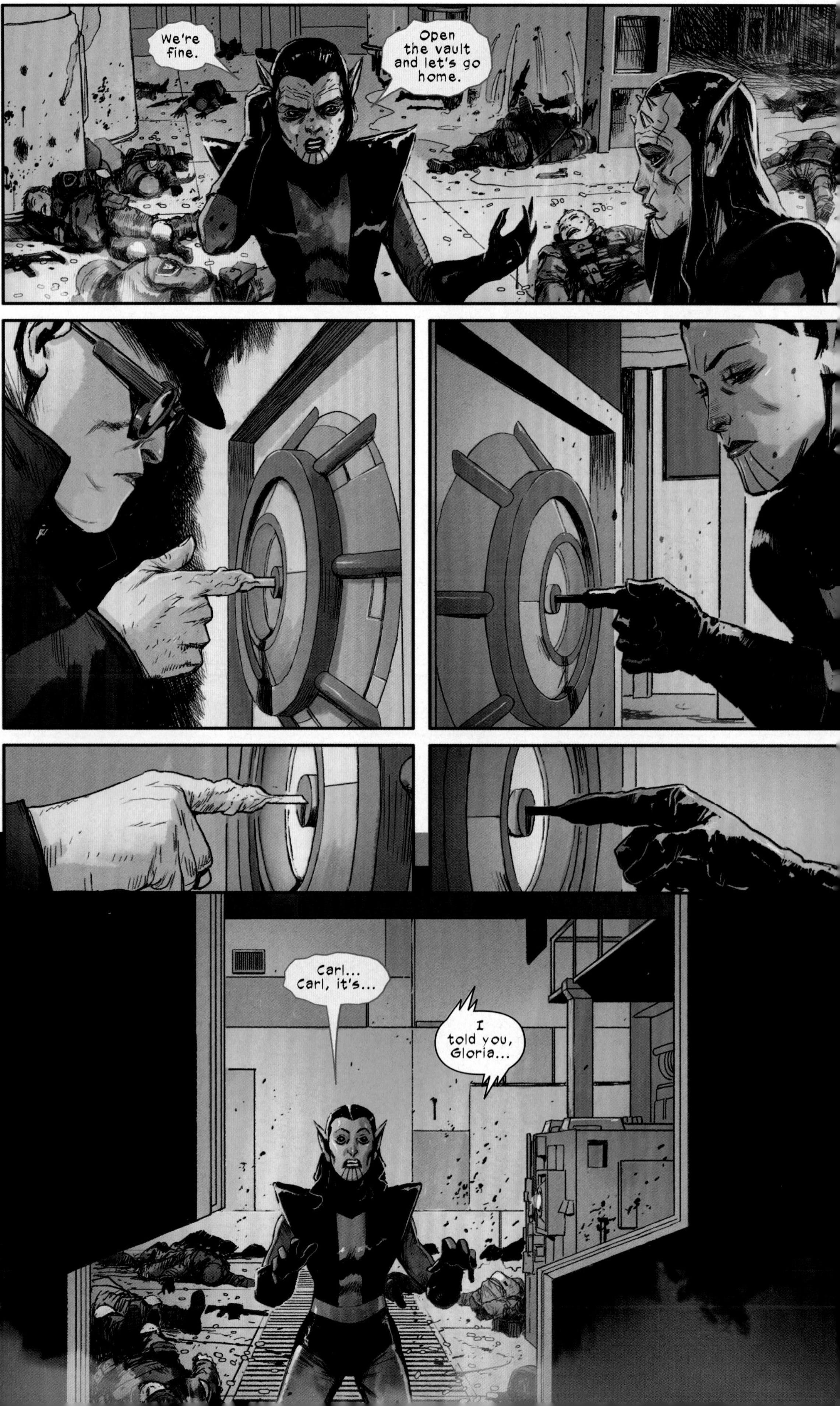
We're fine.
Open the vault and let's go home.
Carl... Carl, it's...
I told you, Gloria...

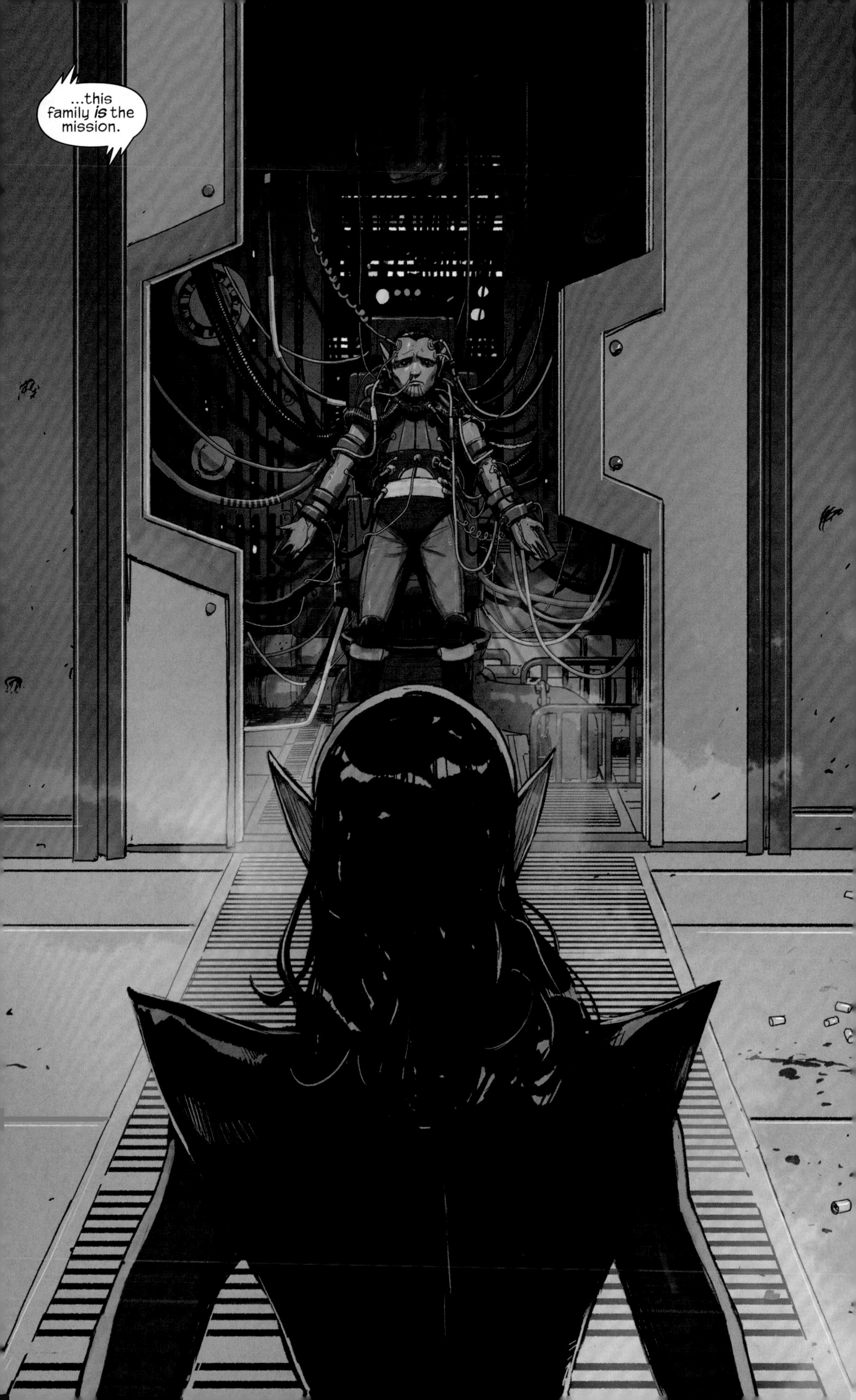
...this family *is* the mission.

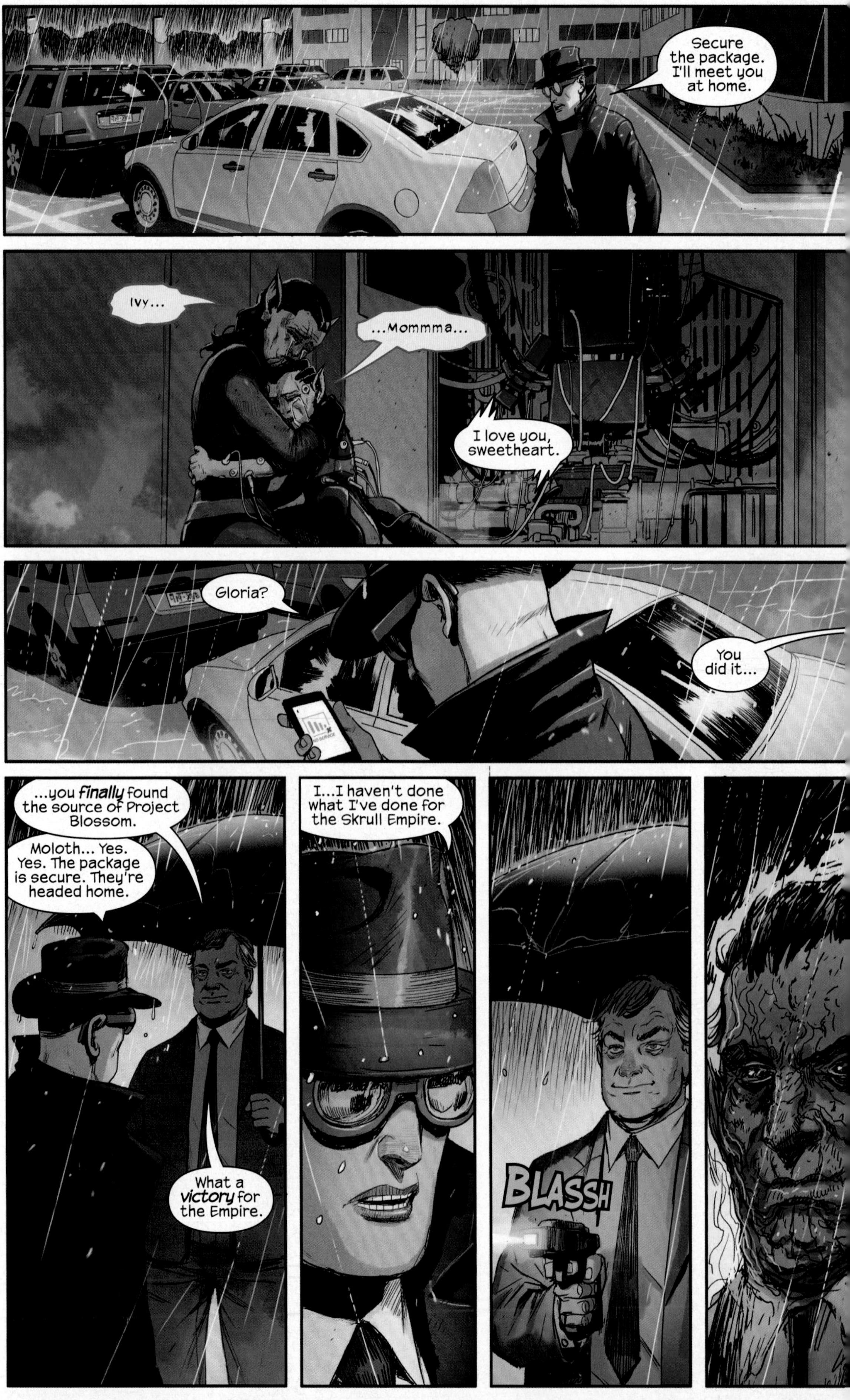
Secure the package. I'll meet you at home.
Ivy...
...Mommma...
I love you, sweetheart.
Gloria?
You did it...
...you finally found the source of Project Blossom.
Moloth... Yes. Yes. The package is secure. They're headed home.
What a victory for the Empire.
I...I haven't done what I've done for the Skrull Empire.
BLASSH

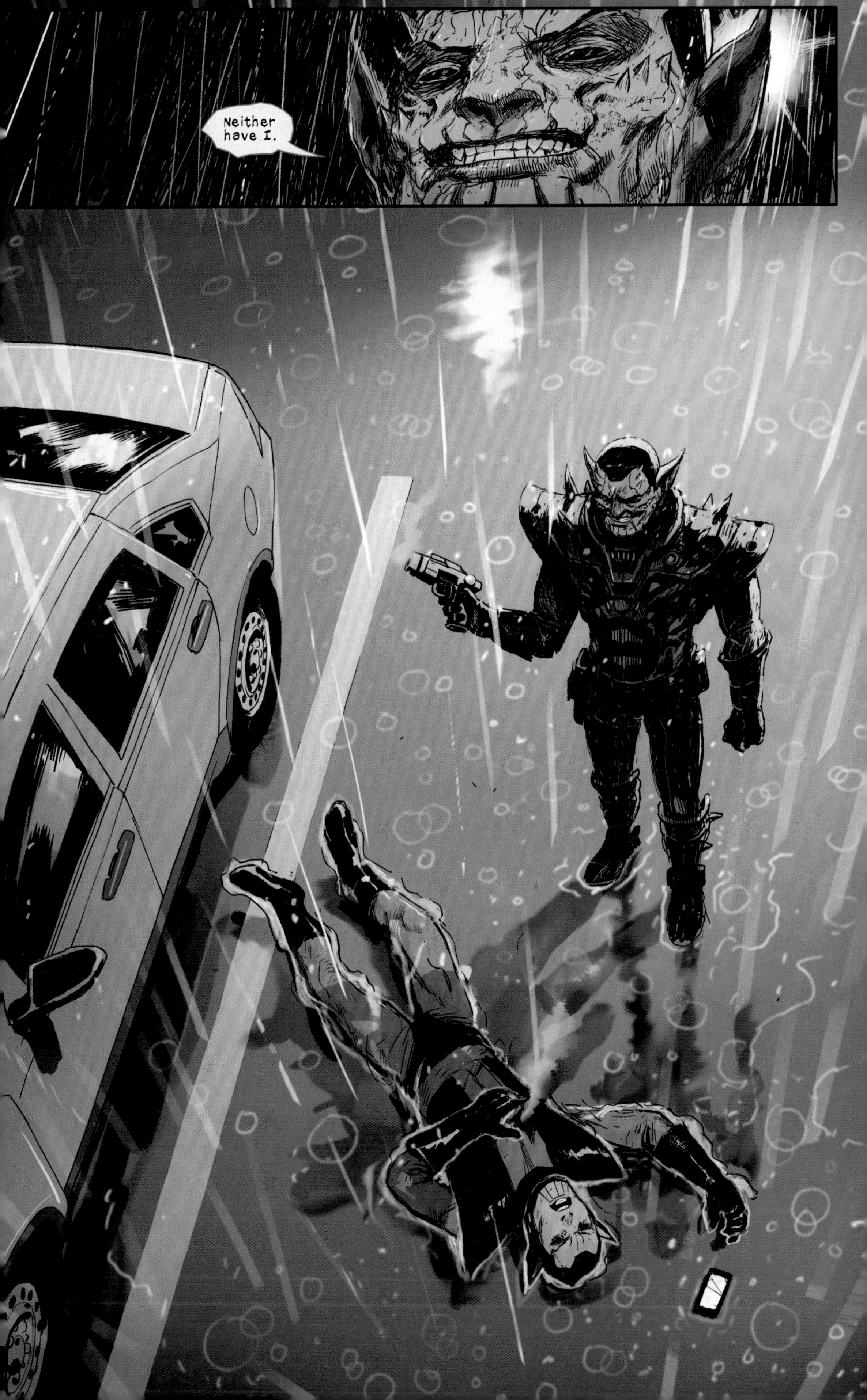
Neither have I.

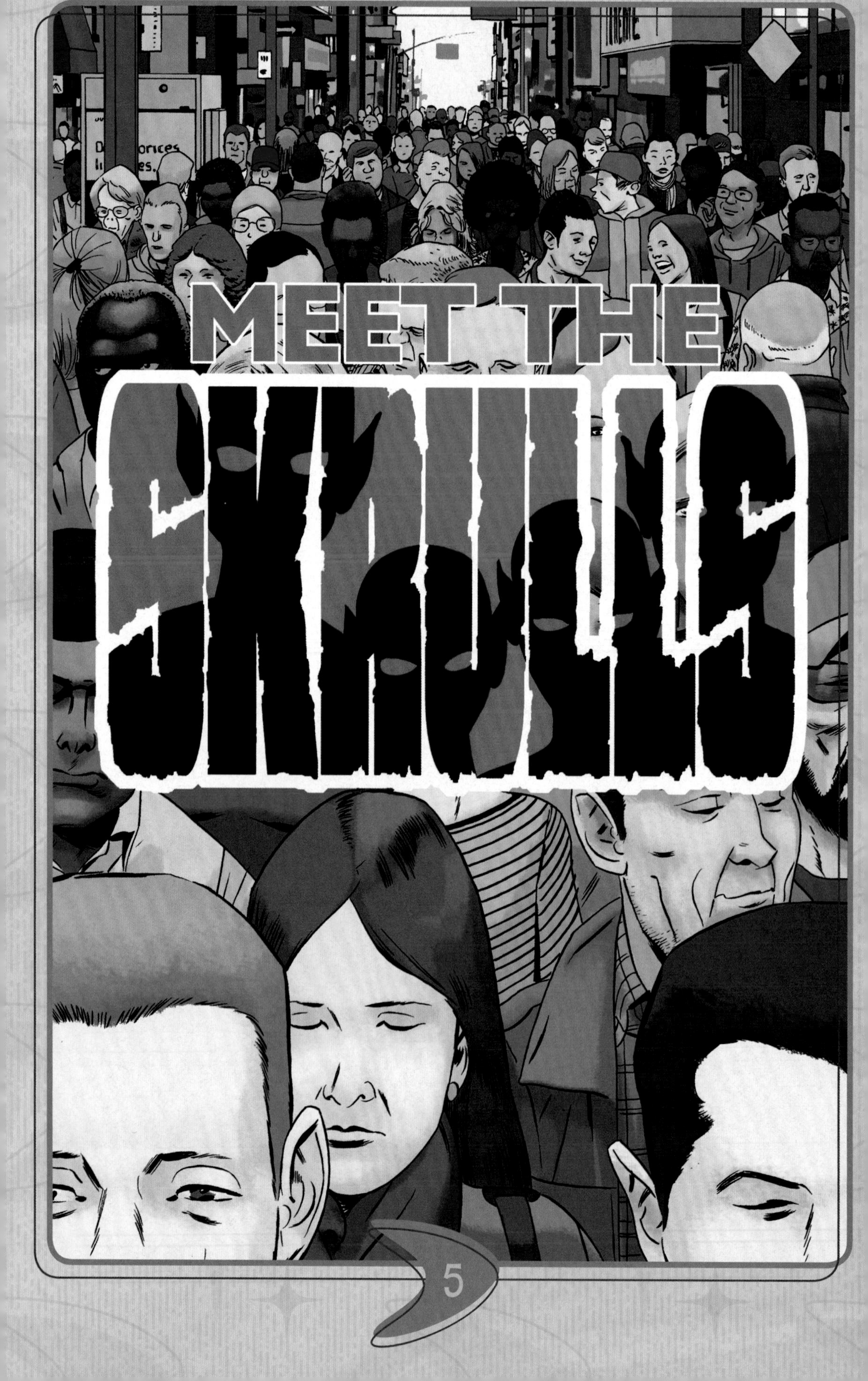
MEET THE
SKRULLS

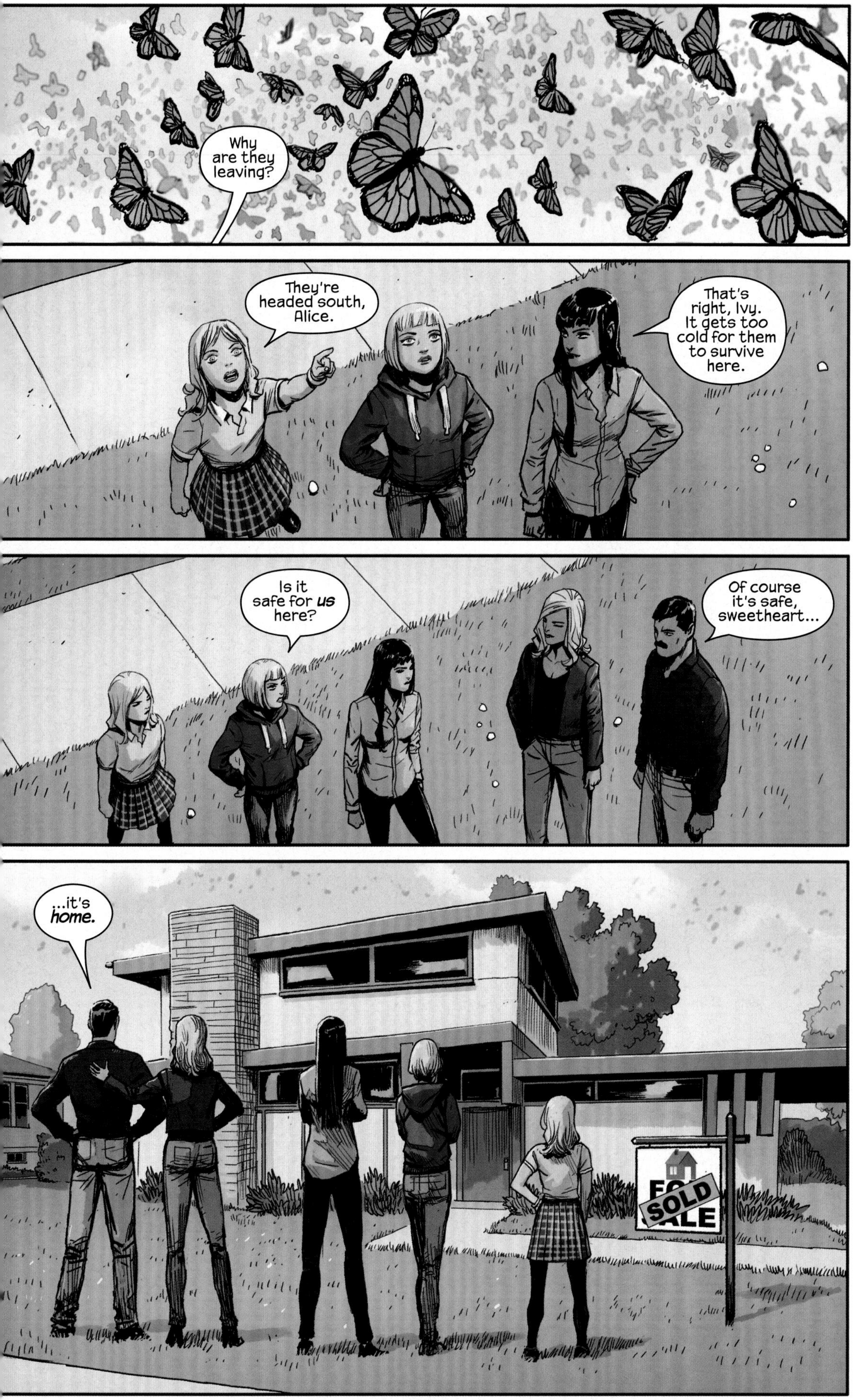
Why are they leaving?
They're headed south, Alice.
That's right, Ivy. It gets too cold for them to survive here.
Is it safe for *us* here?
Of course it's safe, sweetheart...
...it's *home.*
SOLD

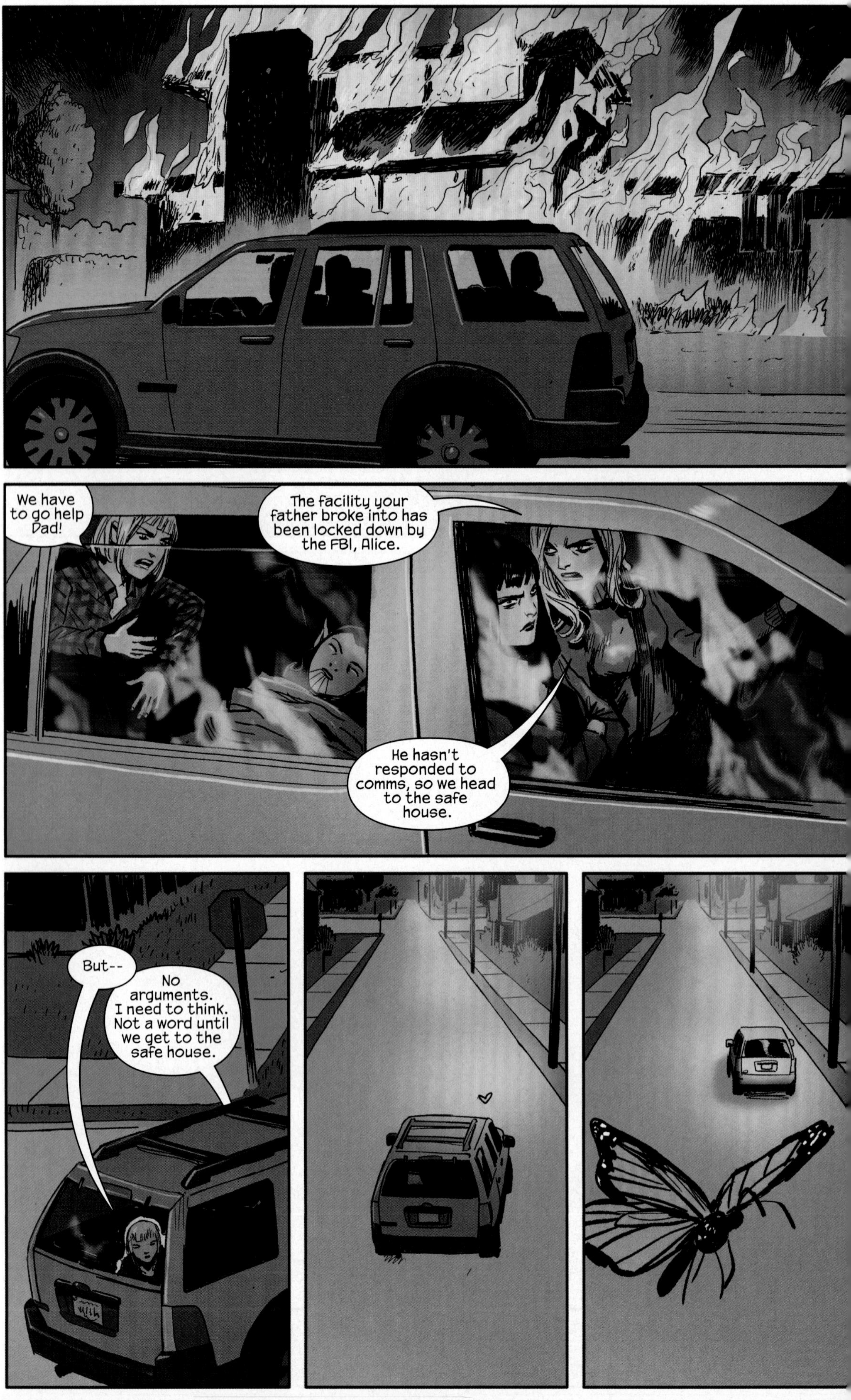
We have to go help Dad!
The facility your father broke into has been locked down by the FBI, Alice.
He hasn't responded to comms, so we head to the safe house.
But--
No arguments. I need to think. Not a word until we get to the safe house.

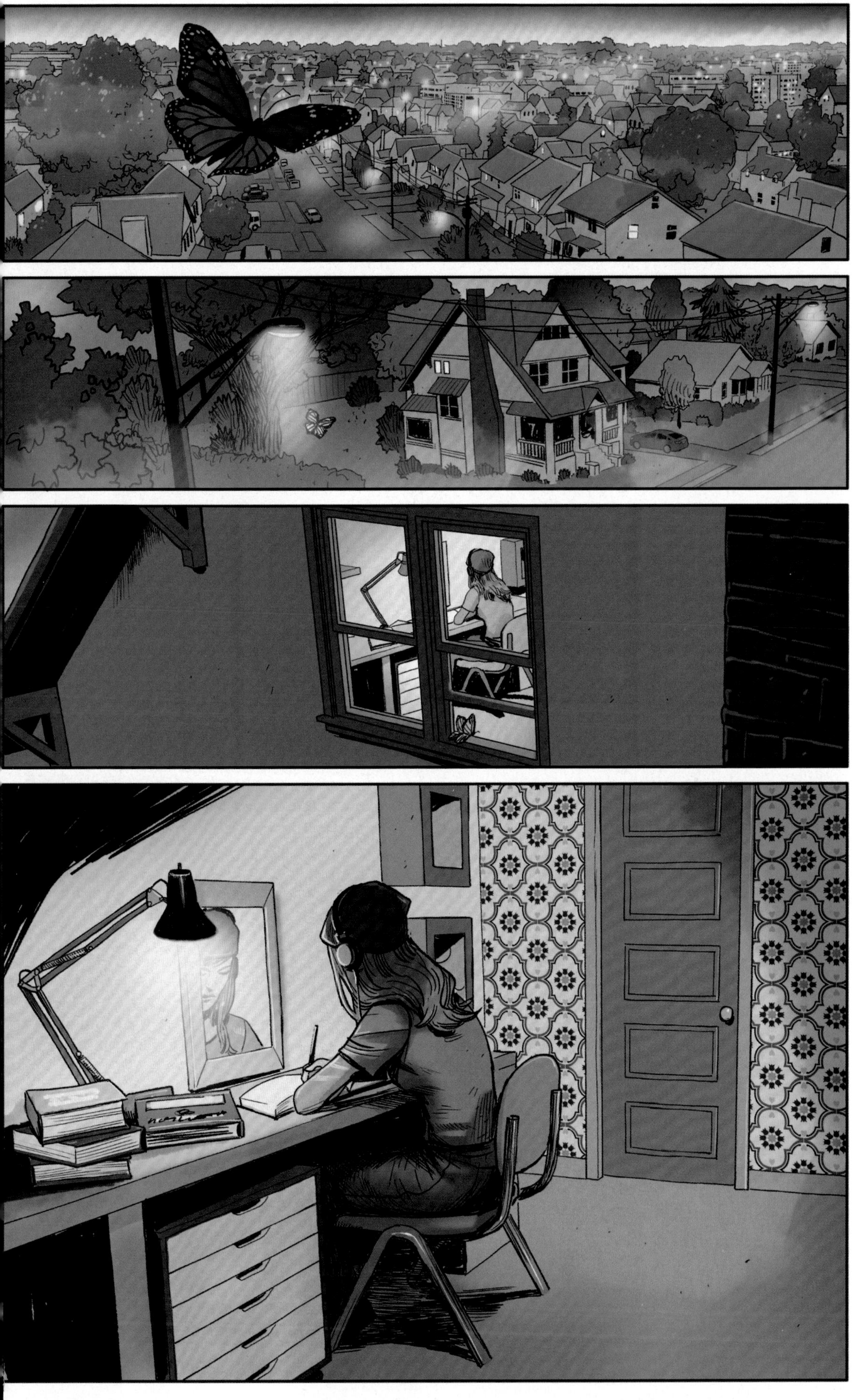

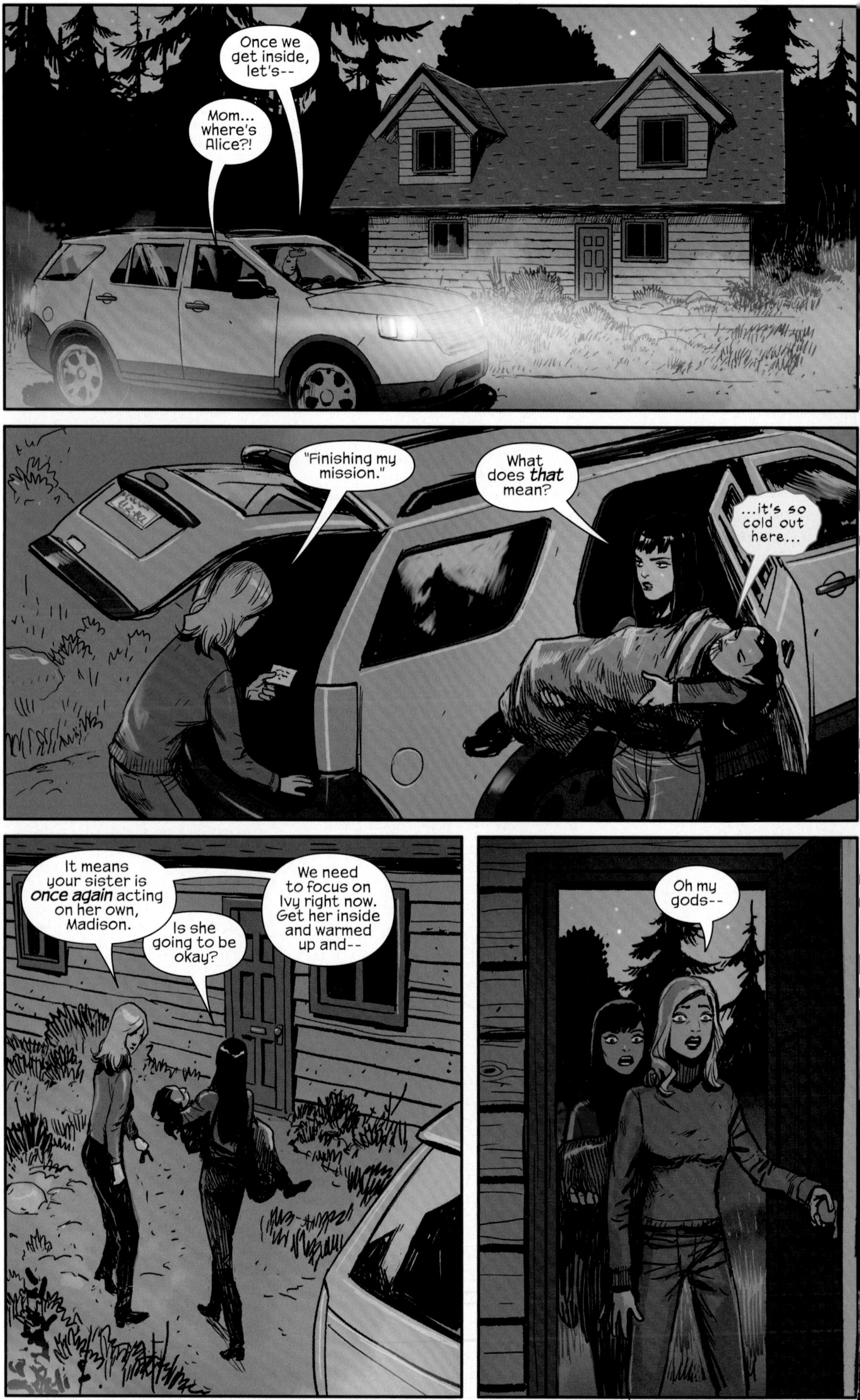
Once we get inside, let's--
Mom... where's Alice?!
"Finishing my mission."
What does *that* mean?
...it's so cold out here...
It means your sister is *once again* acting on her own, Madison.
Is she going to be okay?
We need to focus on Ivy right now. Get her inside and warmed up and--
Oh my gods--

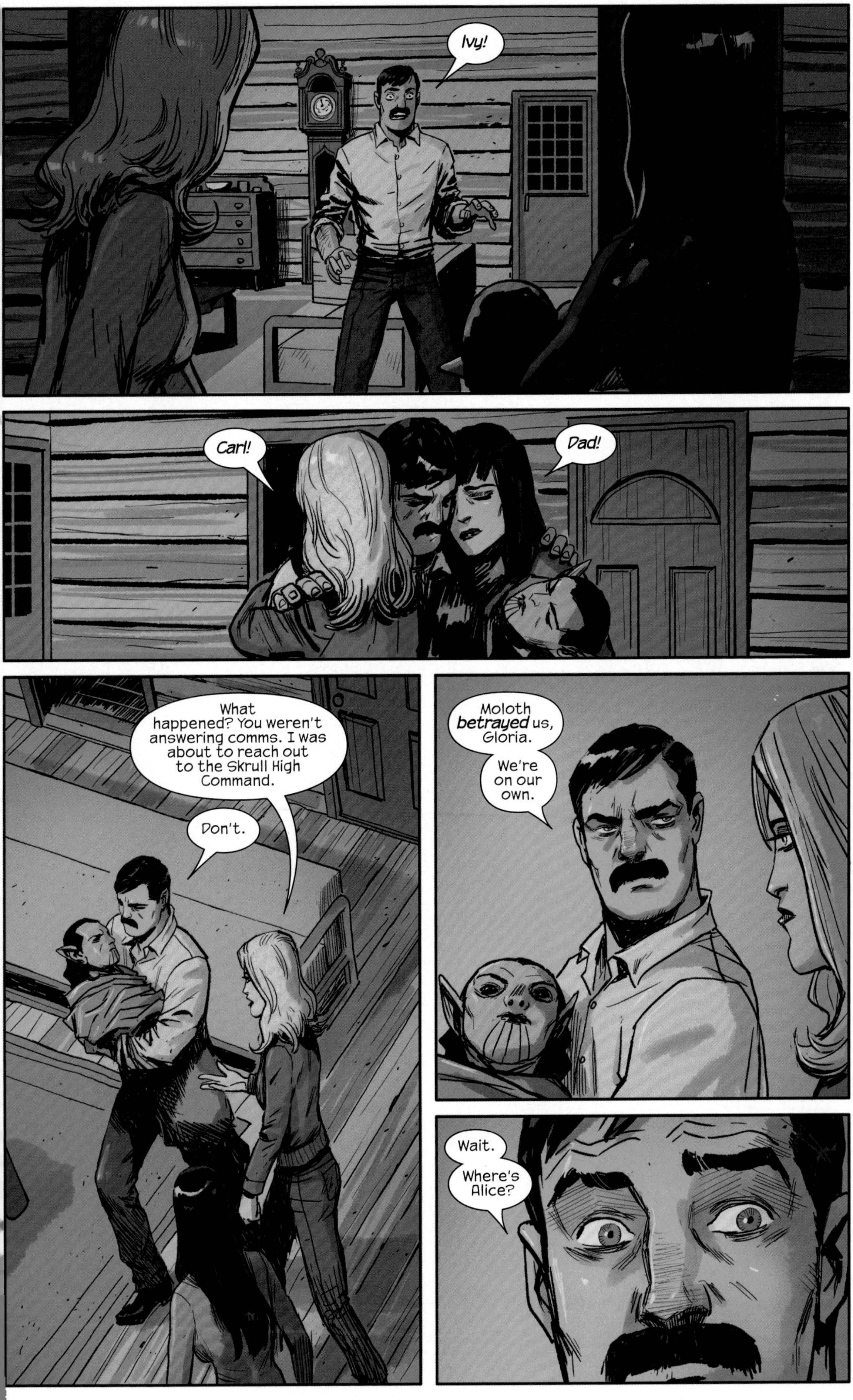
Ivy!
Carl!
Dad!
What happened? You weren't answering comms. I was about to reach out to the Skrull High Command.
Don't.
Moloth **betrayed** us, Gloria.
We're on our own.
Wait.
Where's Alice?

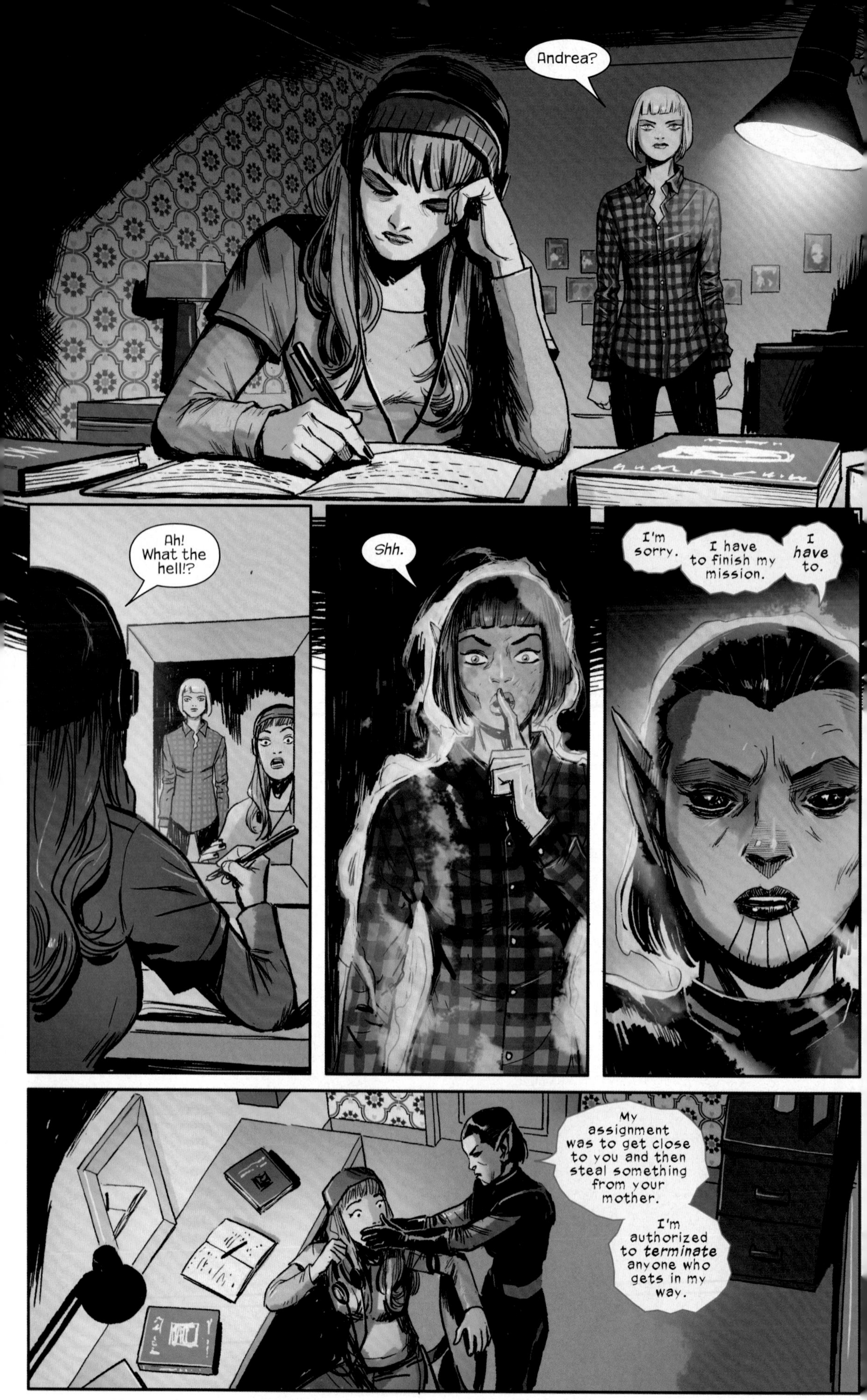
Andrea?
Ah! What the hell!?
Shh.
I'm sorry.
I have to finish my mission.
I have to.
My assignment was to get close to you and then steal something from your mother.
I'm authorized to terminate anyone who gets in my way.

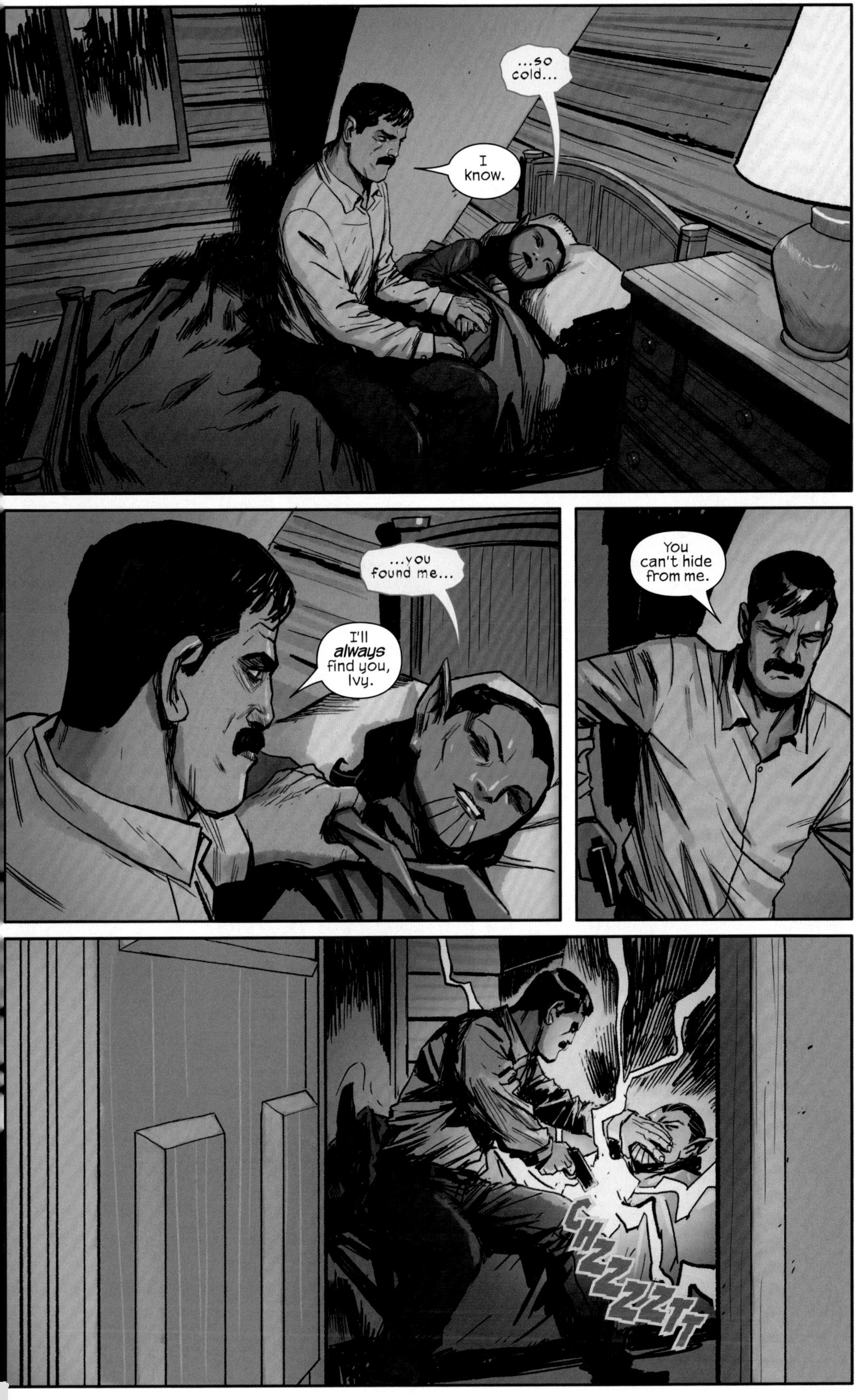

...so cold...
I know.
...you found me...
I'll *always* find you, Ivy.
You can't hide from me.
CHZZZZTT

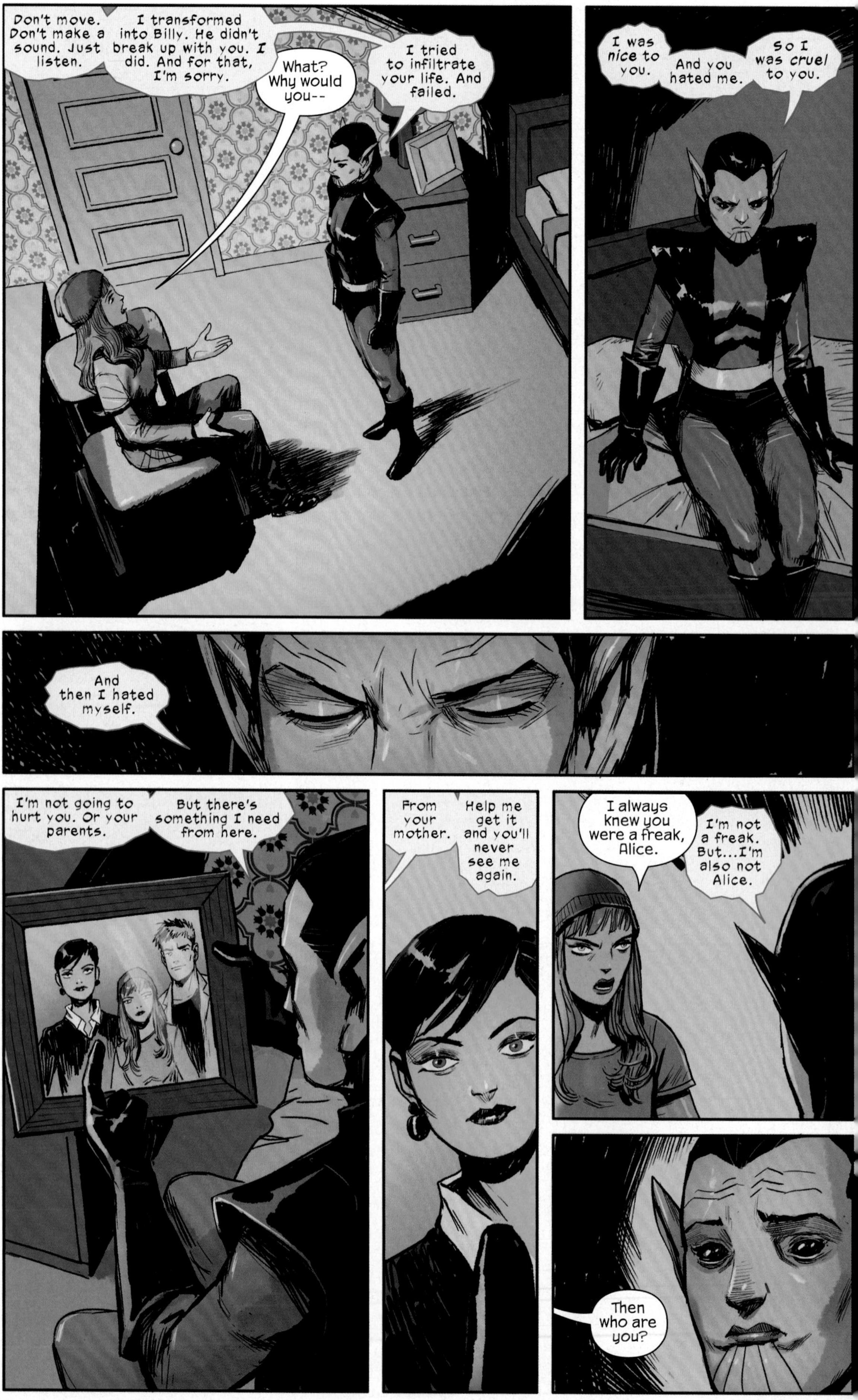

Don't move. Don't make a sound. Just listen.
I transformed into Billy. He didn't break up with you. *I* did. And for that, I'm sorry.
What? Why would you--
I tried to infiltrate your life. And failed.
I was *nice* to you.
And you hated me.
So I was *cruel* to you.
And then I hated myself.
I'm not going to hurt you. Or your parents.
But there's something I need from here.
From your mother.
Help me get it and you'll never see me again.
I always knew you were a freak, Alice.
I'm not a freak. But...I'm also not Alice.
Then who are you?

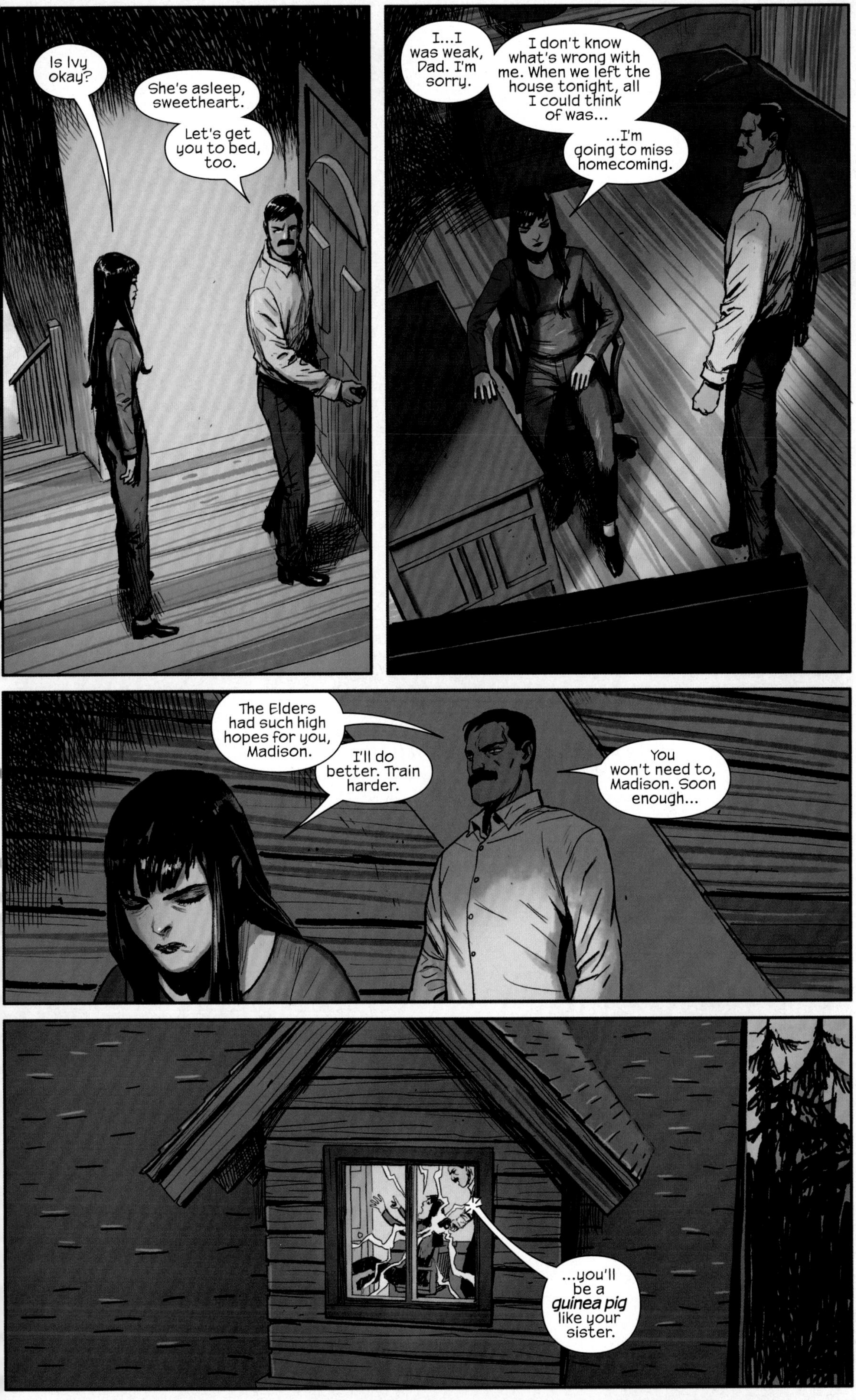
Is Ivy okay?
She's asleep, sweetheart.
Let's get you to bed, too.
I...I was weak, Dad. I'm sorry.
I don't know what's wrong with me. When we left the house tonight, all I could think of was...
...I'm going to miss homecoming.
The Elders had such high hopes for you, Madison.
I'll do better. Train harder.
You won't need to, Madison. Soon enough...
...you'll be a *guinea pig* like your sister.

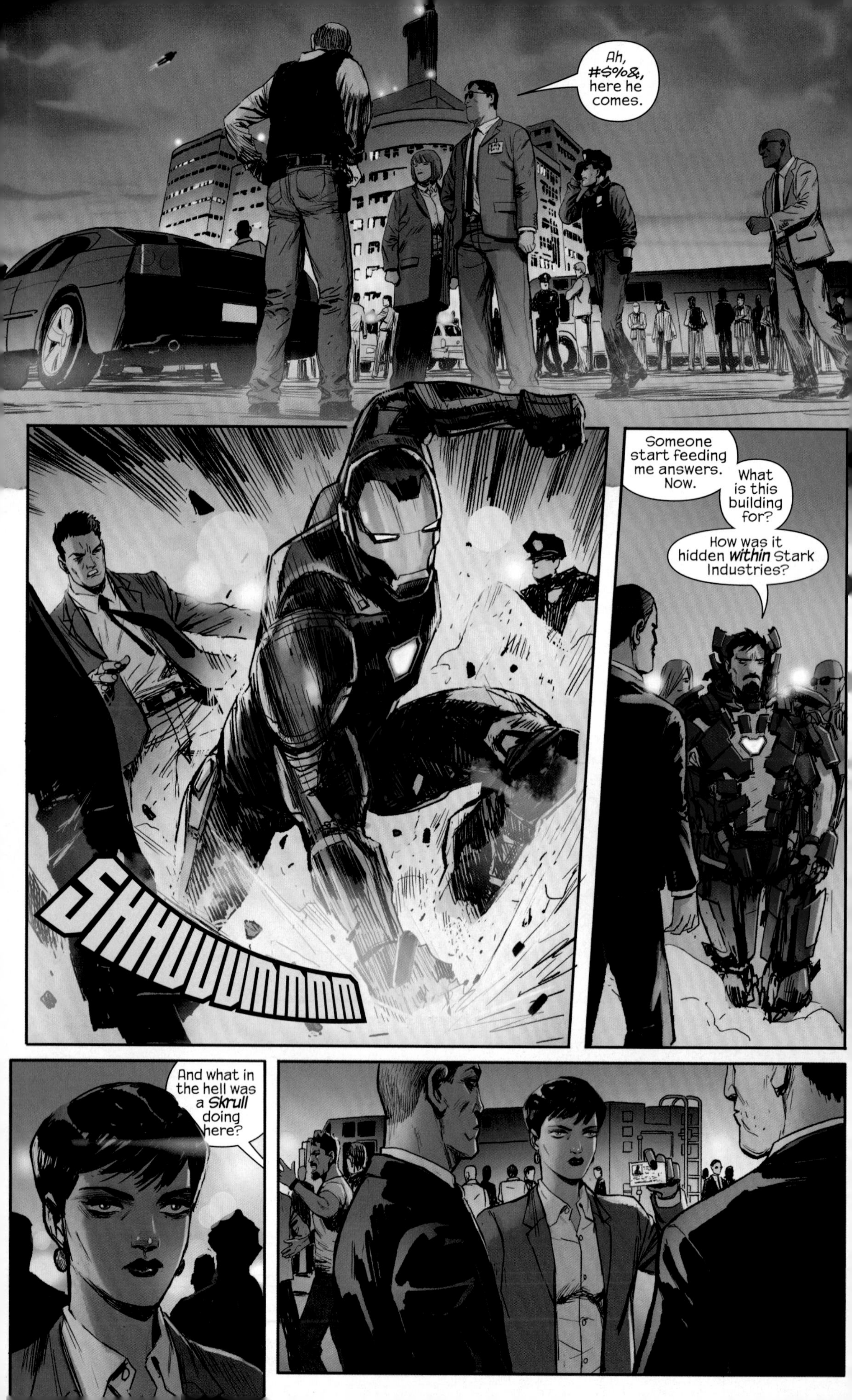
Ah, #$%&, here he comes.
SHHUUUMMMM
Someone start feeding me answers. Now.
What is this building for?
How was it hidden within Stark Industries?
And what in the hell was a Skrull doing here?

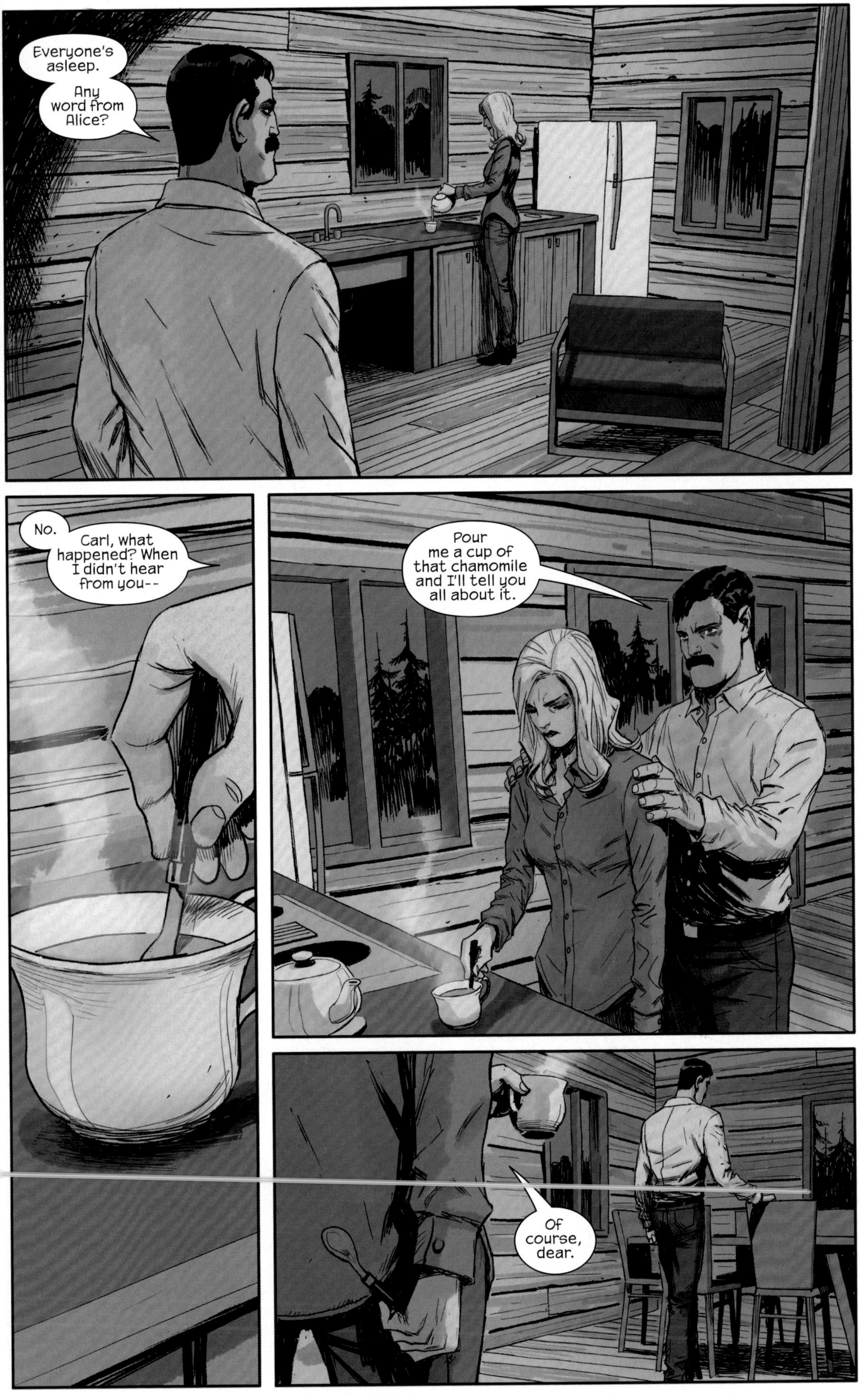
Everyone's asleep.
Any word from Alice?
No.
Carl, what happened? When I didn't hear from you--
Pour me a cup of that chamomile and I'll tell you all about it.
Of course, dear.

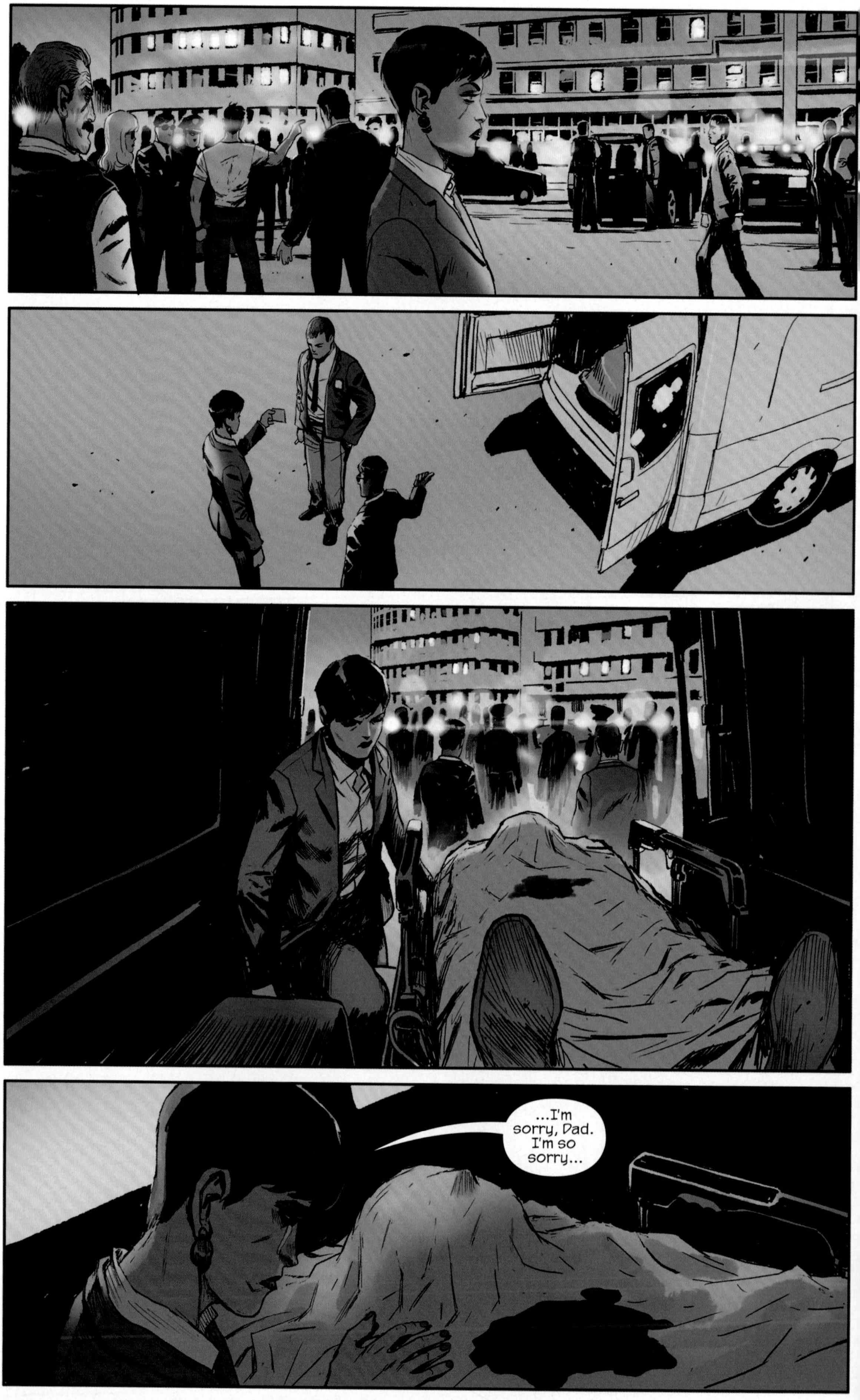
...I'm sorry, Dad. I'm so sorry...

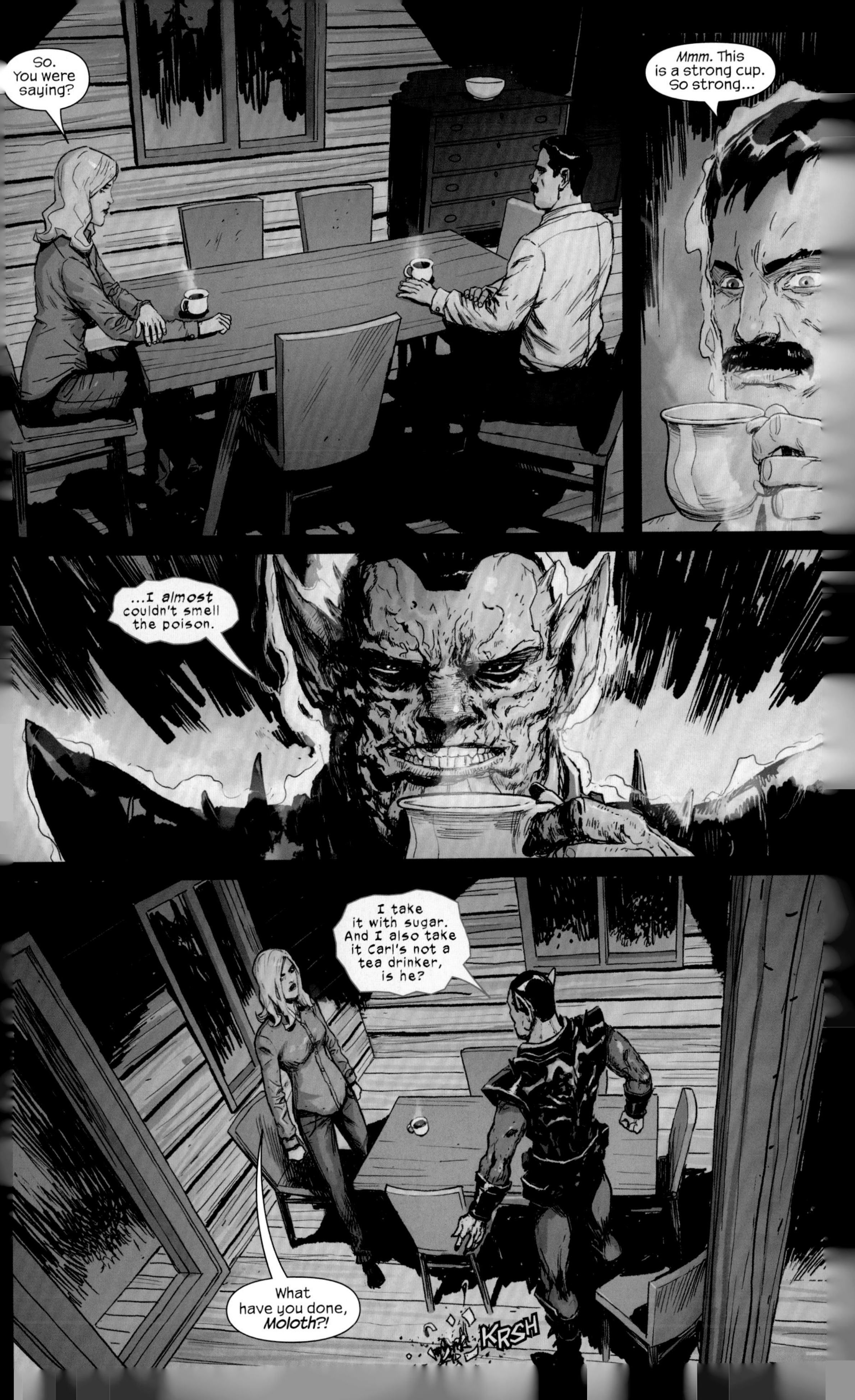
So. You were saying?
Mmm. This is a strong cup. So strong...
...I almost couldn't smell the poison.
I take it with sugar. And I also take it Carl's not a tea drinker, is he?
What have you done, Moloth?!
KRSH

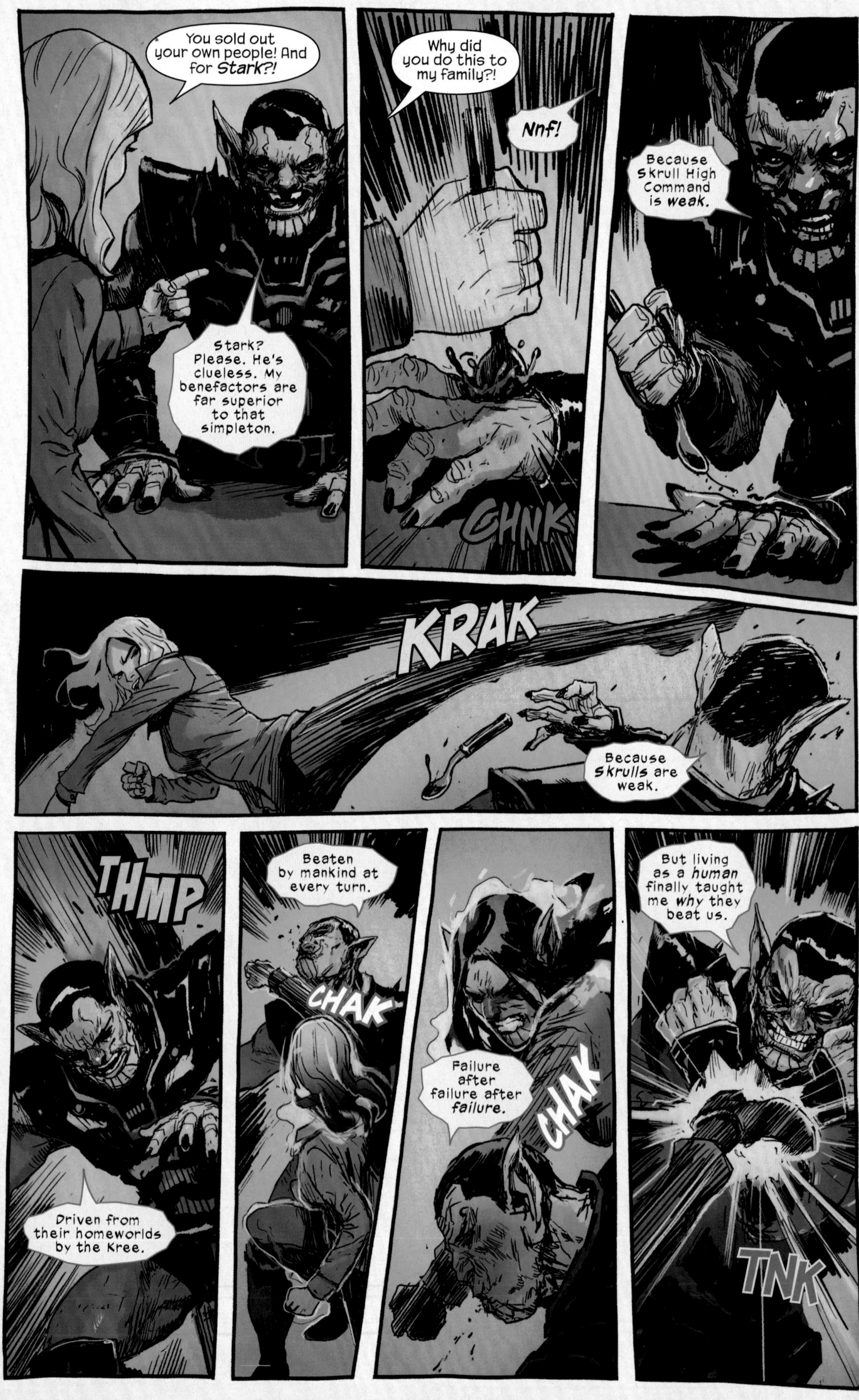
You sold out your own people! And for Stark?!
Stark? Please. He's clueless. My benefactors are far superior to that simpleton.
Why did you do this to my family?!
Nnf!
CHNK
Because Skrull High Command is weak.
KRAK
Because Skrulls are weak.
THMP
Driven from their homeworlds by the Kree.
Beaten by mankind at every turn.
CHAK
Failure after failure after failure.
CHAK
But living as a human finally taught me why they beat us.
TNK

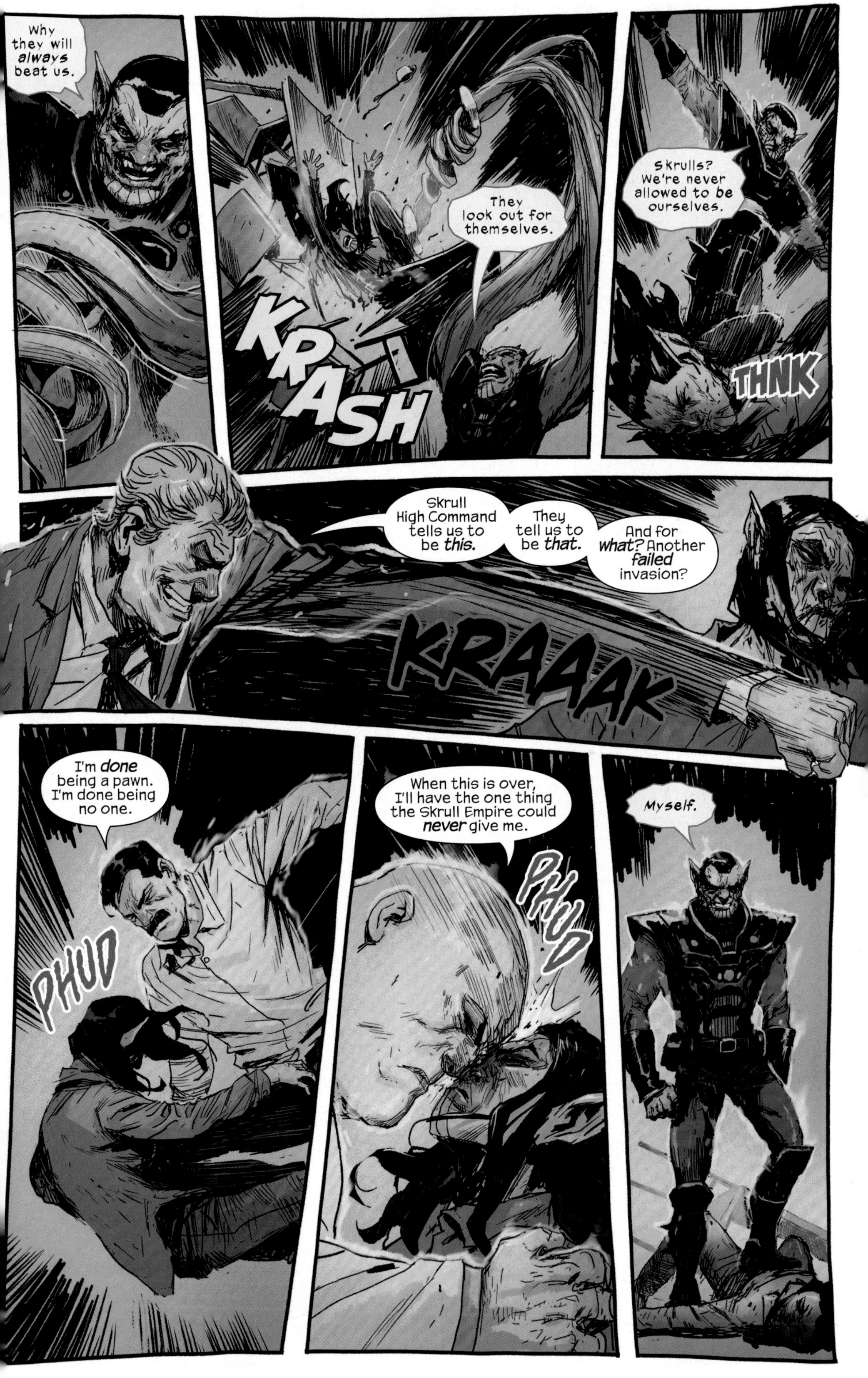
Why they will always beat us.
KRASH
They look out for themselves.
Skrulls? We're never allowed to be ourselves.
THNK
Skrull High Command tells us to be this.
They tell us to be that.
And for what? Another failed invasion?
KRAAAK
I'm done being a pawn. I'm done being no one.
PHUD
When this is over, I'll have the one thing the Skrull Empire could never give me.
PHUD
Myself.

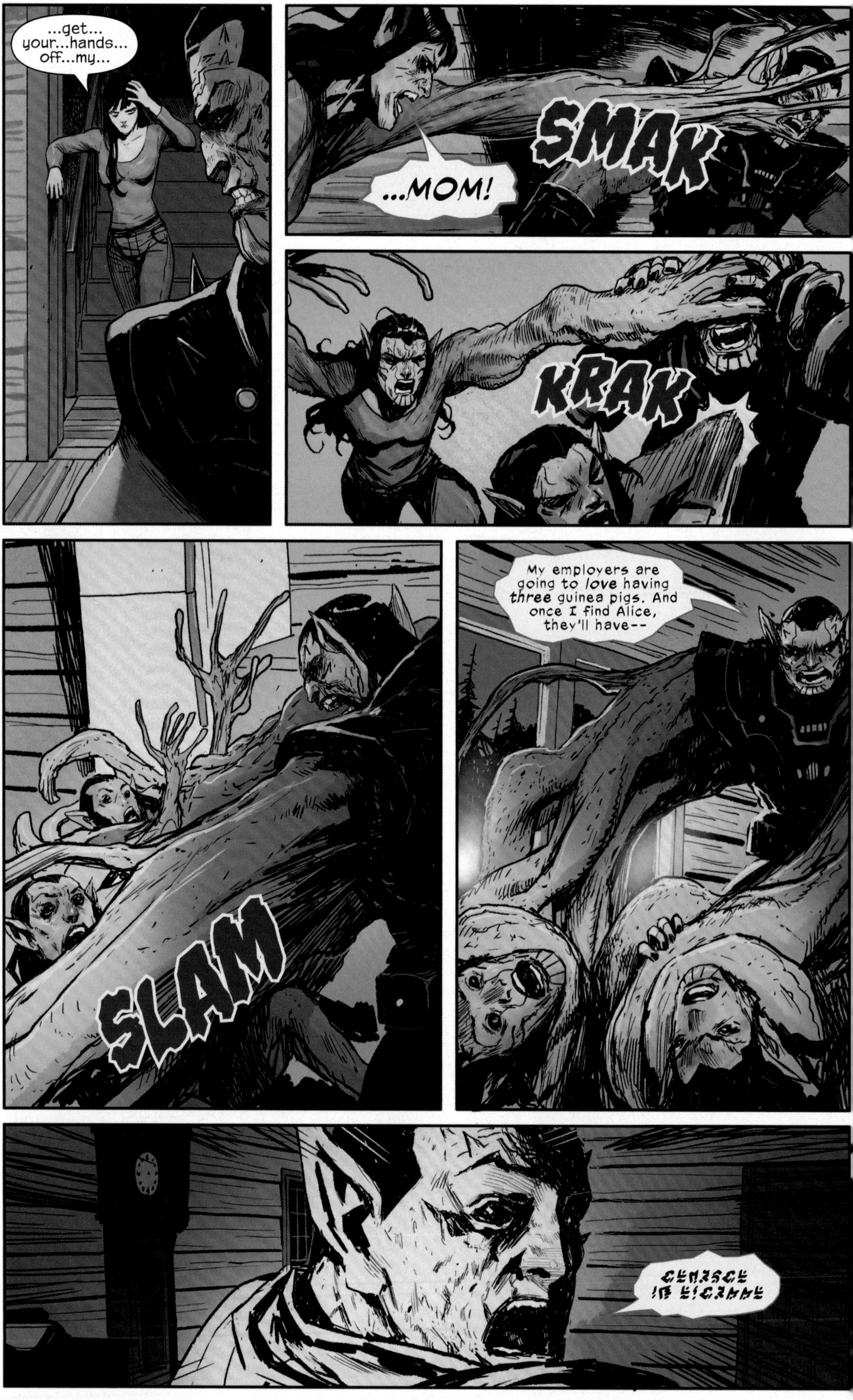
...get... your...hands... off...my...
...MOM!
SMAK
KRAK
SLAM
My employers are going to love having three guinea pigs. And once I find Alice, they'll have--

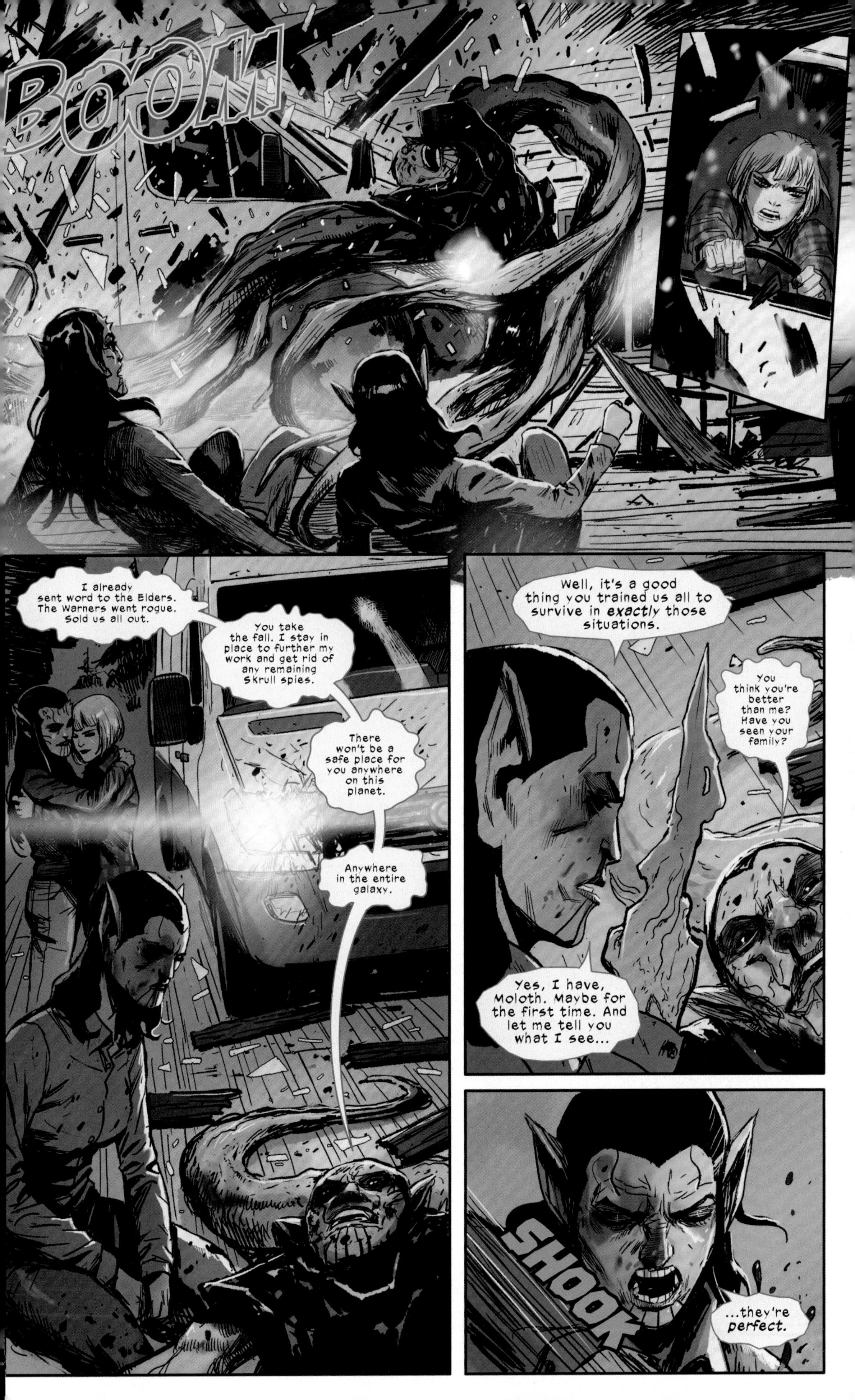
BOOM
I already sent word to the Elders. The Warners went rogue. Sold us all out.
You take the fall. I stay in place to further my work and get rid of any remaining Skrull spies.
There won't be a safe place for you anywhere on this planet.
Anywhere in the entire galaxy.
Well, it's a good thing you trained us all to survive in exactly those situations.
You think you're better than me? Have you seen your family?
Yes, I have, Moloth. Maybe for the first time. And let me tell you what I see...
SHOOK
...they're perfect.

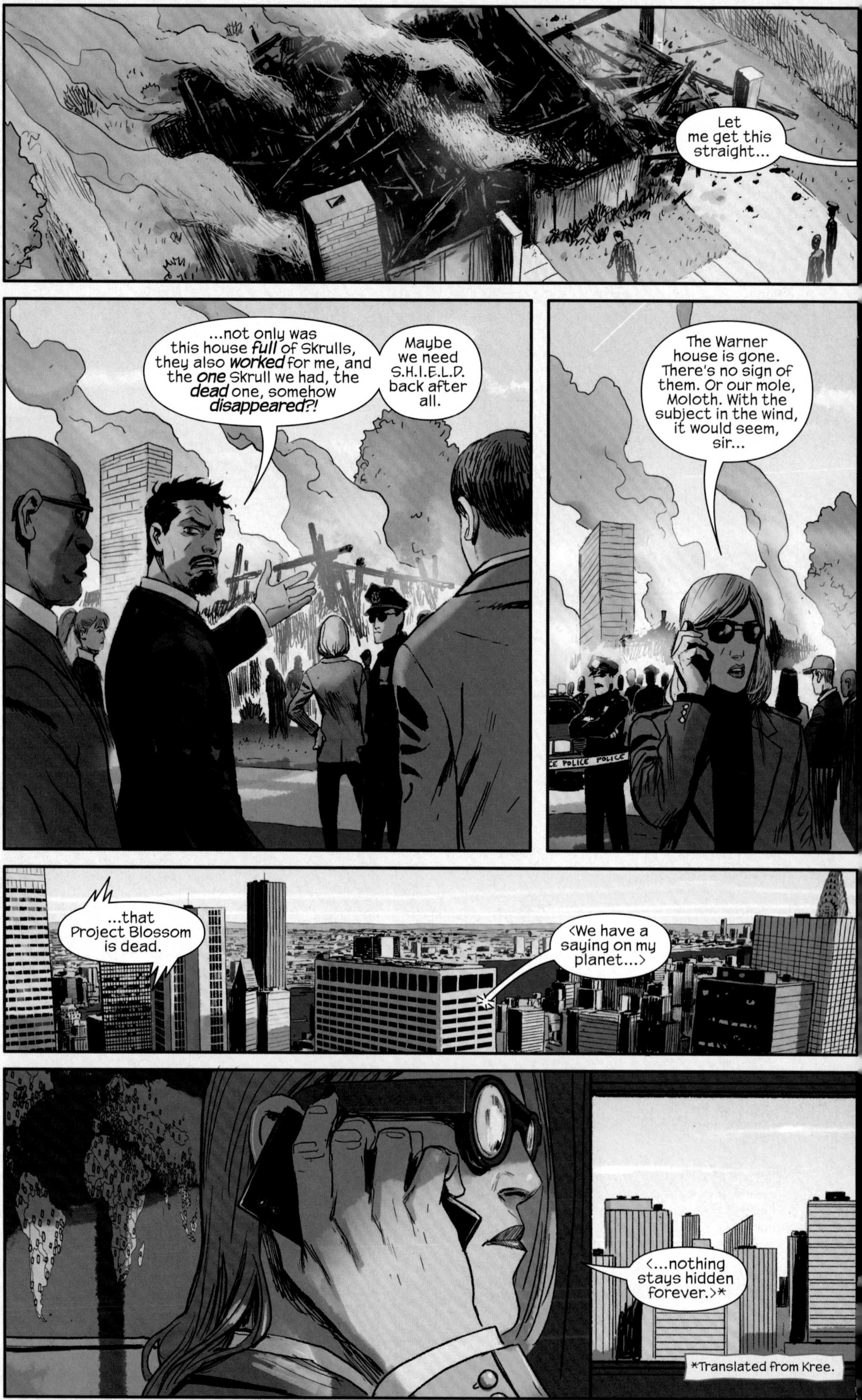
Let me get this straight...
...not only was this house *full* of Skrulls, they also *worked* for me, and the *one* Skrull we had, the *dead* one, somehow *disappeared?!*
Maybe we need S.H.I.E.L.D. back after all.
The Warner house is gone. There's no sign of them. Or our mole, Moloth. With the subject in the wind, it would seem, sir...
POLICE POLICE
...that Project Blossom is dead.
<We have a saying on my planet...>
<...nothing stays hidden forever.>*
*Translated from Kree.

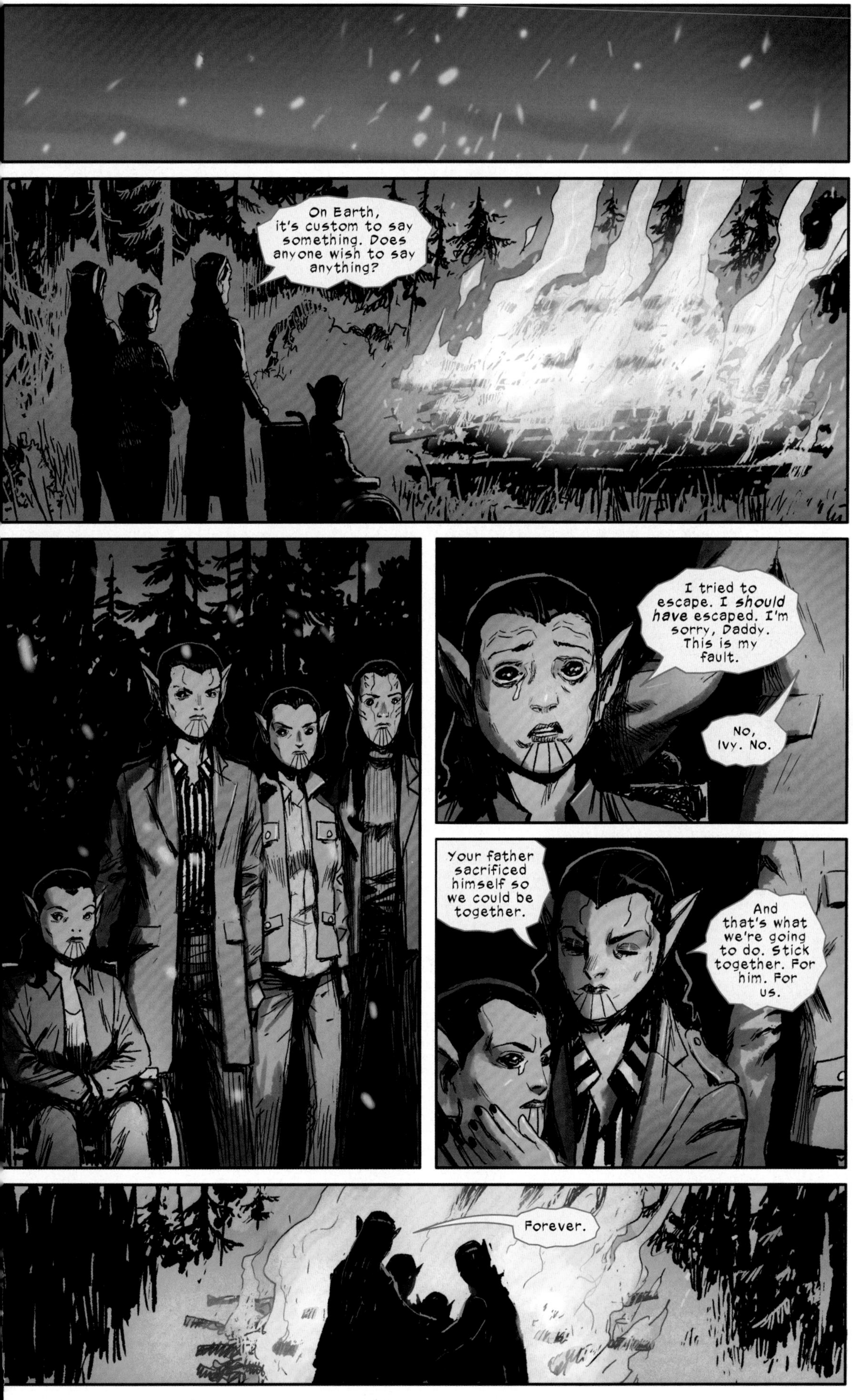
On Earth, it's custom to say something. Does anyone wish to say anything?
I tried to escape. I *should have* escaped. I'm sorry, Daddy. This is my fault.
No, Ivy. No.
Your father sacrificed himself so we could be together.
And that's what we're going to do. Stick together. For him. For us.
Forever.

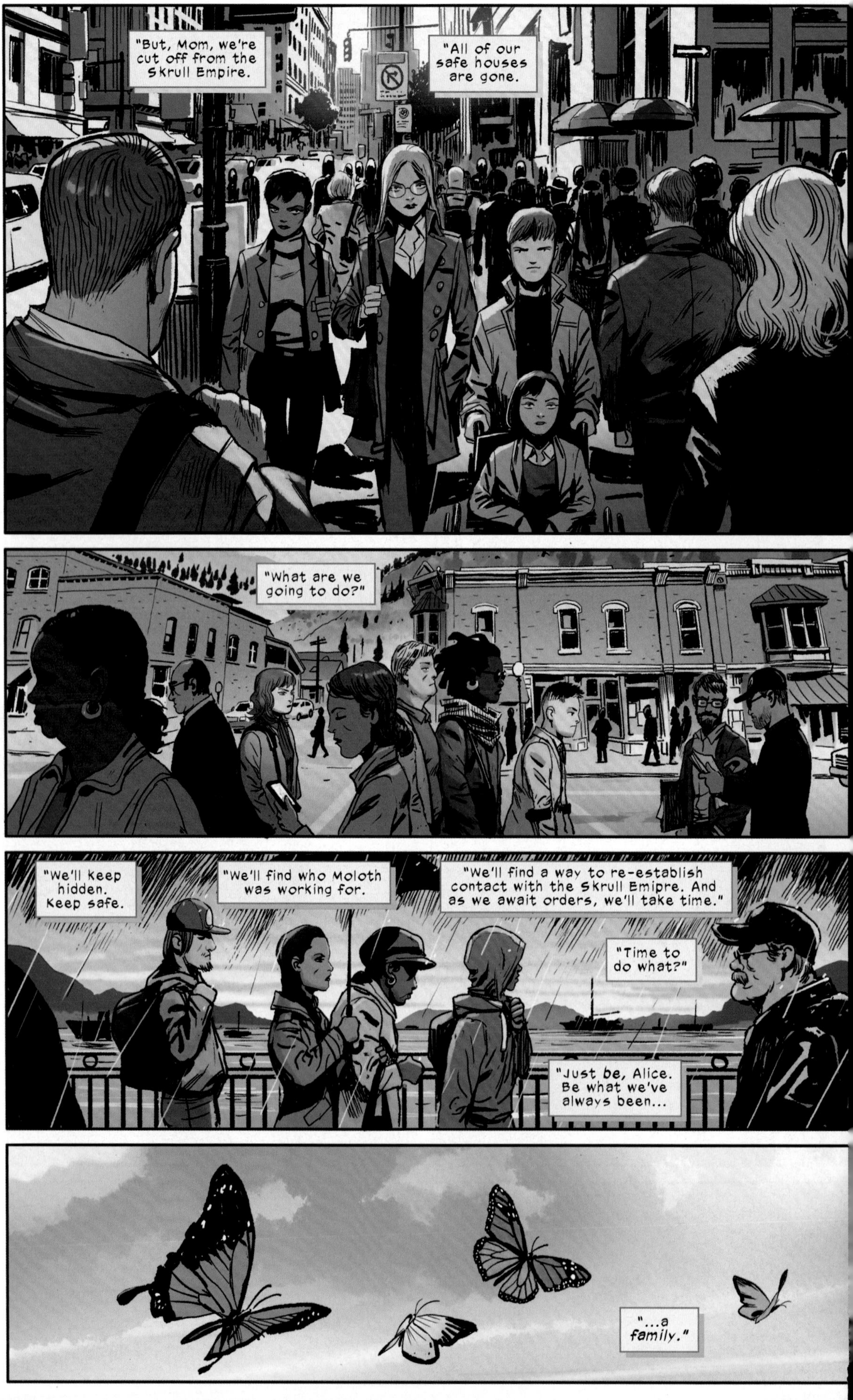
"But, Mom, we're cut off from the Skrull Empire.
"All of our safe houses are gone.
"What are we going to do?"
"We'll keep hidden. Keep safe.
"We'll find who Moloth was working for.
"We'll find a way to re-establish contact with the Skrull Emipre. And as we await orders, we'll take time."
"Time to do what?"
"Just be, Alice. Be what we've always been...
"...a family."

THE END.

WELL, SORT OF. MY NAME IS NICK LOWE, AND I'VE BEEN THE LUCKY PERSON WHO EDITED THIS BOOK. OVER THE YEARS, ROBBIE THOMPSON AND I HAVE TALKED ABOUT DOING BOOKS THAT WERE REALLY DIFFERENT FROM THOSE WE'D BEEN WORKING ON, LIKE *SILK* AND *SPIDEY* AND *SPIDER-MAN/DEADPOOL*. WE TALKED ABOUT A LOT OF CONCEPTS TO TRY TO PUT TOGETHER, BUT WHEN HE HAD THE IDEA OF A SPY FAMILY OF SKRULLS, I WAS HOOKED AND KNEW THAT ROBBIE'S INCREDIBLE VOICE FOR DIALOGUE AND CHARACTERS' INNER LIVES WOULD MAKE IT SING. BUT I ALSO KNEW IT WOULD BE A TOUGH SELL. WHEN I GOT A WALK-THROUGH OF THE CAPTAIN MARVEL FILM AND THE SKRULLS' INVOLVEMENT, WE JUMPED AND GOT THE BOOK APPROVED.

WE TALKED ABOUT ARTISTS, AND I CAN'T REMEMBER WHOSE IDEA IT WAS TO GO TO THE INCREDIBLE NIKO HENRICHON, BUT AS SOON AS WE THOUGHT OF IT WE REALIZED NO ONE ELSE COULD DO IT. FROM *PRIDE OF BAGHDAD*, WHERE I FIRST SAW HIS WORK, TO *DOCTOR STRANGE* AND *NEW MUTANTS*, WHERE WE GOT TO WORK TOGETHER, NIKO SHOWED HE COULD DRAW ANYTHING. USUALLY WHEN YOU SAY THAT, YOU MEAN BIG, CRAZY STUFF, WHICH NIKO CAN CERTAINLY DRAW. BUT IN THIS CASE, COULD HE DRAW A FAMILY IN THEIR LIVING ROOM? MIGHT BE STRANGE TO SAY, BUT NOT EVERY COMIC BOOK ARTIST CAN DRAW THAT AND STILL HAVE IT BE INTERESTING. NIKO EXCELLED AT IT AND THE BIG, CRAZY THINGS HE HAD TO DRAW AS WELL.

THE INCREDIBLE ASSISTANT EDITOR KATHLEEN WISNESKI (WHO IS RESPONSIBLE FOR SO MUCH OF WHAT MAKES THIS BOOK SUBTLE AND POWERFUL) AND I HAD JUST FINISHED WORKING WITH LETTERER TRAVIS LANHAM ON *PETER PARKER: THE SPECTACULAR SPIDER-MAN* AND WANTED A NEW PROJECT WITH HIM. HE IS A TIRELESS WORKER AND SO CREATIVE, SO WE KNEW WE'D BE IN GOOD HANDS. TRAVIS DELIVERED.

LASTLY, WE KNEW THIS WASN'T A CONCEPT THAT WOULD BE EASY TO MAKE JUMP OFF THE SHELVES, SO WE NEEDED THE COVERS TO BE POWERFUL. LUCKILY, ONE OF THE GREATEST COVER ARTISTS OF **ALL TIME**, MARCOS MARTIN, CAME ON BOARD.

IT WAS THESE PEOPLE WHO BROUGHT THE WARNERS TO LIFE AND MADE THEIR LIVES SO RICH, AND I FEEL LUCKY TO HAVE SPENT THESE FIVE ISSUES WITH THEM. AND NOW, IT ENDS. THIS BOOK AND THE WARNERS' STORY IS OVER. THERE'S NO WAY THAT, OVER THE NEXT FEW YEARS, YOU'LL BE SPENDING TIME WITH ONE OF YOUR FAVORITE CHARACTERS IN ONE OF YOUR FAVORITE BOOKS AND COME ACROSS A REVEAL THAT IT'S ACTUALLY ALICE WARNER. NO WAY IS THAT GOING TO HAPPEN. THEIR STORY IS OVER. **THE END**.

NICK LOWE
EDITOR

THIS IS FOR MY FAMILY. THANK YOU FOR MAKING ME WHO I AM.

ROBBIE THOMPSON

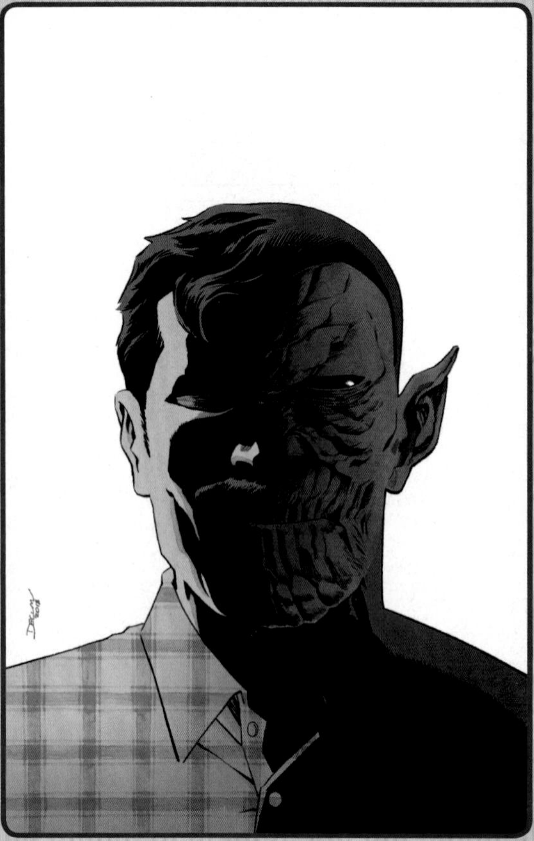

DECLAN SHALVEY
#1 Variant

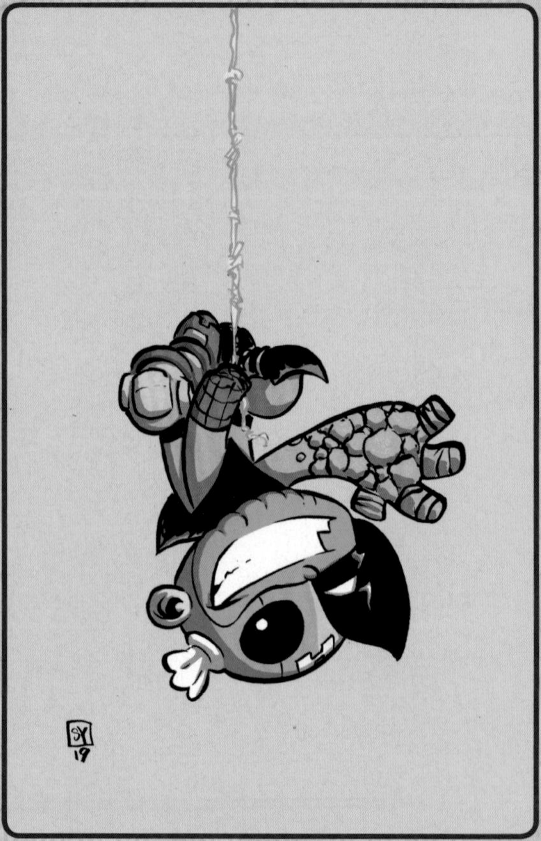

SKOTTIE YOUNG
#1 Variant

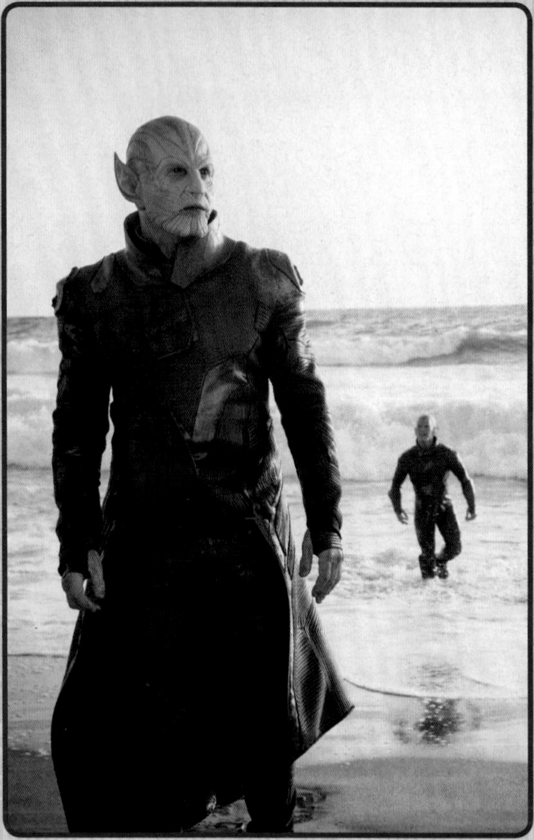

#1 Movie Variant

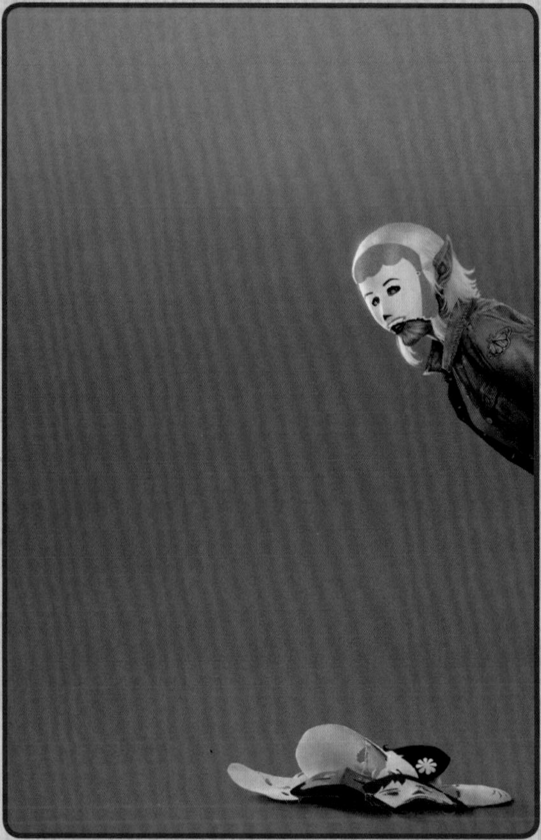

RAHZZAH
#2 Variant